NATIONAL WWII MEMORIAL

Presented in Grateful Appreciation to

BPO Elks Lodge #143
Lafayette, IN

For Your Generous Support of
The National World War II Memorial

TRIBUTE TO A GENERATION

DEDICATION CELEBRATION · **MAY 27-30, 2004**

WORLD WAR II
MEMORIAL CAMPAIGN

Senator Robert J. Dole
National Chairman

Frederick W. Smith
National Co-Chairman
Chairman, President, CEO
FedEx Corporation

The summer of 2004 witnessed a significant national celebration when the World War II Memorial was dedicated on Memorial Day weekend. With an estimated 150,000 people in attendance on the National Mall, and millions gathered in communities and in homes across the nation to view telecasts of the day's events, it was an emotional testimonial to the service and sacrifice of America's World War II generation.

Six decades have passed since the nation united to defeat tyranny in the 1940s. In that time, we have lost three-quarters of the 16 million who served in uniform during the Second World War. We dedicated the memorial in their memory and as a permanent reminder to future generations that a time may come when they, too, are called to sacrifice for a cause greater than themselves. Since the American Battle Monuments Commission opened the memorial to the public in late April, it has bridged generations, prompting youngsters to approach World War II veterans and ask questions about the war years while offering heartfelt thanks.

The memorial could not have been built without your generous support and that of countless other Americans. As a token of appreciation to those who donated $1,000 or more to the memorial fund, we present to you this special edition of *The World War II Memorial: A Grateful Nation Remembers*. It tells the story of the memorial—its history, design, and construction—and stories of the men and women in uniform and at home.

If you have not yet visited the World War II Memorial, we hope you have the opportunity to do so soon. You, too, will be inspired by America's newest symbol of freedom.

Thank you for all you have done to help make the World War II Memorial a reality.

BOB DOLE
National Chairman
World War II Memorial Campaign

FREDERICK W. SMITH
National Co-Chairman
World War II Memorial Campaign

THE DEDICATION

Dedication of the World War II Memorial

David A. Lande

Tribute to a Generation

The national spotlight shone on a generation Memorial Day weekend 2004, when hundreds of thousands of people descended on Washington for a four-day tribute that celebrated the dedication of the World War II Memorial.

Events packed the four days with bittersweet remembrance of the cataclysmic losses of World War II, but celebrated the spectacular victory won by the Greatest Generation. It was an opportunity to renew old friendships, mourn those lost, and pay tribute to the service and sacrifice of all Americans on the home front and battlefront.

The spirit of patriotism and camaraderie permeated the entire city, and signs of it were everywhere. For example, the expansive lobby of the J.W. Marriott hotel in downtown Washington became a portrait gallery with a nostalgic collection of wartime wallet photos reproduced poster size and placed at intervals on easels. Washington's Union Station featured World War II photos from the archives of the Associated Press. And on bustling downtown sidewalks, one could see two or three generations of families wearing T-shirts with silk-screened photos of smiling, fresh-faced youth in uniform along with name, rank and military unit emblazoned on the opposite side, under a proud heading of Dad, Granddad, or even Great-granddad. It was a chance for the generation to witness what *The Washington Post* called "a renaissance of appreciation for their wartime achievements."

Some might say all this was 59 years in the making, but from the point of view of the friends and supporters of the World War II Memorial, it was the culmination of an 11-year effort that started when the monument was authorized by Congress on May 25, 1993.

On April 29, 2004, the American Battle Monuments Commission opened the World War II Memorial to the public—exactly one month before its official dedication. Opening before dedication may be unprecedented for a national monument, but the intent was to afford as many World War II veterans as possible the opportunity to see it. The somber fact is that only a fourth of the 16 million men and women in the armed forces during World War II were alive for the memorial's dedication, according to the Department of Veterans Affairs, and more than 1,000 were dying daily.

From the moment the memorial opened, visitors began laying small tributes to loved ones—flowers, photos, poems, old V-mail letters—at the bases of pillars inscribed with the name of their home states. And they paused to gaze upon the Freedom Wall with its field of 4,000 sculpted gold stars, reflecting on those who didn't come back.

With the dedication of the memorial as its focal point, the "Tribute to a Generation" celebration began on May 27 and continued through May 30. Highlights follow in words and pictures.

NATIONAL WORLD WAR II REUNION

A line-up of vintage military vehicles in the "Motor Pool" included these trucks, along with numerous jeeps and a variety of others, like a 1943 Indian motorcycle, DUKW (duck) amphibious craft, and an observation airplane.

Looking more like a bivouac circa 1944 than Washington in 2004, the National Mall was transformed for the four-day National World War II Reunion organized by the Smithsonian Institution Center for Folklife and Cultural Heritage in partnership with the American Battle Monuments Commission. In a tent city erected on the Mall, scattered servicemen in World War II uniform milled about, as did women in USO, Red Cross, and

"Rosie the Riveter" attire. Some were paid actors in period costume, but more were warriors of six decades ago wearing their own uniforms with pride.

Approaching from the direction of the U.S. Capitol, a first view of the grounds was the "Motor Pool," where a multitude of military vehicles were parked, including jeeps, tracked vehicles like a Sherman tank, trucks of various sizes, a DUKW ("duck") amphibious vehicle, and more.

On the stage of the "Capitol Canteen" tent, musical groups such as the Avi8tors, an ensemble of eight musicians, performed a USO-style show. In the "Wartime Stories" tent, many prominent World War II veterans talked on various topics, such as Navajo Code Talkers explaining their mission in the South Pacific, and actors Ernest Borgnine and Jack Palance swapping war tales.

Between sets of boogie-woogie tunes, a member of the USO Liberty Belles welcomes an Ohio veteran to the reunion.

Credit: Michael Thompson/Center for Folklife and Cultural Heritage, Smithsonian Institution

Next door in the "Reunion Hall" tent, veterans intently scanned eight-foot-tall bulletin boards wallpapered in a solid mass of postings numbering about 10,000 that were tacked up on panels representing 160 military units. Tearful reunions were the order of the day as long-lost buddies were found.

In the "Family Activities" tent, families deciphered secret codes and practiced identifying aircraft silhouettes, but perhaps the most family fun was learning basic swing dance steps to 1940s-era big-band tunes. Music was a major part of the event, with large audiences in attendance at the "Homecoming Stage," where many acts performed, including the Air Force's Airmen of Note, who carry on the musical tradition of legendary Army Air Forces bandleader Glenn Miller.

In quieter spaces of the grounds, volunteers for the Veterans History Project diligently collected 2,865 stories over the reunion's four days. The vast majority were on-the-spot interviews with World War II veterans, but some came in the form of written submissions and memoirs delivered by veterans or their families. About 400 Library of Congress employees and members of the community volunteered their time to do interviews. Library of Congress staff also conducted workshops on how to write, record, audio/videotape, and preserve personal histories, and on the small stage of the Veterans History Project tent, they presented interviews, speakers, and exhibits that showcased firsthand accounts of those who served in uniform and on the home front. By the end of the reunion's four days, the grand total of stories collected by the project surpassed 20,000.

In an adjacent tent with signage for "Preserving Memories," experts from the National Archives, Smithsonian Institution, and Library of Congress conducted workshops on how to preserve veteran's uniforms, documents, photos, medals, and memorabilia.

The "Building the Memorial" tent featured an exhibition on the planning and building of the World War II Memorial, and offered forums with the memorial's architects, engineers, and builders.

The Smithsonian estimated that more than 100,000—a third of the reunion's 315,000 visitors—were from the World War II generation. And many of the generation were veterans, prompting TV and newspaper journalists to venture that Washington hadn't seen so many World War II veterans since the war ended in 1945.

The National WWII Reunion drew some 315,000 people over its four days of World War II-themed events on the National Mall. The reunion had something for everyone—music, dancing, wartime stories, family activities, and camaraderie.

Credit: Andrew Wilson/Center for Folklife and Cultural Heritage, Smithsonian Institution

Navajo Code Talker Sam Billison recounts his experiences with the 5th Marine Division in the Pacific.

Credit: Eric Long/Center for Folklife and Cultural Heritage, Smithsonian Institution

World War II veteran Col. Robert A. Shawn (second from left) poses in front of a vintage staff car with two actors in period uniforms and Lt. Col. Paul Faraci, active duty USAF, during the World War II Reunion, May 29, 2004. Lt. Col. Faraci introduced himself to Col. Shawn, who told about his experience as a fighter pilot in Europe during World War II.

Credit: Ginevra Portlock/Center for Folklife and Cultural Heritage, Smithsonian Institution

Credit: Richard Olsenius

SALUTE TO WORLD WAR II VETERANS

Talented members of America's current armed forces dazzled World War II veterans with a two-hour musical and stage revue. A cast and crew numbering 542 from all branches—U.S. Army, Navy, Marine Corps, Air Force, and Coast Guard—performed for exuberant audiences at four separate shows at Washington's MCI Center on May 28 and 29.

Staged by the Military District of Washington, each performance began with images of World War II service medals on a gigantic 56-by-25-foot video screen, which formed the backdrop for all of the Salute's stage action. The U.S. Army Band played the National Anthem as a multi-service color guard marched across the stage with Old Glory. As the arena darkened, black-and-white video burst onto the screen with paratroopers vaulting out in the slipstream and the Iwo Jima flag-raising, as the revue's title "Remembrance of Things Past" washed over the screen in letters ten feet tall. A series of theatrical vignettes then began, performed entirely by active duty members of the military except for the child actors.

The scene opened with a granddaughter trying to convince her reluctant grandfather to attend the World War II Memorial Dedication. Through flashbacks, the saga of the man's family unfolds, beginning when their lives are transformed by the announcement of the Japanese attack on Pearl Harbor.

By following the lives of the archetypal World War II family, the audience witnessed the grandfather (flashbacked to a young man again) and his

An all active duty military cast "wades ashore" with rifles held high to re-enact the invasion of Tarawa, a climactic battle for the U.S. Marine Corps.

brother enlisting immediately—one in the Army destined for Europe and the other in the Marines bound for the South Pacific; their mother going to work in war industry à la "Rosie the Riveter;" their father, a World War I veteran, appointed to the local draft board; and even their young sister becoming a home front junior air raid warden. Through these characters, the audience had a taste of all branches of the services, the home front, and each major combat theater.

The performance became even more dramatic through the multilayered sights and sounds of war-era music played live by bands just off stage and visuals shown on the giant screen. The experience was enhanced through large video screens off to the left and right of the main screen, enabling the audience to see the nuances of expression on the actors' faces.

Frequent allusions to popular songs, brand names, wartime parlance, and the ever-present Zippo lighter captivated the audience, ushering them back to a time when an entire American generation "pulled itself up by the bootstraps" and responded with a resolute, indomitable, yet often good-humored attitude.

The two sons survive and return home in the end. But they—along with America and the world—are changed forever. A bookend finish returns us to the granddaughter and her grandfather, who has decided he indeed will attend the World War II Memorial Dedication.

A visual blast through 400 military emblems and patches on the giant screen in eight minutes kept the audience riveted and watching for those they recognized and perhaps once distinguished their own uniforms. The show was capped by a set of patriotic music performed by various military bands, with emphasis on swing music by the U.S. Air Force Band's Airmen of Note jazz ensemble. The finale came when drum majors from each service led their musicians out onto the floor and service songs were played in turn for the Coast Guard, Air Force, Navy, Marines, and Army. Many vets stood for their respective branch of service song and applauded. The performance ended with a Navy trumpeter leading off "Amazing Grace" and an Army soloist singing "God Bless America."

According to one veteran, "There wasn't a dry eye anywhere in the auditorium."

A SERVICE OF CELEBRATION

Several hundred veterans along with their families, congressional leaders, and others gathered for an interfaith "Service of Celebration and Thanksgiving to God for the Completion and Dedication of the World War II Memorial on the National Mall" held on the morning of Saturday, May 29, at the Washington National Cathedral. The hour-and-a-quarter service, simulcast on screens on the National Mall, celebrated the dedication of the memorial and remembered those who made the ultimate sacrifice in World War II.

Speaking at the Washington National Cathedral, General John W. Vessey Jr. emphasized "the overwhelming effort of the American people and their armed forces" during World War II.

Credit: Lloyd Johnson/Washington National Cathedral

Military and civilian clergy, as well as World War II dignitaries, participated in the service at the cathedral known as A National House of Prayer for all People. The service included moving tributes by former President George Herbert Walker Bush and General John William Vessey Jr., USA (Ret), former chairman of the Joint Chiefs of Staff.

General Vessey, a veteran of the 34th Infantry Division that fought through North Africa and Italy, recalled how total victory required "enormous effort" that meant "nearly everyone was involved either fighting, supporting the fighters, or supporting those supporting the fighters." He referenced the huge influx of workers that were mostly women, as millions of men went into the armed forces. He emphasized the purpose of the new World War II Memorial as a monument "not to glorify war, but rather to recognize the defining event of the 20th century, and the overwhelming effort of the American people and their armed forces."

Former President Bush, a decorated U.S. Navy pilot in the Pacific, humbly described his generation not as the "greatest," but as "average men and women who lived in extraordinary times" and that "no matter the danger or hardship, they responded with exceptional bravery."

General P. X. Kelley, USMC (Ret), Chairman of the American Battle Monuments Commission, recited a prayer written by George Washington in a 1783 letter to the governors of the 13 United States, as well as an excerpt from Abraham Lincoln's Gettysburg Address. General Kelley asserted that during World War II, America upheld the pledges and ideals of our first and sixteenth Commanders-in-Chief, saying, "…our nation has sent its most precious treasures, its sons and daughters, to human conflicts beyond our shores, not to seize, not to subjugate, not to occupy, but to preserve the inalienable right of all mankind to life, liberty and the pursuit of happiness."

During the Service of Celebration and Thanksgiving, Former President George Herbert Walker Bush reflected on America's "sacred duty to defend freedom," which the World War II Memorial commemorates.

Credit: Lloyd Johnson/
Washington National Cathedral

Prayers, readings, and other parts of the service were delivered by clergy that included the Right Reverend John B. Chane, Bishop of Washington and Dean of the Cathedral; the Right Reverend A. Theodore Eastman, Vicar of the Cathedral; the Right Reverend George E. Packard, Episcopal Bishop Suffragan for Chaplaincies; and the Chief of Chaplains for each of the U.S. Armed Forces.

Masterful musicians, civilian and military, offered moving tributes in song. The United States Marine Chamber Orchestra and the Armed Forces Chorus, along with cathedral choirs, delivered instrumental and vocal preludes and music throughout the service. And the Washington Ringing Society concluded the service with a full peal of the Cathedral's peal bells as the congregation departed.

WORLD WAR II MEMORIAL
DEDICATION CEREMONY

About 117,000 people—more than half of them members of the World War II generation—came with tickets in hand on Saturday, May 29, 2004, for the dedication of the World War II Memorial. Overlooking a stage positioned with the memorial as its dramatic backdrop, attendees were seated on the gentle slope leading down from the Washington Monument and areas spanning the National Mall on a picture-perfect day, with a gentle breeze and high temperature of 74 degrees. Approximately 40,000 others without tickets watched the event live on giant video screens deployed along the Mall in open-air viewing areas.

A certain solemnness was inherent to the day, perhaps felt most vividly in the moment of silence called for by Senator Bob Dole for the more than 400,000 American servicemen and women killed during the war.

But the day was by no means all gravely introspective. Pre-ceremony entertainment kicked off at noon, taking attendees back to the wartime era through music, photo images, newsreel clips, and reminiscences of the time. Lively swing music prompted some attendees to dance in the aisles. Across the country, veterans in Phoenix, Memphis, Modesto, Camden (aboard the USS *New Jersey*), and Milwaukee participated in a two-way satellite transmission.

Postmaster General John E. Potter and John F. Walsh, vice chairman of the U.S. Postal Service Board of Governors, unveiled a new postage stamp depicting the World War II Memorial. Remarks followed by Ohio Congresswoman Marcy Kaptur, who first proposed the legislation in 1987

President Bush congratulates Gen. P. X. Kelley, USMC (Ret), chairman of the American Battle Monuments Commission, on creating a memorial that required, in the President's words, "skill and vision and patience." Several dignitaries in the background look on: (left to right) Presidents Bill Clinton and George H.W. Bush, Chairman of the Memorial Advisory Board Peter Wheeler (over shoulder), Tom Hanks (center), and Archbishop Philip M. Hannan.

to create a national memorial to World War II, which segued into a video chronicling the creation of the memorial.

The formal dedication ceremony began at 2 P.M. with a presentation of state and territory flags and an invocation by Archbishop Philip M. Hannan, a World War II chaplain. General P. X. Kelley, USMC (Ret), in his capacity as chairman of the American Battle Monuments Commission, welcomed everyone to the event at which a "grateful nation remembers the 16 million men and women who wore the uniform of their country, and the 144 million who manned the home front. Let us pray to our chosen God that our nation's memory of their service will never fade."

Other luminaries speaking at the 100-minute dedication included television news anchor Tom Brokaw, who authored three books on "The Greatest Generation," and actor Tom Hanks, who became national spokesman for the World War II Memorial Campaign after starring in the World War II film "*Saving Private Ryan*." Brokaw extolled the sacrifice and valor of the generation he has titled the greatest: "Your lives and how you lived them, the country you defended and loved and cared for the rest of your days, that is the undeniable legacy of you, the men and women I call 'The Greatest Generation.' " Hanks pondered the perspective that time has given the memorial: "As we now live in the third millennium, time demands that more than the fallen be remembered in this place of national honor. Let us remember not just those who lost their lives in the war, but all Americans who were alive, conscientious, and chose to serve as best they could in the years from 1941 to 1945. It is no embellishment to say their lives were interrupted, their futures were altered, their dreams were held in stasis while every minute of their youth was burdened with fear, with loss and with uncertainty. . . Everyday they asked themselves 'what can I do?' and then provided their own answer."

Frederick W. Smith, founder and CEO of FedEx Corporation and national co-chairman of the memorial fund-raising campaign, commented on the very successful fund-raising efforts: "Our fund

Tom Brokaw, a speaker at the ceremony, exchanges greetings with Secretary of State Colin Powell on stage.
Credit: Robert M. Bush/ Congressional Medal of Honor Society

Don Ripper/Latoff & Company/ABMC

raising became a campaign across America from corporate boardrooms to school classrooms; from the largest veterans organizations to the smallest reunion groups; from state legislatures to individual homes."

Former Senator Bob Dole, an Army veteran severely wounded in World War II, recalled poignant personal memories and added: "What we dedicate today is not a memorial to war, rather it's a tribute to the physical and moral courage that makes heroes out of farm and city boys, and that inspires Americans in every generation to lay down their lives for people they will never meet, for ideals that make life itself worth living."

Following these remarks, a Marine bugler played taps inside the memorial. General Kelley then presented the World War II Memorial to President George W. Bush, who received the memorial on behalf of the American people and called it "a fitting tribute, open and expansive, like America; grand and enduring, like the achievements we honor." In speaking to the vast audience on the Mall, one of the largest gatherings ever to hear him in person, the president expressed gratitude on behalf of all Americans: "At this place, at this memorial, we acknowledge a debt of long standing to an entire generation of Americans—those who died, those who fought and worked and grieved and went on. They saved our country, and thereby saved the liberty of mankind. And now I ask every man and woman who saw and lived World War II, every member of that generation, to please rise, as you are able, and receive the thanks of our great nation." As people rose all across the sprawling landscape, so did the two presidents onstage who preceded President Bush—Bill Clinton and President Bush's father, George Herbert Walker Bush. The two stood side by side and applauded.

The ceremony concluded with the world-renowned mezzo-soprano Denyce Graves leading the National Anthem and "God Bless America." Dr. Barry C. Black, Chaplain of the U.S. Senate, offered the closing benediction.

Doris Wilson served as a captain in the Air Transport Command during World War II.

Above: *Opera singer Denyce Graves delivers a moving rendition of the National Anthem at the conclusion of the dedication ceremony.*

Both Photographs Credit: Don Ripper/ Latoff & Company/ABMC

The newly dedicated World War II Memorial was the site for numerous smaller ceremonies during the weekend, such as a long-delayed pinning of a hard-earned Silver Star medal on a World War II combat veteran, and an intimate candlelight memorial service for the American World War II Orphans Network on Memorial Day.

The city of Washington and surrounding communities used the dedication weekend to launch a summer-long celebration called "America Celebrates the Greatest Generation." The 100-day commemoration, sponsored by the Washington D.C. Convention and Tourism Corporation, featured films of the Second World War at the National Theater, Norman Rockwell's famous "Four Freedoms" paintings at the Corcoran Gallery of Art, and more than 140 other exhibits, performances and events—all in celebration of the World War II Memorial taking its place among Washington's defining landmarks.

Perhaps the emotional impact of the memorial dedication and celebration was best expressed by the widow of a World War II veteran: "The memorial and so many events associated with it," wrote Adeline Sunday Allen, wife of the late Colonel Robert Allen, "bring back a flood of memories about the American spirit in World War II—great accomplishments, firm commitment, determined grit and guts, and brains that made victory possible. This tribute to the Greatest Generation and its sacrifices for the greatest country give us an honored closing chapter to our lives."

Wearing Marine dress blues, a World War II veteran bows his head in a moment of silence during the memorial dedication ceremony.

Credit: www.chrischrossphotography.com

THE
WORLD WAR II
MEMORIAL

*We honor those twentieth century Americans who
took up the struggle during the Second World War
and made the sacrifices to perpetuate the gift our
forefathers entrusted to us: A nation conceived in
liberty and justice.*

—FROM THE WORLD WAR II MEMORIAL

KANSAS   NEVADA   COLORADO   SOUTH DAKOTA

THE
WORLD WAR II
MEMORIAL

A Grateful Nation Remembers

Douglas Brinkley, Editor
Foreword by John S.D. Eisenhower
Memorial Photography by Richard Latoff

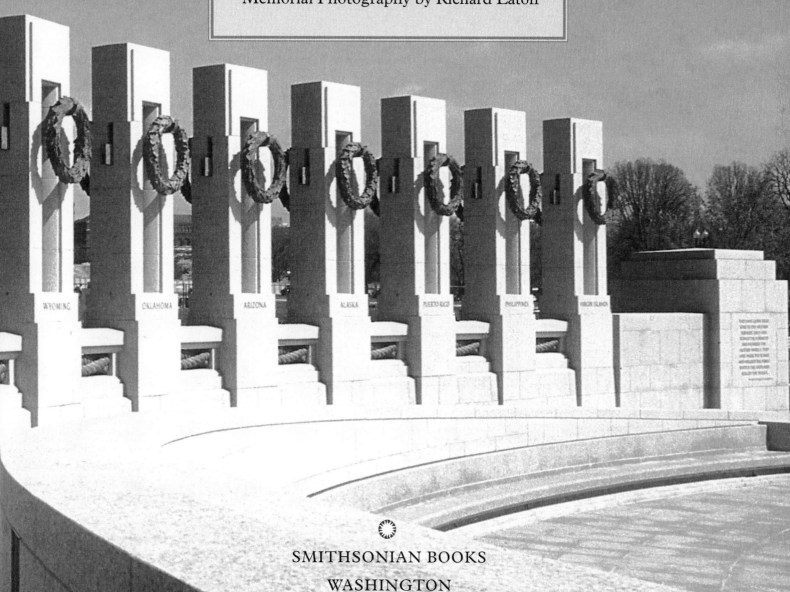

SMITHSONIAN BOOKS

WASHINGTON

ISBN: 1-58834-210-7
Library of Congress Control Number: 2004104628
British Library Cataloguing-in-Publication Data available

Manufactured in the United States of America
10 09 08 07 06 05 04   2 3 4 5

∞ The paper used in this publication meets the minimum requirements of the
American National Standard for Information Sciences--Permanence of Paper
for Printed Library Materials ANSI Z39.48-1992.

For permission to reproduce illustrations appearing in this book, please corre-
spond directly with the owners of the works, as listed in the individual credits.
Smithsonian Books does not retain reproduction rights for these illustrations
individually or maintain a file of addresses for photo sources.

Production—*Elizabeth Publishing*
Graphic Designer—*Virginia Norey*
General Editors—*John W. Wright and Robert Uth*
Senior Editor—*Alan Joyce*
Associate Editor—*Glenn Marcus*
Editorial Assistants—*Michael Noble, Simonida Uth, Lu Ugaz,*
Jason Germeroth, James Garver
Image Research—*Amy Pastan, Teresa Giones*
Sidebars by—*Thomas Lee Wilborn, Lu Ugaz, and Michael Noble.*
Transcripts—*Cece Whittaker*

A companion volume to the PBS documentary,

The World War II Memorial: A Testament to Freedom,

directed by Robert Uth, produced by Glenn Marcus,

and generously underwritten by

The Disabled American Veterans National Service Foundation

and Ford Motor Company

CONTRIBUTORS

Thomas B. Allen has written books and articles on a wide variety of subjects including many on military history. His articles about World War II in National Geographic include pieces on Pearl Harbor, the Battle of Midway, and D-Day; his reference book, *World War II: America at War, 1941–1945*, was a New York Public Library reference book of the year. His most recent books are *George Washington, Spymaster*, and *The Bonus Army: An American Epic*, co-authored with Paul Dickson.

Douglas Brinkley currently serves as director of the Eisenhower Center for American Studies and is a professor of history at the University of New Orleans. His recent publications include *Dean Acheson: The Cold War Years, 1953-71; The Unfinished Presidency: Jimmy Carter's Journey Beyond the White House;* and *FDR and the Creation of the United Nations* with Townsend Hoopes. He has contributed to numerous magazines and journals. His essays on "The Arsenal of Democracy" draw directly from his books *Wheels for the World* (2003) and *Voices of Valor* (2004).

Thomas Childers is a professor of history at the University of Pennsylvania. He is currently completing a trilogy on the Second World War, consisting of *Wings of Morning: The Story of the Last American Bomber Shot Down Over Germany in World War II; We'll Meet Again;* and the forthcoming *The Best Years of Their Lives*, examining the difficulties of veterans returning home from the Second World War. His latest book is *In the Shadows of War: An American Pilot's Odyssey Through Occupied France and the Camps of Nazi Germany.*

Carlo D'Este retired from the Army in 1978 at the rank of Lt. Colonel after tours of duty in Germany and Vietnam. He is the author of six books on military campaigns and biographies including *Decision in Normandy; Bitter Victory: The Battle for Sicily, 1943; World War II in the Mediterranean, 1942-1945; Fatal Decision: Anzio and the Battle for Rome; Patton: A Genius for War;* and *Eisenhower: A Soldier's Life.* He lives in New Seabury, Massachusetts.

Terry Golway is a well-known columnist for and the city editor of the *New York Observer*. He is also the author of *So That Others Might Live: A History of the New York Fire Department*, *For the Cause of Liberty: A Thousand Years of Ireland's Heroes*, and is the principal author of *The Irish in America*.

Allan R. Millett is Raymond E. Mason Jr. Professor of Military History at Ohio State University. He is the author of many books, including *Semper Fidelis: The History of the United States Marine Corps* and *Their War for Korea;* and co-author (with Williamson Murray) of the highly successful military history of World War II, *A War to Be Won*.

Robert Uth is a television producer and writer with New Voyage Communications in Washington, DC. This book is a companion to his most recent work for PBS, *The World War II Memorial: A Testament to Freedom*. Uth's *Korean War Stories*, a 60-minute documentary hosted by Walter Cronkite, tells the story of American veterans during the Korean War. The program won the 2002 National Emmy for "Outstanding Historical Documentary."

Emily Yellin is a journalist, freelance writer, and author of *Our Mothers' War: American Women at Home and at the Front During World War II*.

CONTRIBUTING EDITORS

David A. Lande is the author of seven books about World War II, including *From Somewhere in England: The Life and Times of 8th Air Force Bomber, Fighter and Ground Crews in World War II*. His work has appeared in *MHQ*, *World War II*, and *Aviation History*. He served as a commissioned officer in the air wing of the U.S. Marine Corps.

Lincoln Paine is the author of *Ships of the World: An Historical Encyclopedia*, among other books and articles. He has lectured in the United States and Australia, and has taught global maritime history at the University of Southern Maine. He is currently writing a maritime history of the world.

CONTENTS

FOREWORD

John S.D. Eisenhower

The National World War II Memorial, situated on the Mall in the nation's capital, takes its place between two other edifices that stand for the great milestones of America's history. One is the Washington Monument, which celebrates the nation's founding; the other is the Lincoln Memorial, to the west, which celebrates the preservation of the Union in the great Civil War of 1861–65. To recognize a third great event, the American Battle Monuments Commission has established the World War II Memorial. While a war memorial, this edifice is more than a tribute to the men and women of this country whose bloody struggle loosened the world from tyranny; it marks for all Americans the emergence of the United States as the leader of the Free World in the mid-20th century.

Though our ranks are thinning, many elderly Americans, of whom I am one, carry vivid memories of America as she was before the Second World War and were able to witness the transformation it wrought in our country. For more than a decade preceding the outbreak of war in Europe in 1939, America had undergone a devastating and tragic economic depression. Though Americans, with their basic optimism and trust in their country and their leaders, never lost faith that our society would recover, the personal crises faced by countless individuals and families were so burdensome that the term "depression" applied to the general attitude of the people as well as the state of the nation's economy. As a 17-year-old in 1940, I can well recall standing on a street in Tacoma, Washington, and remarking on the evidence of weariness and sadness that showed on the faces of the people.

Five years later, those same people viewed the future with general optimism, confident in America's role therein. Problems remained, of course. Our people were faced with adjusting to the new challenges of postwar civilian life, financing the rebuilding of Europe and Japan, and confronting our former ally, the Soviet Union, in the 50-year confrontation called the cold war. Still it was a different America, more optimistic than it had been in the days when the Nazi war machine was overrunning France.

Since the Second World War occurred long before most of those who will visit the memorial were born, it might be well to review the sequence of events in a general but far from exhaustive way. The seeds of the conflict were sown long before it officially broke out in Europe in 1939, and some will even attribute the conflict to the draconian provisions of the Treaty of Versailles that ended the First World War two decades earlier. Its economic effects were to lead to the seizure of power in Germany by the dictator Adolf Hitler in 1933. His move toward war seems now to have been all but inevitable. It became a reality on September 3, 1939, two days after Hitler's panzers had crossed the border into Poland. The Soviet Union stood neutral at that moment, but Britain, then France, declared war on Germany.

For more than two years after the war's beginning, everything went badly for the Western Allies. Hitler overran Norway and Denmark in the spring of 1940 and two months later shattered the French Army. Britain stood alone in defiance—the one bright spot—forcing Hitler to turn eastward into the Balkans and, in mid-1941, even the Soviet Union. During those years, America remained aloof, clinging to peace. But we were neutral in name only. Our sympathy for the Western Allied cause was such as to prompt President Franklin Roosevelt to stretch the neutrality laws to give them material support. By the time America was thrust into the war by the Japanese sneak attack on the United States battle fleet at Pearl Harbor, Hawaii, on December 7, 1941, Americans had already exchanged shots with German submarines in the North Atlantic.

With our battle fleet crippled as the result of the Japanese attack, the months after America's entrance into the war produced only a series of costly, tragic, and humiliating defeats in the Pacific. The first loss, to the Americans, was that of the Philippine Islands, which held a "commonwealth" status in preparation for their planned independence from the United States in 1946. Then came losses sustained principally by the British and Dutch—Hong Kong, Indonesia, and the Malay Peninsula, even the supposedly impregnable British bastion of Singapore. The Japanese tide was halted only by the historic battle of Midway in June 1942, where the partially rebuilt American Pacific Fleet, commanded by Admiral Chester Nimitz, virtually destroyed the Japanese carrier fleet. From that time on, Hawaii and the West Coast of the United States were no longer considered in danger. The Pacific offensive began, slowly at first, across the vast ocean spaces toward Japan.

Fortunately for the Americans and British, their two leaders, Prime Minister Winston S. Churchill and President Franklin D. Roosevelt, refused to allow the initial defeats to dampen their faith in ultimate victory or content themselves with planning defensive actions for any great length of time. Even before the fall of the Philippines—right after the Pearl Harbor attack, in fact—the two leaders met with their military staffs in Washington to plan the future conduct of the war. At that meeting, they confirmed earlier planning to concentrate the bulk of Anglo-American forces in Europe first, where American, British, and Russians could concentrate their joint effort against the most dangerous member of the so-called Axis, Nazi Germany. Mussolini's Italy, while one of the targets, was considered of lesser importance. Only after the destruction of Nazi power would the three Allies turn their full power on Japan. That decision required courage on the part of our political leaders, considering that the focus of the American public's anger was directed toward Japan, not Germany.

The turning point of the war is generally accepted to have been reached by events occurring around the end of 1942, the year that had opened with so many Allied defeats. On November 19, 1942, the Red Army, under command of Marshal

Georgy Zhukov, began the siege of the German Sixth Army at Stalingrad, thus marking the end of Nazi offensive action in Russia. About three weeks earlier, on October 31, began the Battle of El Alamein, in the eastern Sahara Desert. There the British forces, under General Sir Harold Alexander and General Sir Bernard Montgomery, dealt the German "Desert Fox," Field Marshal Erwin Rommel, a resounding defeat that sent him reeling westward. On November 8, 1942, British and American forces under General Dwight D. Eisenhower landed in Morocco and Algeria, eventually to join with Montgomery in squeezing Rommel's beleaguered Afrika Korps, resulting in the surrender of some 300,000 Germans and Italians.

In 1943, the European side of the war consisted of a series of amphibious attacks in the Mediterranean. Sicily fell to the Allies, still under Eisenhower, in July; the first invasion of mainland Italy began in September. These Allied victories brought about the ouster of Italian dictator Benito Mussolini and shortly thereafter the surrender of Italy, though the campaign against Italy's German occupiers continued for the duration of the war. One tyrant had been toppled, but there were still two to go. Allied strategic air forces based in Britain and the Mediterranean began the ambitious and costly process of bombarding Germany, both to destroy her war-making power and, in Operation Pointblank, to eliminate the effectiveness of the German Air Force.

In the Pacific, the year 1943 also saw significant advances. Admiral Chester Nimitz's Central Pacific Command began a westward movement, island by island, toward the enemy homeland. Attu in the Aleutians, Makin, and Tarawa fell to his forces during that year. In the Southwest Pacific, General Douglas MacArthur's forces concentrated on clearing New Guinea, an important stepping stone from his base in Australia toward his goal of returning to the Philippines.

The first part of 1944 in Europe saw progress in Italy overshadowed by the buildup in Great Britain of the vast Anglo-American force that would, in the middle of the year, invade northwestern France, in Operation Overlord. On June 6, 1944— known to laymen and historians alike as "D-Day"—American and British forces, under the command of General Dwight D. Eisenhower, crossed the English Channel to begin the long and costly road leading to the final conquest of Nazi Germany. Though many bloody battles were yet to be fought, including Hitler's counteroffensive in the Ardennes (the "Battle of the Bulge"), 11 months after the landings, when Eisenhower was able to report to Roosevelt and Churchill that his mission had been completed. That Allied force amounted to some 90 divisions, 62 of them American. May 8, 1945, was designated as V-E (Victory in Europe) Day.

The task in Europe then turned overnight from conquest to rehabilitation. The elation of victory was diluted by the weight of the Allied casualties and the realization that victory had come too late to prevent the methodical genocidal murder of 6 million Jews and millions of other Europeans in the grisly chapter of history known as the Holocaust.

The war in the Pacific also gained momentum. On October 20, 1944, General Douglas MacArthur set foot on the shore of the Philippine island of Leyte, thus fulfilling a personal promise he had made to the Filipinos two and a half years earlier, "I shall return." Though the fighting in that area would go on for months, a symbolic moment had taken place. In the Central Pacific, forces under Admiral Nimitz took Kwajalein and Saipan.

The year 1945 saw a dramatic close to the Pacific war. On February 19, the United States Marines landed on the heavily defended island of Iwo Jima and the joint Army–Marine Tenth Army landed on Okinawa on April 1. Its commander, General Simon Bolivar Buckner, was mortally wounded by an artillery shell 10 weeks later. Buckner was the only high-ranking American general killed in combat during the war.

On August 6, 1945, a B-29 bomber named *Enola Gay* took off from Tinian carrying a highly secret and incredibly lethal weapon, the first atomic bomb ever to be used in war. The target was Hiroshima, where the successful blast resulted in the deaths of 100,000 Japanese, most of them civilians. The atomic bomb had been under development since 1942, and it was up to the new president, Harry S Truman, to give the agonizing order to drop it. Three days later, another atomic weapon was dropped on the Japanese port of Nagasaki, also resulting in many thousands of deaths. Also on that day the Russians launched a massive attack on Japanese armies. The Japanese high command, seeing the futility of further resistance, surrendered on August 15, 1945. The surrender was formalized in Tokyo Bay aboard the battleship USS *Missouri* on September 2, General MacArthur presiding.

World War II was at an end.

The direction of World War II, as briefly outlined above, was conducted intelligently and often under extreme difficulty and conflicting viewpoints between nations and military services. Millions of words have been written describing them. It is well that historians study and debate the campaigns and the decisions that brought them about, to pinpoint Midway (1942), Stalingrad (1943), D-Day in Europe (1944), and the atomic bomb (1945) as critical moments in the war. The military conduct of the war, however, would never justify the erection of this Memorial, nor would it explain what World War II meant, in broadest terms, to the United States.

The impact of World War II lies chiefly in the effect it had on the Americans who lived through the period, especially those who participated, and the impact it had on American society. That means on the men and women who fought it, not the generals, not the statesmen. To the infantry soldier crouching in his foxhole or charging into an enemy machine-gun nest, to a sailor firing his gun on a hostile shore until he collapses from fatigue, to an airman flying on a bombing mission to Schweinfurt or Ploesti, to a nurse under direct artillery fire on the Anzio beachhead, there is no such thing as a small action. The individual's war is limited to what he or she can see and, more important, can feel. The collective experience, shared by so many, is what makes World War II important.

The National World War II Memorial is designed to preserve just that, the broadest significance of the war experience to all Americans. Visitors coming to see it will be informed, educated, impressed, and most of all, given an appreciation of one of the most significant American experiences of our time.

INTRODUCTION

Douglas Brinkley

Throughout 1941, using Kansas City as his home base, the legendary painter Thomas Hart Benton had traveled throughout the Great Plains praising the canvases of Iowa's Grant Wood while denouncing the modernist conceits of France. No part of American culture was off limits to his imagination. Benton had even taken to playing harmonica at public lectures, recording an album for Decca Records to show off his virtuosity. As President Franklin Roosevelt was drawing the United States into an alliance with Great Britain, the frenetic Benton was reporting on Detroit "sit-down" strikes for *Life*, drawing sketches of southeast Missouri floods for the *St. Louis Post-Dispatch*, writing articles on the Oklahoma oil boom for *Scribner's* magazine, and painting his controversial nude "Susannah and the Elders" to the condemnation of New York art critics. But Pearl Harbor ended his intrepid travels.

On December 7, 1941, the 52-year-old Benton was about to deliver a speech on American Regionalism to a crowd of Cincinnati art mavens when an usher whispered into his ear the cataclysmic news from Hawaii. "I got off promptly, telegraphed my agency to cancel all further engagements and went home," Benton recalled in the second edition of his memoir *An Artist in America*. "I would try to wake up the Middle West to the grimness of our national situation." An unabashed nativist when it came to American art, politically, however, Benton was an internationalist. "As the Nazi power grew and its atrocities multiplied and its influence on some of our South American brothers placed its menace on our very doorsteps I began to favor American intervention," Benton wrote. "By the late autumn of 1941 my mind was so much on the international situation that I found it difficult to concentrate on painting."

In the wake of Pearl Harbor Benton decided to create gigantic propaganda pictures to be hung in Kansas City's Union Station. He wanted to jolt "the milling travelers" about the evils of fascism. Working at breakneck speed, Benton, within six weeks, painted eight brutal works of unbridled violence, which are collectively known as *The Year of Peril* series—"Starry Night," "Again," "Indifference," "Casualty," "The Sowers," "The Harvest," "Invasion," and "Exterminate!" Benton had one overriding objective in mind: to portray America's enemies as genocidal, bloodthirsty maniacs.

Today *The Year of Peril* paintings are housed at the State Historical Society of Missouri in Columbia. They're just one of the myriad examples of artistic endeavors aimed at awakening American isolationists to the grim realities of the Second World War. When the war ended shortly after a nuclear bomb was dropped over Nagasaki, however, the antifascist propaganda came to a grinding halt. Instead, following VJ Day, towns across America started forming commissions to erect marble memorials to honor our brave G.I.s. Virtually every state capital erected a World War II Memorial on their lawns. The grandest of all of these was the United States Marine Memorial (better known as the "Iwo Jima Memorial") next to Arlington National Cemetery. The 32-foot-tall cast bronze statue, taken from the heroic Pulitzer Prize–winning photograph of Associated Press photographer Joe Rosenthal, depicts five Marines and one Navy Corpsman raising the Stars and Stripes on top of Mount Suribachi during the battle for Iwo Jima. Designed by Felix de Weldon— and formally opened in 1954 by President Dwight D. Eisenhower—the memorial, which is the largest cast bronze statue in the world, has for 50 years awed millions of visitors.

Now, a half century later, another World War II memorial is being erected, this one located on the Mall near both the Washington Monument and Lincoln Memorial. Unlike the Iwo Jima Memorial, or hundreds of others in parks and turnabouts scattered across America, this National World War II Memorial is meant to pay homage to an entire generation. As you stand at the Rainbow Pool, you quickly realize the memorial encompasses the totality of the World War II experience in all the theaters of operation. It honors not just the young G.I. storming ashore at Normandy or the admiral deciding how to best win the Battle of Midway, but the American people as a whole. The memorial salutes the tireless women who worked in the textile mills to make parachutes and the world-class engineers who designed essential new parts for the B-24 bomber. It is, at its essence, a glorious memorial that pays homage to Franklin D. Roosevelt's Four Freedoms, a national shrine for the enduring triumph of Jeffersonian-Hamiltonian Democracy.

This edited volume—*The World War II Memorial: A Grateful Nation Remembers*—is a commemorative book to mark the ribbon cutting. It is meant to both celebrate the Allied victory and to ponder the tremendous cost of war. When trying to decide who should write the foreword, John S.D. Eisenhower became the obvious choice. A first-rate historian, his surname is synonymous with the Second World War. Eisenhower, in other words, is shorthand for Allied Victory. Over the decades, John Eisenhower—a retired Brigadier General in the Army Reserve and former U.S. Ambassador to Belgium—has written a number of excellent history books, including a riveting narrative study of the Battle of the Bulge. He is a national treasure, and we are grateful for his contribution.

The final part of this volume offers the readers a brief synopsis of how the World War II Memorial came to fruition. It emanates from a line John Steinbeck crafted to start his collection of World War II letters: "There was a war, long ago—once upon a time…" To Americans old enough to have lived through the cataclysms of World War II this playful line is wildly ironic, a coy jest by an able novelist. World War II is still so seared into their memories that it's impossible to forget. But in truth, most Americans have no direct memory of the Second World War. The postwar generations garner their historical information about World War II from Steven Spielberg movies, TV documentaries and, with luck, accurate textbooks. Given this growing generation gap, it makes sense for our own nation to declare a few acres on our National Mall as sacred ground for remembering World War II. While learning comes in many guises, the creation of an elegant memorial is a time-honored way to pay tribute to past deeds. Most of us, for example, don't think about Abraham Lincoln too often. But when you come to Washington, D.C., and stand in front of sculptor Daniel Chester French's 19-foot statue at the Lincoln Memorial, you realize our 16th president was truly a man for all ages. If you shut your eyes, you can almost hear him delivering the Gettysburg Address.

As Hugh Hardy makes clear in his evocative essay about the value of Friedrich St.Florian's design for the World War II Memorial—like the Lincoln Memorial—was conceived for future generations to think about the past. As a design-architect, St.Florian is world class. He was, in fact, unanimously selected from 400 entrants to design the memorial. While some concerned citizens believed that a memorial at the center line of the National Mall was unnecessary, that it destroyed green space, Hardy believes otherwise. He explains not just the rationale behind erecting the memorial, but justifies the plaza configuration, colonnades, sculptures, fountains, and pavilions. The memorial, it is clear, was designed to be part of the National Mall, not a disruption of its hallowed grounds. Of particular interest is St.Florian's wise decision to use classical forms and materials like granite and bronze. He wanted to honor the old memorial traditions, not experiment with postmodern minimalist abstractions. His respect for earlier American memorial architecture is most appreciated.

The second—and longest section—of this volume tackles the theme of America at war from a scholarly perspective. During the immediate decades following World War II, most G.I.s—and home front workers, for that matter—didn't want to discuss the global cataclysm. They wanted to return to a normal America that built cars, not tanks. "Instead of talking about it," novelist James Jones, author of *From Here to Eternity* explained, "most Americans didn't talk about it."

Once World War II ended, people wanted to forget. That may have been a normal instinct, but it was an impossible task. How do you forget your legs being blown off by a land mine in the Philippines? How do you forget seeing human ovens at Auschwitz? How do you forget working 12-hour shifts at the Norfolk Naval Shipyard while trying to keep a family clothed and fed? The official task of remembering the past falls upon the historians. And so we commissioned a handful of essays from several World War II scholars to explain various aspects of America at war. Almost every facet of the war is addressed in this section, including a wide-ranging essay on the role women played, by historian and journalist Emily Yellin. The home front is covered in two separate essays, one by Terry Golway, and another by myself on the building of what President Franklin Roosevelt called the "Arsenal of Democracy" and the crucial role played by the Ford Motor Company. For the war itself, we were fortunate to have the acclaimed biographer of General Patton, Carlo D'Este, for "Victory in Europe." His section also includes eyewitness testimonies from Yogi Berra, Robert Dole, Daniel Inouye, and Warren Spahn, as well as a portrait of Audie Murphy, our most decorated soldier. Allan R. Millett, a highly respected military historian, has written with great insight about "The Land War with Japan." First-person reminiscences are offered by Jay J. Rebstock, Jr., a veteran of the Iwo Jima campaign, and a selection on Okinawa from a searing memoir by the recently deceased U.S. Marine, E.B. Sledge. Thomas B. Allen, the author of numerous books on the war, illuminates the origins of America's participation in the war in the Pacific and describes the Navy's crucial role in attaining victory. Finally, in an essay by the distinguished historian Thomas Childers, you will read not only the extraordinary story of how air power changed warfare forever, but also about the terrible price paid by the men who flew on dangerous missions over Europe, Japan, and the Pacific Ocean. A poignant reminiscence by U.S. Senator George McGovern about his experiences as a bomber pilot is complemented by two interviews with fighter pilots, including one of the famed Tuskegee Airmen, Howard Baugh.

The history of the war is followed by an authoritative recounting of how the World War II Memorial came to fruition, as well as background on the hallowed ground we call the National Mall. It is written by Emmy Award winning producer and director Robert Uth. Having filmed most of the memorial's construction, Uth conceived this book as a companion volume to his PBS documentary, *The World War II Memorial: A Testament to Freedom*. A great deal of the technical detail and most of the interviews with veterans contained herein are the result of that effort, which was sponsored by the Disabled American Veterans National Service Foundation, and Ford Motor Company.

By no means is this book meant to be a comprehensive history of World War II. It is a selective group of essays meant to illuminate the major events and topics of the war. As a memorial remembrance, it serves as a reminder that some 60 million people died in World War II, the United States losing over 400,000. This does not include the millions of others who were physically and psychologically damaged by the global conflict. But out of such a blaze of horrors came valor. As a society, the United States understood that freedom didn't come cheap. This book—and the memorial—are modest "thank-yous" from one generation to another.

So let the history books show that in 2004 the American people, recognizing the essential role the World War II generation played in saving our democracy, erected a sublime memorial. Building the memorial—and editing this volume—are modest deeds to be sure, but they're clearly preferable to deciding to forget. They were not conceived out of outrage, as Benton's *The Year of Peril* paintings were. They were designed as heartfelt prayers of national gratitude.

Douglas Brinkley, Director of the Eisenhower Center
for American Studies at the University of New Orleans
April 5, 2004

PART I
THE MEMORIAL

THE WORLD WAR II MEMORIAL

WELCOME

The World War II Memorial is a lasting symbol of national unity and the American spirit, and stands as a timeless reminder of service and sacrifice for generations to come. Representing the collective will of the American people to sacrifice for the ideals that shaped our foundation and guide our future, the World War II Memorial has assumed its deserving place in American history.

THE WWII MEMORIAL SITE

The National Mall is America's village green, the place we gather to celebrate our heritage among the cherished icons to our nation's democratic ideals. Just as their forefathers fought to establish and then reunite our nation, the World War II generation fought to preserve freedom itself.

The memorial rests on one of America's preeminent public spaces, the 7.4-acre Rainbow Pool site. One of eight locations considered, the Rainbow Pool site was deemed most worthy for America's commemoration of what most believe is the defining event of the 20th century.

This historic location at the east end of the Reflecting Pool between the Lincoln Memorial and the Washington Monument was dedicated on Veterans Day 1995 with the sprinkling of soil from the nation's 14 overseas World War II cemeteries maintained by the American Battle Monuments Commission.

The prominent site is commensurate with the historical importance and lasting significance of World War II to America and the world. In the immediate vicinity are the Washington Monument, the Lincoln Memorial, the Jefferson Memorial, Constitution Gardens, the District of Columbia World War I Memorial, the Franklin D. Roosevelt Memorial, the Korean War Veterans Memorial, and the Vietnam Veterans Memorial.

I hope the memorial will tell the world that there was a generation of Americans, who through their gallantry and courage and conviction truly changed the course of world history, and that we must forever remember them.

—Friedrich St. Florian,
Design Architect

DESIGN

The design of the memorial is an inspiring testimony to the passion, optimism, courage, and heroism of the World War II generation of Americans. It creates a place of beauty that is a stage for remembrance and celebration of the principles and values fought for and defended in the Second Word War. The classical architecture complements the major monuments and memorials in the vicinity. Constructed around a restored Rainbow Pool, it creates a public forum that is distinct, memorable, evocative, and serene.

The design is sensitive to its site and surroundings, preserving the open vista between the Lincoln Memorial and the Washington Monument, and views across the memorial in all directions. Its vertical dimensions celebrate victory, yet remain modest in relation to the principal visual features of the Mall: the elms, the Lincoln Memorial, the Reflecting Pool, the Washington Monument, and the Mall itself.

ENTRANCES

The memorial is located on the center line of the National Mall. Adjacent to the Reflecting Pool and cradled within the elm walks, the memorial has both a distinctive north-south and east-west axis. The ceremonial entrance is located on 17th Street, immediately across from the Washington Monument grounds. Visitors can also enter the memorial from the elm walks through the arched pavilions on the north or south. Gently sloped ramps allow visitors access to the Memorial Plaza. All of the memorial entrances are fully accessible.

MATERIALS

Granite was chosen for its aesthetic appeal and durability. More permanent than marble, it has been used for thousands of centuries. The two principal stones are Kershaw for the walls and vertical elements, and Green County for the main plaza paving stone. Two green stones, Rio Verde and Moss Green, were used for accent paving on the plaza. Academy Black and Mount Airy were used to reconstruct the Rainbow Pool. Mount Airy is the original coping stone of the Lincoln Memorial's Reflecting Pool. There are more than 200 separate pieces of bronze sculpture for the memorial. Bronze is a traditional material used in memorials. It is warm in appearance, and looks better with age. A bluish-green patina was applied to the sculpture to create a 'cool' color relationship with the granite.

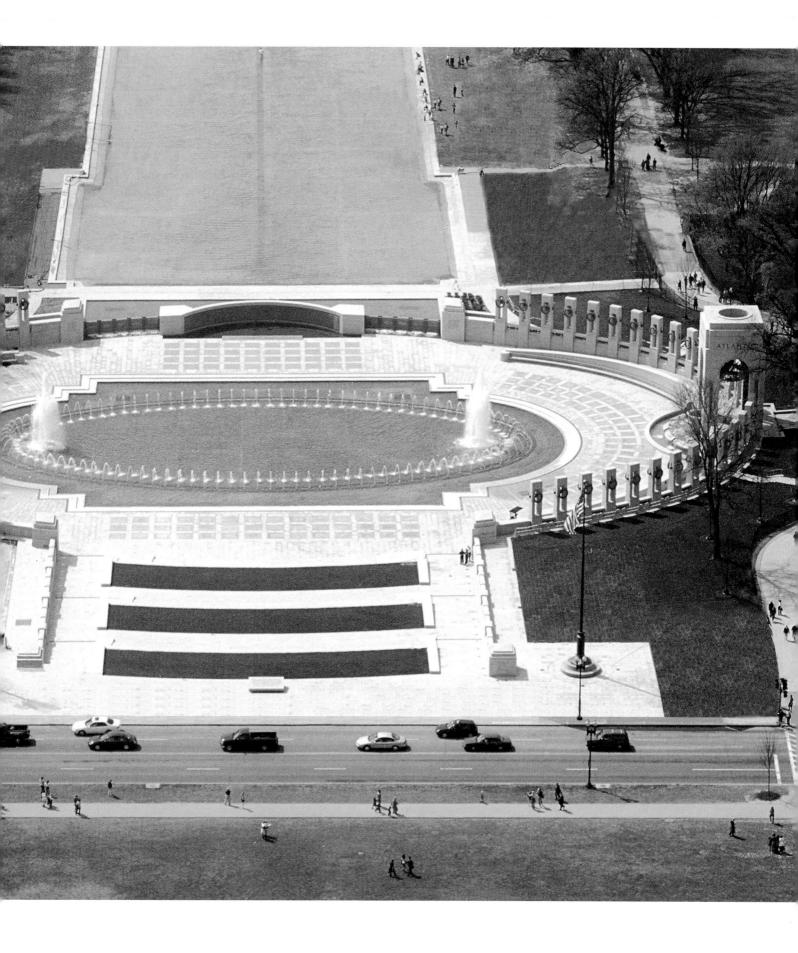

CEREMONIAL ENTRANCE

Centered at the ceremonial entrance on 17th Street, an announcement stone provides context for the purpose and location of the memorial.

HERE IN THE PRESENCE OF WASHINGTON AND LINCOLN, ONE THE EIGHTEENTH CENTURY FATHER AND THE OTHER THE NINETEENTH CENTURY PRESERVER OF OUR NATION, WE HONOR THOSE TWENTIETH CENTURY AMERICANS WHO TOOK UP THE STRUGGLE DURING THE SECOND WORLD WAR AND MADE THE SACRIFICES TO PERPETUATE THE GIFT OUR FOREFATHERS ENTRUSTED TO US: A NATION CONCEIVED IN LIBERTY AND JUSTICE.

Two flagpoles frame the entrance. The bases of granite and bronze contain the seals of the Army, Navy, Marine Corps, Army Air Forces, Coast Guard, and Merchant Marine. Inscribed on the granite benches that encircle the flagpole bases are the words:

AMERICANS CAME TO LIBERATE, NOT TO CONQUER,
TO RESTORE FREEDOM AND TO END TYRANNY

BAS-RELIEF PANELS

Ceremonial steps and ramps lead from 17th Street into the lowered plaza. A series of bronze bas-relief panels along the ceremonial entrance balustrades depict America's war years, at home and overseas. There are 24 separate panels: 12 on the north depict the Atlantic Front, while 12 on the south portray the Pacific Front. The unifying theme of the panels is the transformation of America caused by the country's total immersion in World War II. They depict the all-out mobilization of America's agricultural, industrial, and military resources that transformed the country into the arsenal of democracy as well as the breadbasket of the world.

These raised panels evoke the human drama of war and bring a literal, storytelling dimension to the memorial. The unity of purpose unique to this time in America is captured by placing the visual emphasis on the individual with a style of sculpture that dates back to ancient times. All details, scenes, and equipment are subordinate to the human figure.

Atlantic Front panels include: *Lend Lease, Enlistment, Women in the Military, Rosie the Riveter/Aircraft Construction, Battle of the Atlantic, Air*

Submarine Warfare

Shipbuilding

Normandy Beach Landing

*Rosie the Riveter/
Aircraft Construction*

War/B-17, Paratroopers, Normandy Beach Landing, Tanks in Combat, Medics in the Field, Battle of the Bulge, and Russians Meet Americans at the Elbe.

Pacific Front panels include: Pearl Harbor, Bond Drive, Embarkation, Shipbuilding, Agriculture, Submarine Warfare, Navy in Action, Amphibious Landing, Jungle Warfare, Field Burial, Liberation, and V-J Day.

At the base of the ceremonial entrance, two inscriptions describe the magnitude and toll of America's war effort.

WOMEN WHO STEPPED UP WERE MEASURED AS CITIZENS OF THE NATION, NOT AS WOMEN. . . THIS WAS A PEOPLE'S WAR, AND EVERYONE WAS IN IT.

—*Colonel Oveta Culp Hobby*

THEY FOUGHT TOGETHER AS BROTHERS-IN-ARMS. THEY DIED TOGETHER AND NOW THEY SLEEP SIDE BY SIDE. TO THEM WE HAVE A SOLEMN OBLIGATION.

—*Admiral Chester A. Nimitz*

MEMORIAL PLAZA
AND RAINBOW POOL

The Memorial Plaza and Rainbow Pool are the principal design features of the memorial, unifying all other elements. The plaza is lowered six feet below the level of the Reflecting Pool to give the memorial its own sense of place and to preserve the Mall vistas. The layout of the plaza is an oval with paving stones of gray and light green that form a visually distinctive radial pattern. Seating for visitors is provided on benches along the rampart walls and around the coping of the Rainbow Pool.

The historic waterworks of the Rainbow Pool have been restored and contribute to the celebratory nature of the memorial. Semicircular fountains at the base of the two memorial pavilions and waterfalls flanking the Freedom Wall complement the waterworks in the Rainbow Pool. The dancing water throughout the memorial creates a sense of light and life.

INSCRIPTIONS

On the Plaza's corners and rampart walls, inscriptions recall the words of America's political and military leaders during the war. They evoke the spirit, courage, and sacrifice of Americans overseas and at home, and pay tribute to our allies.

PEARL HARBOR

DECEMBER 7, 1941, A DATE WHICH WILL LIVE IN INFAMY. . .
NO MATTER HOW LONG IT MAY TAKE US TO OVERCOME
THIS PREMEDITATED INVASION, THE AMERICAN PEOPLE,
IN THEIR RIGHTEOUS MIGHT, WILL WIN THROUGH TO
ABSOLUTE VICTORY.

—President Franklin D. Roosevelt

THEY HAVE GIVEN THEIR SONS TO THE MILITARY SERVICES.
THEY HAVE STOKED THE FURNACES AND HURRIED THE
FACTORY WHEELS. THEY HAVE MADE THE PLANES AND
WELDED THE TANKS, RIVETED THE SHIPS AND ROLLED
THE SHELLS.

—President Franklin D. Roosevelt

BATTLE OF MIDWAY JUNE 4–7, 1942

THEY HAD NO RIGHT TO WIN. YET THEY DID, AND IN DOING SO THEY CHANGED THE COURSE OF A WAR. . . EVEN AGAINST THE GREATEST OF ODDS, THERE IS SOMETHING IN THE HUMAN SPIRIT— A MAGIC BLEND OF SKILL, FAITH AND VALOR—THAT CAN LIFT MEN FROM CERTAIN DEFEAT TO INCREDIBLE VICTORY.

—Walter Lord, Author

❦

D-DAY JUNE 6, 1944

YOU ARE ABOUT TO EMBARK UPON THE GREAT CRUSADE, TOWARD WHICH WE HAVE STRIVEN THESE MANY MONTHS. THE EYES OF THE WORLD ARE UPON YOU...I HAVE FULL CONFIDENCE IN YOUR COURAGE, DEVOTION TO DUTY AND SKILL IN BATTLE.

—General Dwight D. Eisenhower

❦

WE ARE DETERMINED THAT BEFORE THE SUN SETS ON THIS TERRIBLE STRUGGLE OUR FLAG WILL BE RECOGNIZED THROUGHOUT THE WORLD AS A SYMBOL OF FREEDOM ON THE ONE HAND AND OF OVERWHELMING FORCE ON THE OTHER.

—General George C. Marshall

❦

THE WAR'S END

TODAY THE GUNS ARE SILENT. A GREAT TRAGEDY HAS ENDED. A GREAT VICTORY HAS BEEN WON. THE SKIES NO LONGER RAIN DEATH—THE SEAS BEAR ONLY COMMERCE— MEN EVERYWHERE WALK UPRIGHT IN THE SUNLIGHT. THE ENTIRE WORLD IS QUIETLY AT PEACE.

—General Douglas MacArthur

The principal element of a memorial should not be a building, but a forum, a public space, a plaza, as I call it. And the idea behind that is that the forum, in classical terms, was always a gathering place, a place where people can meet and communicate with each other. It seemed very important, that what we really celebrate, what is the essence of our victory in the Second World War, was the fact that it allowed the free world to continue to be a free world. That we could live in peace and under democratic rules, that we could openly speak to each other, exchange our ideas without fears.

—Friedrich St.Florian, Design Architect

OUR DEBT TO THE HEROIC MEN AND VALIANT WOMEN IN THE SERVICE OF OUR COUNTRY CAN NEVER BE REPAID. THEY HAVE EARNED OUR UNDYING GRATITUDE. AMERICA WILL NEVER FORGET THEIR SACRIFICES.

—President Harry S Truman

THE HEROISM OF OUR OWN TROOPS. . . WAS MATCHED BY THAT OF THE ARMED FORCES OF THE NATIONS THAT FOUGHT BY OUR SIDE. . . THEY ABSORBED THE BLOWS. . . AND THEY SHARED TO THE FULL IN THE ULTIMATE DESTRUCTION OF THE ENEMY.

—President Harry S Truman

THE MEMORIAL AT NIGHT

Many visitors will see the memorial at night. It is illuminated with hundreds of light fixtures, all computer-controlled to alter the overall lighting effect. Memorial lighting creates a secure and dramatic environment for nighttime visitors, focusing the most intense light inside the memorial pavilions. From a distance, the memorial appears as a soft glow, allowing the image of the Washington Monument to appear clearly within the Reflecting Pool.

Sculpture

- ✦ 4 bronze columns, 4 bronze eagles and 1 bronze laurel within each arch
- ✦ 24 bronze bas-relief sculptures along the ceremonial entrance (12 on each side)
- ✦ 4,000 sculpted gold stars on the Freedom Wall
- ✦ 112 bronze wreaths with armatures (2 wreaths on each pillar, one on each side)
- ✦ 52 bronze intertwined sculpted ropes between the pillars

MEMORIAL PAVILIONS

Two 43-foot-tall pavilions on the north and south ends of the plaza commemorate the victory of democracy over tyranny and serve as markers and entries to the plaza. The south pavilion commemorates the Pacific theater of war, and the north pavilion the Atlantic theater. A vertical split in the piers of the pavilions received a semi-columnar treatment similar to that of the memorial's pillars, giving them a family-like resemblance as well as increased transparency.

Bronze baldacchinos (a sculptural canopy) are an integral part of the pavilions's design. Four bronze columns support four American eagles that hold a suspended bronze laurel, the traditional symbol of victory. Inlaid on the floor of the arches is a bronze World War II victory medal surrounded by these words, also inlaid in bronze:

1941–1945 VICTORY ON LAND VICTORY AT SEA

VICTORY IN THE AIR

This is not a museum to explain the whys and wherefores of World War II. . . it's to make people think about World War II, to elicit some emotional response at the enormity of the event, at the sacrifice and at the unity of the nation, but not to tell them what to think. I'll know the memorial is a success if I see people stunned into silence when they enter the memorial precinct.

—Ray Kaskey,
Sculptor

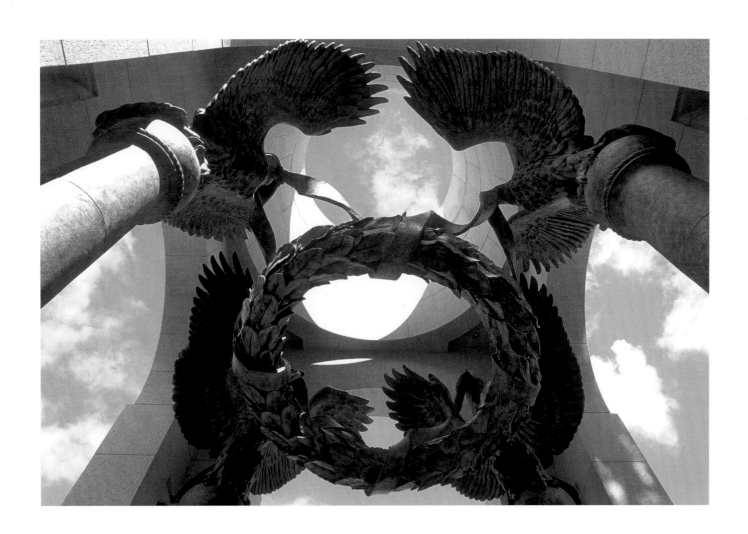

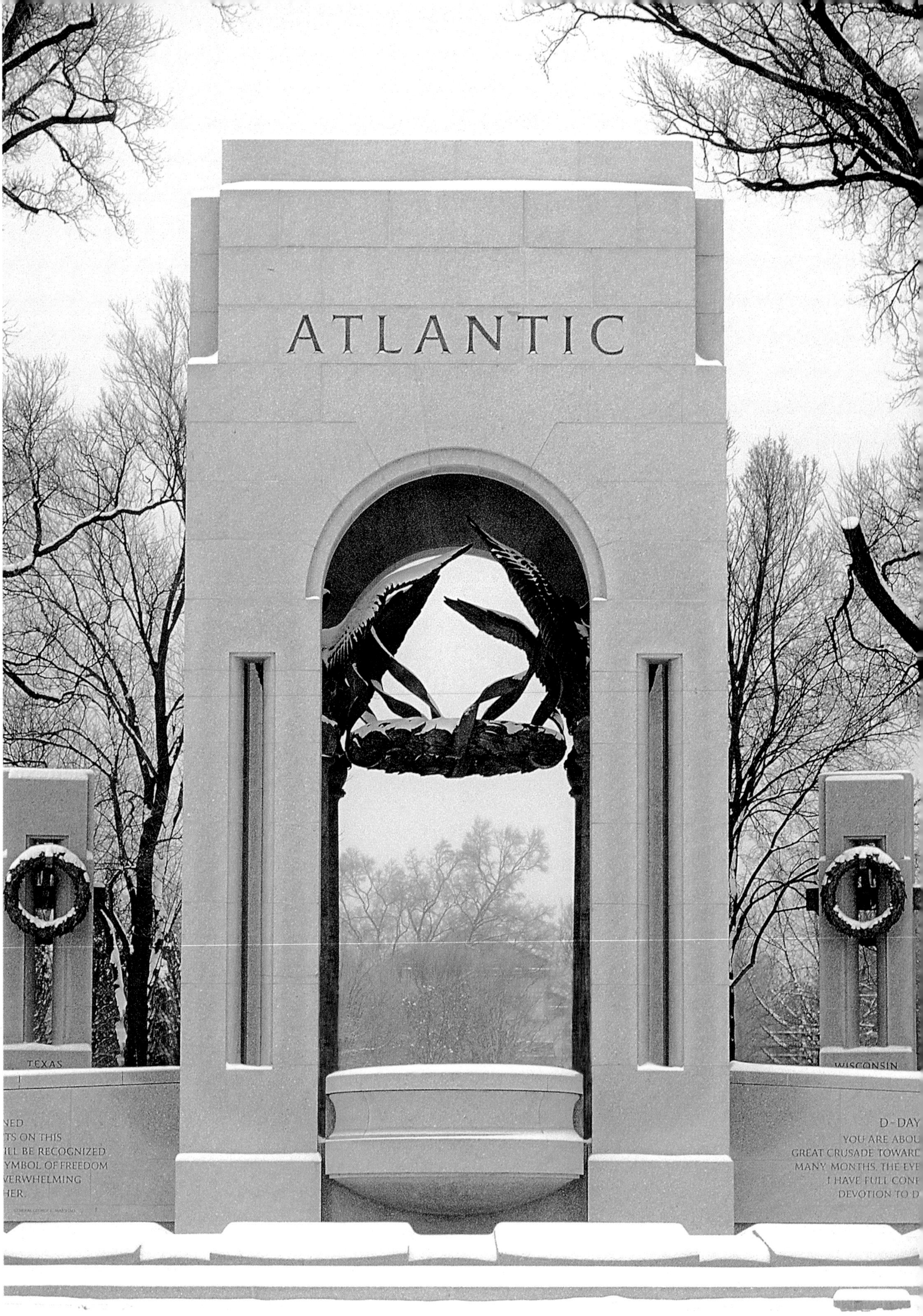

ATLANTIC

TEXAS

WISCONSIN

NED
TS ON THIS
ILL BE RECOGNIZED
YMBOL OF FREEDOM
VERWHELMING
HER.

GENERAL GEORGE C. MARSHALL

D-DAY
YOU ARE ABOU
GREAT CRUSADE TOWARE
MANY MONTHS, THE EYE
I HAVE FULL CONF
DEVOTION TO D

At the base of the Atlantic and Pacific pavilions, along the fountain copings, are inscribed theaters of war and the names of battles and places that resonate as chronicles of a global war.

On the Atlantic side of the memorial plaza, the following are inscribed on the upper and lower copings of the fountain:

NORTH AFRICA   SOUTHERN EUROPE   WESTERN EUROPE
CENTRAL EUROPE

BATTLE OF THE ATLANTIC ★ MURMANSK RUN ★ TUNISIA
★ SICILY SALERNO ANZIO ROME PO VALLEY ★ NORMANDY ★
ST.LO ★ AIR WAR IN EUROPE ★ ALSACE ★ RHINELAND
★ HUERTGEN FOREST ★ BATTLE OF THE BULGE ★
REMAGEN BRIDGE ★ GERMANY

On the fountain copings on the Pacific side of the plaza are inscribed:

CHINA   BURMA   INDIA   SOUTHWEST PACIFIC
CENTRAL PACIFIC   NORTH PACIFIC

PEARL HARBOR ★ WAKE ISLAND ★ BATAAN CORREGIDOR ★
CORAL SEA ★ MIDWAY ★ GUADALCANAL ★ NEW GUINEA
★ BUNA ★ TARAWA ★ KWAJALEIN ★ ATTU ★
SAIPAN TINIAN GUAM ★ PHILIPPINE SEA ★ PELELIU
★ LEYTE GULF ★ LUZON ★ MANILA ★ IWO JIMA ★
OKINAWA ★ JAPAN

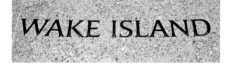

PILLARS, ROPES AND WREATHS

Fifty-six granite pillars embrace the memorial plaza in semicircular colonnades, 14 on each side of the Atlantic pavilion and 14 on each side of the Pacific pavilion. The 17-foot pillars are open in the center for greater transparency, and ample space between each allows viewing into and across the memorial.

Individually, the pillars represent the 48 states, seven territories and the District of Columbia that made up the United States during the war. They are arranged in order of precedence of entry into the union, with the name of each state, territory, or district inscribed on both sides of the pillar.

Collectively, the pillars celebrate the unprecedented unity of the nation during the Second World War and the bonding of the nation. The symbolism of "bonding" is visually reinforced by bronze, intertwined ropes that appear in the balustrade between the pillars.

Oak and wheat wreaths hang on opposite sides of each pillar. The oak, a symbol of strength used in military ornamentation, represents the military and industrial might the United States brought to bear in World War II. The wheat represents agricultural power and the nation's role during the war as the breadbasket of democracy.

The symbolism of "bonding" is visually reinforced by bronze, intertwined ropes that appear in the balustrade between the pillars.

—Friedrich St. Florian,
Design Architect

COMMEMORATIVE AREA

A commemorative area at the western side of the memorial recognizes the ultimate sacrifice of America's servicemen and women. A field of 4,000 sculpted gold stars on the Freedom Wall honors the more than 400,000 Americans who gave their lives, each star representing approximately 100 deaths.

During World War II, families hung blue stars in their windows to reflect a family member serving in uniform. When a loved one was killed, the star was changed to gold, the symbol of a family's sacrifice. On a raised coping along the edge of a quiet pool beneath the Field of Stars appears this simple yet poignant message:

HERE WE MARK THE PRICE OF FREEDOM

NATIONAL SYMBOL

The World War II Memorial has taken its rightful place among the other great monuments and memorials in the nation's capital. Through its granite structures, its bronze sculpture, and its words carved in stone, the memorial preserves the memory of a generation of Americans who, in the mid-twentieth century during the world's darkest hours, sacrificed their lives and their self-interest for the greater cause of freedom. For generations to come, this will be the World War II Memorial's commemorative message.

Dimensions

✦ Length (back of arch to back of arch): 384′

✦ Width (Freedom Wall to bottom of ceremonial entrance): 279′

✦ Plaza: 337′-10″ long; 240′-2″ wide; 6′ below grade

✦ Rainbow Pool: 246′-9″ long; 147′-8″ wide

✦ Ceremonial entrance: 148′-3″ wide; 147′-8″ long (curb to plaza)

✦ 2 Pavilions: 43′ above grade; 23′ square

✦ 56 Pillars: 17′ above grade; 4′4″ wide; 3′ deep

✦ Freedom Wall: 84′-8″ wide; 9′ high from plaza floor; 41′-9″ radius

THE WORLD WAR II MEMORIAL

AN ARCHITECTURAL PERSPECTIVE

Hugh Hardy, FAIA

The World War II Memorial has been built on the Mall in Washington, D.C., to permanently evoke memories of a global conflict that occurred more than half a century ago. It represents the hope that one generation can clarify its ambitions and accomplishments for those that follow, those who have no memory of this war's cataclysmic events, of its appalling loss of life, or the enormous sacrifices required of ordinary citizens on the home front. It commemorates years of national deprivation and commitment that produced a unity of purpose rarely seen in America.

THE DESIGN CHALLENGE

The story of the memorial's design is long and difficult. Successful remembrance of the Second World War required agreement about the memorial's purpose and location, together with consensus about its architectural language. This war's transformation of political structures and its scope of destruction were vast, and had little historical precedent. Therefore, the memorial could not depict a single encounter, nor could it be limited to statues of heroic, battle-clad figures or inscriptions on a free-standing monument. A general on horseback or a pylon with engraved names can serve the tradition of identifying a specific battle, but such artifacts cannot reflect the full power of this defining event of the 20th century. Even a tomb for the fallen could not by itself convey ideas of national unity or home-front sacrifice or the supporting role of our Allies.

Although our military presence eventually triumphed, it was equipment and provisions that came from all across America that made victory possible. Direct involvement of the nation's women, of those too old, too young, or too infirm to fight is as much a part of the story as that of the soldiers, sailors, and airmen themselves. The large, complex equestrian groupings of

HERE WE MARK THE PRICE OF FREEDOM

the Civil War Memorial at the base of the U.S. Capitol represent the effort and stress of combat and celebrate the preservation of the Union. But portrayals of human figures or sculptural representations, even of military leaders, are now regarded as too sentimental and simplistic to encompass the enormity of the Second World War. But then, what language is appropriate?

Great size by itself is not a cogent design idea for this memorial. Mt. Rushmore is an unmistakable monument, a mountain of granite carved into presidential likenesses. But it serves no commemorative purpose other than to acknowledge that these four officeholders once existed. Eero Saarinen's great 630-foot-tall arch in St. Louis is a triumph of abstract design and technology, but much of its impact derives from the time-honored symbolism of the gateway. This triumphal arch's gossamer profile looks nothing like a memorial made in Rome, but it conjures the ceremony of ancient celebrations. The USS *Arizona* Memorial at Pearl Harbor, a sunken battleship in which 1,102 sailors are entombed, serves as both a memorial and a gravesite, its sobering appearance the direct result of battle. But there is no single artifact that can give meaning to this solemn site.

As efforts to acknowledge the disaster of September 11, 2001, in New York, suggest, contemporary architectural consciousness of memorial design now resides in a modernist language, one in which forms and landscape are shorn of historical associations. Maya Lin's design for the Vietnam Veterans Memorial successfully challenges the use of historical references and heroic statuary. Traditional symbols of victory and valor do not apply to the Vietnam War, and it is generally agreed that Lin's abstract language conveys in terms appropriate to this troublesome encounter the loss and sorrow represented by a battle monument. However, despite the success of this achievement, it offers no precedent for presenting the many facets of the Second World War.

THE SITE

The memorial's site is as important as its visual language. Writing in the *New York Times*, Michael Kimmelman noted:

> Memorials seem to exist outside time. They should alter our sense of the clock, slow things down, give us a larger sense of history. While we are experiencing them, we should feel that we leave the present to consider the past and future. Perception and recollection should become synonymous, so we simultaneously sublimate death and exult in being alive. Our sense of time is the key. It cannot be rushed.

The World War II Memorial calls for creation of a place of contemplation that consciously links present with past and future, a process that would be made all but impossible by an abstract design vocabulary. Such an approach would deliberately disconnect the memorial from the context of this symbolically charged landscape.

The memorial's placement on the Mall is clearly justified. Intended as a place for reflection, it becomes important to all visitors, whether they stay only briefly or give long consideration to its configuration and topography. Suggested alternative locations, such as Constitution Gardens or a space in Freedom Plaza on Pennsylvania Avenue, could not compare. The American Battle Monuments Commission and the U.S. Commission of Fine Arts chose well. The site, once an open expanse of grass and trees surrounding the Rainbow Pool, enjoys a conspicuous location guaranteed to give the Second World War the prominence it deserves. To the east stands the Washington Monument, a 555-foot-tall marble obelisk commemorating our founding president and the formation of the Union in the 18th century. This monument's simplicity, isolation, and classical associations give it distinction. To the west sits Abraham Lincoln, surveying the Reflecting Pool and symbolizing the reuniting of the states and the abolition of slavery in the 19th century. The elegance of Henry Bacon's Doric temple coupled with the eloquence of Lincoln's words, the raised site, and the skill of the sculpture by Daniel Chester French gives this memorial a powerful presence. The World War II Memorial is complemented by comparison with these two neighbors that celebrate the accomplishments of previous centuries, and it is appropriate to commemorate America's leadership role in the 20th century on this site.

ORIGINS OF THE MEMORIAL

Program ideas for the memorial were outlined in a 1996 call for entries in a two-stage design program. The designer was asked to provide physical forms that expressed abstract ideas. The call stated that the memorial's design should:

✦ Convey a sense of remembrance and national pride in the fortitude, valor, suffering, and sacrifice of its fighting forces and their heroic accomplishments.

✦ Acknowledge and honor the Nation at Large, the patriotism and vigorous, spirited commitment of the American people to the war effort and the Home Front's vital contribution to the victory won.

✦ Stand for all time as an important symbol of American national unity, a timeless reminder of the moral strength and awesome power that can flow when a free people are at once united and bonded together in a common and just cause.

✦ Strive to capture in architectural form, memorial art, inscribed words, and landscaped setting, the stirring spirit and meaning of this unique moment in American history, a moment in time which, in profound ways, changed forever the face of American life and the direction of world history.

As the design progressed, program elements, plaza configuration, and sculptural concepts were adjusted. Sloping earthen mounds beyond the two colonnades, containing galleries, public facilities, and an auditorium, were removed from the Rainbow Pool site, but these omissions did not change the integrity of St. Florian's design. In fact, the newfound openness that resulted only increased the grandeur of the memorial when approached from north or south. In the semicircular colonnade's evolution from classically inspired abstract shafts without capitals to open-slotted granite piers, the geometry of the design remains intact. Further adjustments in the landscape, paving, and height of the plaza and Rainbow Pool have strengthened the design's clarity.

CLASSICAL ALLUSIONS

It was Thomas Jefferson who determined that the architecture of Washington, D.C., should make a conscious attempt to identify our new democracy with that of ancient Greece and early Rome. Subsequently, architects in the 18th, 19th, and 20th centuries have created in Washington an urban composition of classical elements—columns and cornices, pediments and domes—that unite our capital city. The central Mall, the landscaped vista through Washington's monumental core proposed in Senator James McMillan's 1901 Plan, establishes the capital as a place of honor, built to house cultural institutions and impressive monuments of national significance. Contemporary design theory accepts the axial plan but suggests the Mall's future architecture should abandon the classical tradition, replacing it with an abstract language free of historical reference. For some this is the *only* expression appropriate to our time. However, such an approach would isolate the World War II Memorial from its monumental neighbors, breaking with the historical values they represent, announcing that new values are in play which deny the historical linkages that have long characterized Washington's architecture.

The original instructions to entrants in the competition stated:

> The monuments and buildings in and around the Mall are for the most part classical in character. The strong presence of the Washington Monument, the Lincoln and Jefferson Memorials, the White House and its grounds, and the Mall itself, provide a formal context to which the designer of the WWII Memorial may wish to respond, but the choice of design philosophy and style guiding the proposed memorial design are to be the prerogative of the designer. The resulting work, however, must be respectful of and compatible in configuration and quality with its historic surroundings.

Entrants were therefore free to explore an abstract style if it was "respectful and compatible." Many did. In fact, of the six final designs, only Friedrich St.Florian's held any overt classical references. By complementing the original McMillan plan for the Mall through landscape and classical references, his approach created significant associations with the other monuments and traditions found in Washington. Even though no single element of the memorial directly replicates a classical form, the design resonates with the Mall's architectural traditions. More important, it was the making of a place, not the creation of an object, that was St.Florian's goal. In the end, the jury selected his design unanimously.

St.Florian's materials for the World War II Memorial speak of permanence. By using granite and bronze, he connects his design with the classical vocabulary of Washington, emphasizing a continuity of expression that extends back to the origins of Western architecture. His design presents our wartime victory as a continuation of the "American Experiment," founded when General Washington took office, tested under Abraham Lincoln, and validated by the Second World War. The memorial is a complex amalgam, one that overlays abstract classical forms on a strong, simple geometric premise. Its intent is abstract: to symbolize significant events that happened in more than one place and time, all culminating with victory. It celebrates a great conflict that galvanized the United States's resolve to defend our democratic society.

A FITTING DESIGN

The World War II Memorial translates historical memory into built forms that now become a permanent part of the Mall's landscape. It consists of 56 granite pillars (representing all states, territories, and the District of Columbia) set in two arcs, each containing a central pavilion. These arcs define a sunken plaza set with a central ornamental pool through which pass the major axis of the Mall and a minor north-south axis connecting to the surrounding landscape. Taken all together, these elements define a new public precinct.

This achievement, of a recessed plaza symmetrically set on the Mall's major axis, makes the smallest possible intrusion on views from either of the two adjacent monuments, but it also contributes a contemplative space of powerful meaning. Its broken embrace set with two arcs of pillars suggests the home front's coming together to realize strength in unity. Two small pavilions, one to the north and the other to the south, contain the sculptor Ray Kaskey's victorious eagles carrying in their beaks a beribboned wreath, symbolizing victory in the Atlantic and Pacific theaters. Overlooking fountains and inscriptions, these pavilions emphasize the global aspect of the conflict. Finally, central to the composition, the Freedom Wall contains 4,000 gold stars honoring the 400,000 fallen Americans.

Sculptural detail by Kaskey is omnipresent, both embellishing and humanizing the memorial. Classical precedents—wreaths, eagles, entwined ropes, bas reliefs, and emblems—give human scale to vast stone surfaces, providing decorative texture that also encourages a welcome play of light and shade. These sculptural elements are set apart from the more abstract blocks of stone, providing further links with the Mall's classical imagery. Their presence gives the total composition clear association with ideas of valor, and it honors the transforming events represented by the memorial.

Drawing on 19th-century tradition, Kaskey's work employs literary allusion and sculptural motifs to represent human virtues and heroic concepts. For instance, eagles represent America, and oak-leaf wreaths have funereal associations. Both are used to embellish St. Florian's design, while gold stars represent those killed in battle, and intertwined ropes symbolize the union of the states on the home front. Such elements can be "read" by the public and are an intrinsic part of the memorial's language.

Twenty-four bronze panels line the walls of the ceremonial entrance, giving an element of narrative to the design. These panels provide a chronology of the war, and although such elements are familiar, their execution does not yield to cliché. Rather, their clear composition permits the public to easily understand their narrative intent. Aside from the visual language used in the memorial, actual carved words—battle names and inscriptions—attest to the war's scope and progress. Quotations by presidents and military leaders are engraved in the granite, memorializing the war's aspirations and accomplishments and supporting the design as a whole. In the Rainbow Pool, the reintroduction of a curtain of water produces rainbows with its spray on sunny days; and jets of water add a welcoming sense of light and life.

Night illumination of the memorial also forms an essential ingredient of its design, whether one is outside the site looking in, or within looking out. Fixtures unobtrusively tucked into its surfaces provide a wash of lighting that permits essential features of the memorial to be seen, glowing in the blackness of night. In the evening, along 17th Street, the framed view of the Lincoln Memorial across the Reflecting Pool is one of the great sights in Washington; it is unimpeded by the World War II Memorial.

The grand sweep of achievement represented by the Second World War more than justifies this memorial's prominence on the Mall with an architecture that attests to our republic's longevity. Although physically changeless, it will become a place whose meaning only deepens over time. This accomplishment creates a place for contemplation and inspiration by combining ambitious physical scope, handsome materials, clear symbolism, eloquent inscriptions, and the beauty of an unequalled site.

PART II
AMERICA
AT WAR

★

VICTORY
AT SEA

Thomas B. Allen

"December 7, 1941, a date which will live in infamy . . . No matter how long it may take us to overcome this premeditated invasion, the American people in their righteous might will win through to absolute victory."

—President Franklin D. Roosevelt

BIRTH OF THE TWO-OCEAN NAVY

Spread across Tokyo Bay on September 2, 1945, was the mightiest display of sea power ever seen. Beyond the battleship *Missouri*, where the Japanese signed the surrender document, were seven more U.S. Navy battleships, including the *West Virginia*, which Japanese bombs and torpedoes had seemingly doomed 44 months before. There were two U.S. aircraft carriers, 11 U.S. cruisers, 47 destroyers and destroyer escorts, 12 submarines, 12 minesweepers, 12 high-speed transports, and dozens of the landing craft that had carried Marines and sailors to blood-stained beaches.

Beneath the broad Pacific were Japanese carriers, cruisers, destroyers, and the pride of the Imperial Japanese Navy, the superbattleships *Musashi* and *Yamato*, the largest dreadnoughts ever built. The biggest Japanese warship still afloat was the battered battleship *Nagato*, once the flagship of Admiral Isoroku Yamamoto, the architect of the attack on Pearl Harbor. In July 1946 she would be towed to Bikini Atoll and used as a target in a test of atomic bombs.

Only a decade earlier the armada arrayed in Toyko Bay had been a mere dream of American naval leaders. The U.S. Navy then was second-rate and fading away. From 1929 to 1933, not a single U.S. warship had been built. Then, in 1933, despite the Great Depression, America's shipbuilders and aviation plants began getting Navy contracts. The National Industrial Recovery Act authorized the building of carriers, cruisers, submarines, destroyers, and aircraft. The Roosevelt Administration, reacting to Japanese expansion in the Pacific, was bringing back the Navy.

The renaissance of the U.S. Navy began in the summer of 1933 when Congress allotted $238 million for new naval construction. Nearly $40 million of that money went to the building of two aircraft carriers, the *Yorktown*, whose keel was laid on May 21, 1934, and the *Enterprise*, whose keel was laid two months later. The men who built them included workers paid by the Works Progress Administration, a New Deal employment program.

Although the Navy still revered the battleship, the building of the carriers signaled the start of U.S. airpower at sea. Carrier aircraft would defy the vastness of the Pacific, challenging the Japanese as they extended their empire and imposed a "new order" in the form of the Greater East Asia Co-prosperity Sphere. Japan's thrust into Asia, especially into China, inspired America's decision to build up the Navy. But it would be in the Atlantic that the U.S. Navy would first encounter Japan's ally, Nazi Germany.

AN UNEASY NEUTRALITY

For the U.S. Navy, World War II started not on December 7, 1941, but when American warships joined the Royal Navy and the Royal Canadian Navy in the Battle of the Atlantic, the longest battle of the war—a struggle for Britain's survival that began on September 3, 1939, the day Great Britain and France declared war against Germany in response to Hitler's invasion of their ally, Poland. On that opening day, in the Atlantic northwest of Ireland, the captain of the German submarine U-30 fired torpedoes without warning at the British passenger liner *Athenia*, which was carrying 1,100 passengers to the United States; 112 lives were lost, including 28 Americans. The sinking symbolized what was to come: Although war raged in both Asia and Europe, the United States could not be isolated from that war. Americans, entering a war zone on a passenger liner, had died in a war that was not yet theirs.

Within days, President Franklin D. Roosevelt ordered the U.S. Navy to begin a Neutrality Patrol, which would track—but not attack—any "belligerent" surface ship, submarine, or warplane approaching the U.S. Atlantic coast. Theoretically, Britain and France were just as much belligerent nations as Germany, but in reality Roosevelt was girding the nation for potential war against Nazi Germany. "This nation will remain a neutral nation," Roosevelt said, "but I cannot ask that every American remain neutral in thought as well." From then until December 7, 1941, the Navy was a seagoing instrument of America's "all aid short of war" policy.

On September 8, Roosevelt proclaimed a "limited national emergency," hoping that the flow of U.S. arms to Britain would be enough for them to defeat Germany. But his hope was slight. The United States, he knew, could not long remain on the sidelines of the war. On September 13 he called Congress into special session to add a "cash-and-carry" provision to the Neutrality Act: Belligerents could purchase arms as long as they paid in cash and carried off the arms in their own ships. Technically, the law authorized the sales of arms to any belligerent nation, but clearly Congress' intent was the legalizing of arms sales to England and France for their war against Germany.

Two days before calling Congress into session, Roosevelt began a long

(Previous page)
Task Force 38 of the U.S. Third Fleet maneuvering off the coast of Japan, August 17, 1945—two days after Japan agreed to surrender. The aircraft carrier in lower right is USS Wasp *(CV-18). Also present in the formation are five other Essex class carriers, four light carriers, at least three battleships, plus several cruisers and destroyers.*

Officers on the bridge of a destroyer, escorting a large convoy of ships, keep a sharp lookout for attacking submarines, ca. 1942

private correspondence with Winston Churchill. The foundation of what would become a warm friendship was their affection for their navies. During World War I Roosevelt had served as Assistant Secretary of the Navy and Churchill had been First Lord of the Admiralty. In 1939 Churchill again had been appointed to that post—prompting Royal Navy officers to display "Winston's back!" on many signal halyards.

In the first few months of the war, there were no ground battles in western Europe. U.S. and British journalists called the lull the Phony War. But it was a real war for the Royal Navy, British merchant ships, and the ships of the U.S. Neutrality Patrol. By the end of the first month of the war, U-boats had sunk 41 merchant ships and the First Lord knew that his island nation's fate would be determined by how much material aid the British could receive from the United States and Canada. By Churchill's reckoning, each day about 120,000 tons of cargo—at least 20 ships—had to arrive in British ports for his country to survive and defeat Nazi Germany.

In May 1940, the Phony War suddenly ended when a German blitzkrieg roared through the Low Countries and into France. British Prime Minister Neville Chamberlain, who had proclaimed "peace for our time" after appeasing Adolf Hitler in 1938, immediately resigned, and Churchill became prime minister. Belgium, the Netherlands, Norway, and Denmark fell before the Nazi onslaught. French forces fought bravely in the face of overwhelming odds but after suffering 300,000 casualties, including 120,000 killed, in only a few weeks, France surrendered on June 24th. Britain stood alone as, night after night, bombs fell on London.

U-boats, now slipping out of bombproof pens on the French coast, had a more direct access to shipping lanes and victorious German armies faced an isolated, poorly armed Britain across the English Channel. On July 16, 1940, Hitler issued a directive: "As England, in spite of the hopelessness of her military situation, has so far shown herself unwilling to come to any compromise, I have therefore decided to begin to prepare for, and, if necessary, to carry out, an invasion of England."

Churchill, running the war from his London air-raid shelter—the Cabinet War Rooms, in a basement deep below Whitehall—watched a map of the Atlantic dotted with more and more pins that marked lost ships and their precious cargoes. He beseeched Roosevelt for destroyers to be manned by the Royal Navy as escorts for convoys sailing from Halifax to Britain. "It has now become most urgent for you to let us have the destroyers," he wrote to Roosevelt in June 1940. ". . . Mr. President, with great respect I must tell you that in the long history of the world this is a thing to do now."

Many members of Congress, as well as many U.S. Navy officers, were against giving warships to a belligerent nation, for they saw it as a move that would drag the United States into the European war. But Roosevelt persevered, transforming the would-be gift into an extraordinary swap: 50 overage destroyers to Britain in exchange for 99-year leases on British naval and air bases in the Western Hemisphere. The first eight ships were handed over to British crews at Halifax on September 9; the others followed rapidly. All were crammed with provisions, ammunition, depth charges, and torpedoes.

Later that month, Roosevelt signed into law the first peacetime draft in U.S. history. Meanwhile, Germany, Italy, and Japan signed the Tripartite Pact and became the Axis powers, agreeing to come to each other's aid if attacked by any nation not yet in the war. Roosevelt explained the significance of the pact in one of his "fireside chats," as he called his radio speeches. "Never before," he said on December 29, 1940, ". . . has our American civilization been in such danger as now. By an agreement signed in Berlin, three powerful nations, two in Europe and one in Asia, joined themselves together" in "a program aimed against the United States." To thwart the plans of the Axis, he said, "We must be the great arsenal of democracy."

Congress, which had authorized the naval elements of that arsenal during the Depression, in June 1940 passed what became known as the "Two-Ocean Navy" act. The Navy immediately began awarding contracts for warships that would include 12 aircraft carriers and seven battleships.

PRELUDE TO WAR

By the beginning of 1941, the United States was on the threshold of war. Roosevelt won from Congress a new law dubbed the Lend-Lease Act, which gave him the power to "sell, transfer title to, exchange, lease, lend, or otherwise dispose of" any matériel whose transfer would, in his opinion, help U.S. defense. Three hours after signing the act into law, Roosevelt ordered 28 PT

Admiral Ernest J. King

Gunners from the British Navy are instructed by American Naval gunners in the operation of a secret device that is part of the guns aboard destroyers turned over to Britain as part of the Lend-Lease Act, September 12, 1940.

boats and submarine chasers turned over to the Royal Navy. Churchill called Lend-Lease "Hitler's death warrant."

At Churchill's request, Roosevelt sent Marines to Iceland, replacing British solders needed to defend the British Isles. Marines were sent because they were volunteers, unlike the newest members of the U.S. Army: draftees, who could not be ordered overseas. (To prevent the Germans from gaining a foothold in the Western Hemisphere, British troops had begun occupying Iceland, a Danish colony, after Germany invaded Denmark.)

For five days in August, Churchill and Roosevelt secretly met in Placentia Bay, Newfoundland, alternating their sessions between the U.S. cruiser Augusta and the British battleship *Prince of Wales*. They signed the Atlantic Charter, which proclaimed that their nations were united to fight the Axis "to ensure life, liberty, independence and religious freedom and to preserve the rights of man and justice." The charter, which came close to a joint declaration of war, said that aggressor nations must be disarmed. (The charter's principles laid the foundation for the United Nations.)

The U.S. Atlantic Fleet was under the command of Admiral Ernest J. King, a tough, stubborn, and brilliant officer. Later, when he became Chief of Naval Operations, he explained his advancements in these words: "When they get in trouble, they send for us sons-of-bitches." His order to the Neutrality Patrol was characteristically terse: "Destroy hostile forces that threaten shipping."

On September 4, about 200 miles southwest of Iceland, the U.S. destroyer *Greer* was steaming alone when a British aircraft spotted a German

U-boat on the surface and notified the *Greer*. The destroyer went to general quarters, caught up with the submarine, and maintained sonar contact. The aircraft dropped depth charges at random and flew off. The U-boat, apparently believing that the *Greer* had attacked, turned on the destroyer, firing a single torpedo. The *Greer* counter-attacked with depth charges, and the U-boat fired a second torpedo at the destroyer. Both ships then broke off contact.

President Roosevelt told the nation about the encounter in a radio address, saying, "It was not the first nor the last act of piracy which the Nazi Government has committed against the American flag in this war." He described several other incidents at sea and called on Americans "to stop being deluded by the romantic notion

"Sub Commander"

I graduated from the Naval Academy in June of 1938, and at that point I decided I wanted to get into submarines. So after I graduated in September of 1940, I was ordered to the submarine R4, SS #81, a small non-air conditioned World War I type submarine, barely able to make a trip from New London to Key West without stopping en route. I spent a year in her and during that time, I married the girl across the river, Sylvia, and we're still married after 62 years (see her interview in "Women in World War II"). Then I was ordered to Portsmouth, New Hampshire, to assist in commissioning the USS *Drum*, the lead ship of a new class of submarines being built in Portsmouth. I was assigned as the torpedo and gunnery officer.

On Sunday morning December 7th, 1941, my wife was listening to the radio and said, "My gosh, listen to this!" We heard the attack on Pearl Harbor. I rushed back to the shipyard. She went on home. On February 17th, we headed for Pearl Harbor. The impact of the Japanese surprise attack on Pearl Harbor made a strong impression on all of the junior officers on the *Drum*.

We were out there to fire torpedoes and sink ships. Early in the war, torpedo performance was poor; some ran too deep and therefore didn't explode; some exploded as soon as they were armed, like at 400 yards, and that was a big jolt. We had one case where we had a single ship off the coast of Japan, like a sitting duck, but the skipper saw the torpedo hit the side of the ship, bounce up and break in half, and there was no explosion.

We got our indoctrination on the very first night that we entered Japanese waters south of Tokyo. In the full moon we sighted a very large ship and in seven minutes we fired our first torpedoes, on the surface, something that submarines never did before World War II, never. We succeeded in hitting this ship, but as a result, his escorts became very angry and forced us down. They counter-attacked, and for the next 22 hours, dropped sporadic depth charges, these were the first that the officers and crew had ever heard in combat. Now a depth charge is a difficult weapon to counter. You never were sure exactly when they were going to drop. As time passed during the war, we learned that if you could hear the detonator of the depth charge go off before the main charge exploded, you knew it was very close. And the submarine was evading, changing course, speed and depth. We probably heard 100 depth charges that night. It was clear to me and I'm sure to everyone else, that where the last depth charge went off was not important, the question was, where was the next one going to go off? Most of the submarines that were lost in actual combat were lost to depth charges.

By the middle of 1944, I was commanding officer of the *Drum*. We were ordered north to the Luzon Straits, which is the area between the north end of the Philippines and Taiwan Island. And the very next day, MacArthur came with hundreds of ships and made his landing and uttered his famous remark, "I have returned." *Drum* got to an area in the Luzon Straits, and in 48 hours, we fired 24 torpedoes, sank three ships and damaged three more. That won me my Navy Cross.

Admiral Morris H. Rindskopf

On several of our successful attacks during the war, we had been alerted to a target coming our way because the Navy was intercepting Japanese operational traffic under a system which was highly classified, known as Ultra. Only the skipper and the executive officer were privy to the messages. Ultra was a significant element in the success of submarine force.

Once I decoded a message and it said that along about 10:00 that morning, we should see a ship was at a certain place, a certain course, certain speed. I went to my state room and donned a yellow Aloha shirt. About 10:00, battle stations were sounded. We attacked the ship and we sank it. And nobody asked me any questions about the Aloha shirt, but we chalked up one more ship. On the next patrol, the same thing happened. I put on my yellow Aloha shirt and lo and behold, every crew member put on a yellow Aloha shirt, and again we were successful and sank the ship.

that the Americas can go on living happily and peacefully in a Nazi-dominated world."

American, Canadian, and British navies had established a handing-off process for protecting British-bound convoys. Royal Canadian Navy corvettes escorted merchant ships from Halifax to the Western Ocean Meeting Point, south of Newfoundland. From there, the U.S. Navy took over, shepherding convoys to the Mid-Ocean Meeting Point, where Royal Navy ships, based in Iceland, picked up the convoy. On October 17, the U.S. destroyer *Kearny* was in her hand-off zone when a torpedo hit and ripped open her starboard side. Eleven men were killed and 24 wounded. "The shooting war has started," Roosevelt declared. Two weeks later, another U.S. destroyer, the *Reuben James*, was escorting a convoy when a torpedo struck her, setting off ammunition in the forward magazine and splitting the ship in two. The forward section sank with all hands. Depth charges in the stern section exploded as it sank. The concussions killed men in the water hoping for rescue. Other destroyers saved 46 men, but 115 lives were lost.

Americans now were dying in the Atlantic in the undeclared war with Germany. In the Pacific, America had long been confronting another member of the Axis, imperial Japan. And, while America girded for a war across the Atlantic, Japan was preparing for war against America.

THE RISING SUN

Japan's first armed aggression against the United States came on December 12, 1937, when Japanese warplanes bombed the U.S. river gunboat *Panay* on the Yangtze River. She was the first U.S. warship sunk by enemy action in the 20th century. The *Panay* had originally been sent to China as part of the U.S. Navy's Yangtze Patrol to combat pirates and warlords who were interfering with American interests and commercial shipping. After the Japanese invaded China in November 1937, the *Panay* and other U.S. vessels evacuated most of the American Embassy staff from the capital of Nanking (now Nanjing). On December 11th the last Americans from the embassy came on board the *Panay*, as did several newsmen and a few foreigners. She then moved upriver to avoid becoming involved in the fighting around the capital. Three American merchant tankers moved upstream with her. The senior Japanese naval commander in Shanghai was informed of this movement, a precaution taken to avoid accidental attacks by Japanese forces.

Next day, nine Japanese naval bombers bombed and sank the *Panay*, which had two large American flags spread out on her awnings. Three U.S. sailors and an Italian on the ship were killed and 43 other Navy men and five civilians were wounded. On the same day, Japanese bombers also attacked two American merchant ships and a Japanese Army artillery regiment shelled a British gunboat and took her into custody.

In April 1938, when the Japanese government paid an indemnity of $2.2

million, both nations officially closed the incident. But the sinking of the *Panay* angered many Americans and strengthened a U.S. policy that tilted toward China in its war against Japan. Little more than a year after the *Panay* sinking, the United States said that it would probably allow its commercial treaty with Japan to expire in January 1940—a move that would have disastrous consequences for a nation poor in resources. Japan had become extraordinarily dependent upon the United States, which supplied Japan with 66 percent of its oil, virtually all of its aviation fuel, 91 percent of its copper, and 90 percent of the metal scrap that Japan vitally needed in lieu of iron in its own soil.

Although the United States assured Japan that U.S.-Japanese trade could continue without the treaty, Japan, worried about its future, looked to another source: the Asian colonies controlled by France and the Netherlands, now conquered by Germany. As a member of the Axis, Japan won from Germany the right to occupy French Indochina, where Japan would find bases for further expansion and acquisition of Southeast Asia's oil, rubber, tin, quinine and timber. In September 1940, Japanese troops marched into Indochina and planned the seizure of the oil-rich Dutch East Indies (now Indonesia). The United States responded by cutting off exports of oil, iron, steel, and rubber to Japan.

In April 1940, U.S. warships participated in exercises, using the naval base at Pearl Harbor, on the Hawaiian island of Oahu. When the exercise ended, the warships were to return to their home ports in California. But as

Navy fighter pilots in the ready room of their aircraft carrier before a strike in the Pacific.

a deterrent to Japanese moves against Indochina, President Roosevelt ordered them to remain at Pearl Harbor, which became headquarters of the newly constituted Pacific Fleet in February 1941. When Admiral James O. Richardson, commander in chief of the fleet, protested, Roosevelt fired him. Roosevelt named Rear Admiral Husband E. Kimmel as Richardson's replacement and promoted him to full admiral.

By the fall of 1941, diplomatic relations between Japan and the United States had cooled over such issues as the Japanese invasion of Indochina, U.S. aid to China, and the cutting off of U.S. resources. With only a six months' supply of petroleum available in Japan, the Cabinet fell and the Minister of War, General Hideki Tojo, became prime minister. More soldier than statesman, Tojo oversaw a nation mobilizing for war. Gasoline was rationed, prices fixed, newspapers censored, and secret police were enforcing laws against "dangerous thoughts." If the Japanese people "merge into one in iron solidarity," Tojo said after his appointment, "nothing can stop us.... Wars can be fought with ease."

With Japan's military primed for war, Tojo reiterated Japanese demands: the United States must end aid to China, accept the Japanese seizure of Indochina, resume normal trade, and not reinforce U.S. bases in the Far East. He publicly maintained that the demands were not negotiable and set a deadline for American acceptance. But, unaware that U.S. code-breakers were reading Japanese diplomatic dispatches, he told the Japanese ambassador to the United States, Kichisaburo Nomura, that negotiations were still possible.

Talks between Secretary of State Cordell Hull and Nomura, aided by special envoy Saburo Kurusu, showed that the two nations were at an impasse. On November 26, Hull once more stated the U.S. position, which centered on a Japanese withdrawal from China and Indochina. Viewing Hull's statement as an "ultimatum," Tojo cocked the gun of war.

LAUNCHING OPERATION HAWAII

Of all Japanese military leaders, Admiral Isoruku Yamamoto, Commander in Chief of the Japanese Combined Fleet, was perhaps the most aware of the quality and the industrial capacity of the enemy he would face if Japan went to war against the United States. He had been a member of an advisory team that accompanied Navy Minister Tomasaburo Kato to the 1921–22 naval conference in Washington, D.C. He had studied English at Harvard and later served as Japanese naval attaché in Washington. Like most Japanese admirals, he knew that Japan could never match the United States in resources.

If "hostilities break out between Japan and the United States," he said, "it would not be enough that we take Guam and the Philippines, nor even Hawaii and San Francisco. To make victory certain, we would have to march into Washington and dictate the terms of peace in the White House. I wonder whether the politicians of the day really have the willingness to make sacrifices, and the confidence, that this would entail." Despite his reluctance, Yamamoto went ahead with his plan. He was a fervent gambler, and he heeded his instinct for high-stakes rolls of the dice by conceiving the idea of a preemptive attack on the U.S. Pacific Fleet at Pearl Harbor. He believed that if he could destroy the U.S. battleships and aircraft carriers, there would be no interference with Japanese offensive actions in the Pacific for six months. Tojo agreed to the plan, and on the southern Japanese island of Kyushu, carrier pilots began practicing attacks on simulated targets in Kagoshima Bay, which resembled Pearl Harbor.

In mid-November, ships of the Operation Hawaii strike force converged at Hitokappu Bay on the island of Etorofu in the bleak Kuril Islands, north of Japan's Home Islands. There were six large carriers with almost 400 aircraft, two battleships, three cruisers, and nine destroyers. The warships were loaded with drums of fuel oil, and fuel was carried in the double bottoms of the carriers, a practice usually forbidden. There were also eight oilers for refueling. Three large fleet submarines accompanied the surface ships. On November 26, with radio transmitters sealed to ensure radio silence, the strike force headed east. Twenty-seven other fleet submarines separately headed for Oahu to torpedo any U.S. warships that managed to escape from the aerial onslaught on Pearl Harbor. Five of these submarines carried two-man midget submarines to slip into the harbor before the air attack and add to the devastation. While the ships of the Hawaii Operation headed toward Pearl Harbor, ships of the Southern Operation, coordinated to strike immediately after the Pearl Harbor attack, left Japan for invasions of the U.S. colony of the Philippines, British Malaya, and the Dutch East Indies.

On December 2 (Tokyo time), Yamamoto sent the strike force a message: CLIMB MOUNT NIITAKA 1208. The message, naming Japan's highest mountain (on Taiwan, then part of Japan), authorized the attack and ordered its date: December 8. At Pearl Harbor that date would be Sunday, December 7, 1941.

Admiral Kimmel had received a "war warning" from Washington on November 27. The same day, Lieutenant General Walter C. Short, commander of U.S. Army forces in Hawaii, received a message from Washington saying "Japanese . . . hostile action possible at any moment." Kimmel, not wishing to frighten Hawaii's civilians, did not raise the alert status. But, in an offensive move, he sent the carriers *Enterprise* and *Lexington*, with escorts, to deliver warplanes to Midway Island, about 1,300 miles west of Pearl Harbor, and Wake Island, about 650 miles west of Midway. Following Army doctrine to defend against sabotage, Short massed Army aircraft in wingtip-to-wingtip arrays.

On December 2, Kimmel was reading a report from his intelligence officer. He looked up from the paper and said to the officer, "What! You don't know where the carriers are?" The officer told about a baffling lull in Japanese fleet radio traffic. Kimmel asked, "Do you mean to say they could be rounding Diamond Head and you wouldn't know it?" The officer said he hoped that the carriers would be spotted by the time they reached that Oahu landmark

On one of those vanished Japanese carriers, the *Akagi*, Commander

(Next page)
Photograph taken from a Japanese plane during the torpedo attack on ships moored on both sides of Ford Island. View looks about east, with the supply depot, submarine base and fuel tank farm in the right center distance.
A torpedo has just hit USS West Virginia *on the far side of Ford Island (center). Other battleships moored nearby are (from left):* Nevada, Arizona, Tennessee *(inboard of* West Virginia*),* Oklahoma *(torpedoed and listing) alongside* Maryland, *and* California. *On the near side of Ford Island, to the left, are light cruisers* Detroit *and* Raleigh, *target and training ship* Utah *and seaplane tender* Tangier. Raleigh *and* Utah *have been torpedoed, and* Utah *is listing sharply to port. A Japanese plane is visible in the right center (over Ford Island).*

Mitsuo Fuchida, who would lead the attack on Pearl Harbor, worked out signals for his bombers. Their radios had telegraph keys, not microphones. Using the Japanese phonetic-symbol adaptation to Morse code, Fuchida would send two easily recognized signals: .. _ .. (to), meaning the attack was launched and _ _ _ (ra), meaning it was a "surprise." Coincidentally, *tora* means "tiger" in Japanese.

DECEMBER 7, 1941

At 6:45 a.m. on December 7, Pearl Harbor time, the destroyer *Ward* spotted a small submarine on the surface and moved in for the kill. Her captain, Lieutenant William W. Outerbridge, who had been in command for only two days, ordered his men to commence firing. The first shot missed. The second struck at the waterline and the submarine heeled over and sank. Outerbridge reported the attack, in code, to headquarters at Pearl Harbor. By the time the decrypted message reached Kimmel, the Japanese strike force was 230 miles north of Oahu and the first wave of 183 planes, led by Fuchida, had taken off from the pitching decks of the Japanese carriers.

Around the time the *Ward* fired the first shots of the war against Japan, Washington clocks struck noon. That morning, U.S. code breakers had deciphered the last part of a 14-part message sent from Tokyo to the Japanese Embassy in Washington. The message ended with a notice that U.S.-Japanese negotiations, which had been going on since November 27, were to be broken off at 1 P.M. Washington time (7:30 A.M. Hawaii time).

On Oahu, at 7:02, a radar station picked up blips indicating that a large number of planes were approaching the northern coast. One of the radar operators reported the sighting by telephone to a duty officer who dismissed the report. When he hung up, the blips showed the planes were 88 miles away.

The first wave of 183 Japanese planes struck at 7:55 A.M. Most of the U.S. Pacific Fleet was at anchor at Pearl Harbor, including eight of the fleet's nine battleships, moored along Battleship Row. At airfields around Oahu, there were some 250 Navy, Marine, and Army Air Corps planes, most of them wingtip-to-wingtip in neat lines. Fuchida sent the message: *to ra to ra to ra.* A surprise attack.

The first wave swooped down on the battleships and airfields; a second wave would strike other ships and shipyard facilities. Bombs and torpedoes smashed into the battleships, and one by one they sank at their berths. The *Oklahoma*, struck by as many as seven torpedoes, rolled over, her masts digging into the harbor's mud bottom and hundreds of men trapped within her hull. A bomb hit the main deck of the battleship *Arizona* and penetrated into the forward magazine, where it exploded. In less than nine minutes, she sank with 1,177 of her crew. The *Utah*, a target ship that attackers had been told to ignore, was hit by two torpedoes and capsized, killing at least 58 men. Two torpedoes and a bomb hit the *California*, which settled on the bottom. The *Pennsylvania*, in drydock, was slightly damaged when a 551-pound bomb went through two decks and exploded. Two duds bounded onto the *Tennessee*. One bomb hit the *Maryland*.

(Previous pages, 56-57)
The forward magazine of USS Shaw explodes during the second Japanese attack wave at Pearl Harbor. To the left of the explosion, Shaw's stern is visible, at the end of floating drydock YFD-2. At right is the bow of USS Nevada, with a tug alongside fighting fires.
(58-59)
Sailors stand amid wrecked planes at the Ford Island seaplane base, watching as USS Shaw explodes in the center background. USS Nevada is also visible in the middle background, with her bow headed toward the left. Planes present include PBY Catalina, OS2U Kingfisher, and SOC Seagull types. Wrecked wing in the foreground is from a PBY.

Battleships West Virginia *(sunken at left) and* Tennessee *shrouded in smoke following the Japanese air raid.*

Two bombs and six or seven torpedoes hit the *West Virginia* on her port side, knocking out all power. Her captain, Mervyn S. Bennion, struck by shrapnel, lay on the bridge, giving orders until he died. As the ship listed and threatened to capsize, crewmen managed to open valves for counter-flooding. She settled into the ooze of the seafloor. Of the more than 1,400 men on board, 105 were lost; of the 87 officers, 52 were wounded.

The *Nevada*, holed by one torpedo, got underway during the attack, and, as she slowly groped toward the harbor's entrance, planes of the second Japanese wave pounced on her, hoping to block the channel. Badly battered, she was intentionally run aground to keep her from sinking.

The attack killed 2,390 Americans and wounded 1,178. (All but the *Arizona*, the *Utah*, and the *Oklahoma* were salvaged and returned to sea.) The three U.S. aircraft carriers of the Pacific Fleet, the prime target of the original Operation Hawaii plan, escaped the attack. The *Lexington* and *Enterprise* were at sea west of Hawaii, and the *Saratoga* was in San Diego.

A JAPANESE BLITZKREIG

On December 8, President Roosevelt, calling December 7 "a date which will live in infamy," asked Congress for a declaration of war against Japan. But what of Germany? How could the United States go to war against the Nazis and save Britain? On December 11 came the answer: Hitler, in a long, rambling speech, declared war against the United States, as did Italy.

Japan followed the attack on Pearl Harbor with a stunning sweep across the Pacific, seizing the Gilbert Islands and the U.S. island bases of Guam

and Wake. Off Malaya, Japanese bombers sank the British battleship *Prince of Wales* and the battle cruiser *Repulse*, the first capital ships ever to be sunk by air attack at sea. In the five days following Pearl Harbor, Japanese troops, in quick succession, invaded the Philippines, Hong Kong, Singapore, Malaya, Burma, and the Dutch East Indies.

As a Japanese invasion armada approached Java in January 1942, a hastily assembled American-British-Dutch-Australian fleet of cruisers and destroyers—with no air cover—raced to intercept the invaders. In fierce fighting that continued for four days, Japanese gunfire, bombs, and torpedoes sank five Allied destroyers and four cruisers, including the *Houston*, flagship of the U.S. Asiatic Fleet and the largest U.S. warship in the Far East. The Japanese lost four transports and a minesweeper; six other ships were damaged. The costly Allied action had delayed the invasion only for a few hours.

The Japanese took Hong Kong and drove U.S. and Filipino troops down the rugged Bataan Peninsula toward the U.S. fortress of Corregidor, which would hold out until May. Singapore, the British colony known as "The Gibraltar of the East," fell with the surrender of 80,000 defenders. By the spring of 1942 Japan had gained control of the entire Western Pacific, and had a massive foothold in China, Indochina, Malaya, and Burma. Japanese losses had been minimal—a few dozen planes, a few hundred troops, and several warships, the largest of which were destroyers.

The only good news in those months of loss and despair came from a daring raid on Tokyo. At a White House meeting on January 4, 1942, President Roosevelt had asked his senior military leaders to find a way to bolster American morale by striking back at Japan. The response was a plan for an air raid on Japan by Army twin-engine B-25 Mitchell bombers taking off from a Navy aircraft carrier. Lieutenant Colonel Jimmy Doolittle, a racing pilot in civilian life, and Lieutenant Hank Miller, a Navy carrier pilot, taught Army pilots how to take off with a run of only 350 feet—about a quarter of a typical runway for a bomb-laden B-25. They were not taught to land on a carrier because not even Jimmy Doolittle could do that. (See "Victory in the Air")

In May, 1942 Japan sent an invasion force of 70 ships, including two large carriers, toward Port Moresby, on the south coast of New Guinea. The port would be the launch site for a thrust into Australia. U.S. Navy code-breakers learned about the operation, which Admiral Chester W. Nimitz, who had relieved Kimmel as commander of U.S. naval forces in the Pacific, wanted to foil. But all he had available were the aircraft carriers *Lexington* and *Yorktown* and some destroyers and cruisers.

THE BATTLE OF THE CORAL SEA

The Japanese landed some troops on the island of Tulagi, off Guadalcanal in the Solomon Islands east of New Guinea. Aircraft from the *Yorktown*, hunting for the main Japanese force in the Coral Sea between the Solomons and Australia, found only minor Japanese ships off Tulagi. The American pilots sank three minesweepers, fatally struck a destroyer, and damaged several other ships. In their search for carriers, the Japanese aircraft found and sunk an oiler and a destroyer. Americans, however, found bigger quarry on their next search: the light carrier *Shoho* and her escorts. Ninety-three planes headed for the carrier, and within minutes she went down, hit by 13 bombs and seven torpedoes. As the *Shoho* sunk, Lieutenant Commander Robert E. Dixon of the *Lexington* radioed back a message that became famous: "Scratch one flattop!"

Frustrated by bad weather, Japanese pilots finally gave up their search, jettisoning their bombs and torpedoes and heading back toward their carriers. U.S. fighters spotted them and shot down 10 planes while losing two. The dogfight ended well past sunset. In the darkness, some Japanese pilots mistook the *Yorktown* for one of their own. As pilots prepared to land on the carrier, the lead pilot discovered his error, frantically gave his plane full power, and started climbing amidst a barrage of anti-aircraft fire. The surviving planes finally found their carriers, which turned on searchlights to guide their warriors home.

The next day, 69 Japanese planes finally found the American carriers. A bomb pierced the *Yorktown's* flight deck and went through to the fourth deck before exploding. Torpedo planes streaked down on both sides of the *Lexington*. Two torpedoes struck her on the port side. Five bombs also hurtled down on her. At first the *Lexington* appeared seaworthy. Then gasoline-fed fires roared out of control, and she was abandoned by 2,735 of her officers and men and scuttled. The *Lexington*, who went down with 216 of her men, was the first U.S. aircraft carrier lost in World War II.

Aircraft from the *Yorktown*, meanwhile, sighted the two Japanese carriers and, in a coordinated torpedo and bombing run, attacked the *Shokaku*. All the torpedoes either missed or, if any hit, failed to explode—not an unusual occurrence for U.S. torpedoes early in the war. Only two bombs hit. *Lexington* planes in a subsequent strike again failed in a torpedo attack but did hit the *Shokaku* with one bomb.

The Battle of the Coral Sea was the first in which the participating warships were not in visual range of their opponents. It was the first naval battle to be fought entirely by carrier aircraft. By the tally of ship losses, the U.S. Navy appeared to have lost. But this was a strategic victory for the Allies because it forced the Japanese to abandon their invasion of Port Moresby. Several months later the Japanese would attempt to take Port Moresby by an overland route and would be decisively defeated.

THE BATTLE OF MIDWAY

Admiral Yamamoto, the Japanese Navy's chief strategist, believed that Japan had to annihilate the U.S. Pacific Fleet in 1942 or lose the war. He correctly assumed that an assault on Midway would force Admiral Nimitz to use everything he had to defend Midway, which was vital to the defense of

Pearl Harbor. For Operation Mi, an assault on both Midway and the Aleutian Islands, Yamamoto drew upon virtually every ship Japan had. He planned to open his operation with carrier air strikes on Dutch Harbor, a U.S. naval base in the Aleutians, followed by amphibious landings on the islands of Adak and Kiska. This phase of the operation was designed to distract U.S. attention from Midway.

The actual attack on Midway would begin with carrier aircraft smashing the island's defenses and wiping out its aircraft. The next day the Japanese occupied tiny Kure Island, 60 miles northwest of Midway, and established a base for seaplanes to support the Midway invasion. Japanese submarines were fanned out to thwart the probable paths of U.S. ships expected to steam from Pearl Harbor to Midway and the Aleutians.

What Yamamoto did not know was that U.S. Navy code-breakers had been piecing together a relatively accurate picture of his plan. Since the Pearl Harbor attack, U.S. cryptanalysts had been chipping away at the Imperial Navy's most secret communications. The code breakers did their secret work in a basement room at the naval headquarters building in Pearl Harbor, a dank, dark place known as "the dungeon." Ruling the room in 1942 was the genius of the code breakers, Lieutenant Commander Joseph J. Rochefort, tall, thin, and usually disheveled. Rarely sleeping or eating, he paced the windowless room in his shabby red smoking jacket and carpet slippers, puffing on a cigar and downing cups of coffee. He supervised a complex operation that began with the interception of Japanese military radio traffic by eavesdropping stations around the Pacific. Code breakers, routinely working 84-hour weeks, wrested words out of the interceptors' code groups by endless analysis. Aiding them in their secret room were ancestors of today's computers—big, noisy IBM tabulating machines that sorted the cryptanalysts' punch cards. Translators put the decrypts into English sentences.

In late April 1942, code-breakers picked up repeated mentions of "AF," a place that Rochefort deduced to be Midway. To prove it, he told operators in Midway to transmit to Pearl Harbor radio messages about a water problem, both in clear text and in a low-level code that he knew the Japanese could read. The ruse worked. Japanese Naval Intelligence, in a message heard by U.S. interceptors, sent a message on May 22 reporting a water problem on AF. So AF was Midway.

Rochefort had enough information to tell Nimitz that the Japanese would attack the Aleutians on June 3 and begin an invasion of Midway the next day. Nimitz believed Rochefort's analysis and decided to act. Against four Japanese carriers and their invasion fleet, Nimitz had two seaworthy carriers—the *Enterprise* and the *Hornet*—and the *Yorktown*, battered in the Battle of the Coral Sea. She limped into Pearl Harbor on May 27, a stream of leaking oil spreading ten miles behind her. Crewmen expected that, after temporary repairs in a Pearl Harbor dry dock, she would be ordered to the U.S. West Coast for overhaul. But Nimitz, after personally inspecting her in dry dock, ordered her patched and readied for battle in three days. Some 1,500

(Next page)
A Japanese Mogami-class heavy cruiser after bombing by U.S. carrier-based naval aircraft in the Battle of Midway, June 1942.

yard workers swarmed over her, welding steel plates on her hull and shoring up her collapsed bulkheads with timber.

The *Enterprise* and *Hornet* left Pearl Harbor on May 28. Two days later came the patched-up *Yorktown*, with an air group formed of planes from the three carriers. The carriers and their support ships rendezvoused at a spot Nimitz called Point Luck, about 325 miles northeast of Midway.

On June 3, the two Japanese carriers in Alaskan waters launched planes that bombed Dutch Harbor, just as Rochefort had predicted. His other forecast came true the next day when four other Japanese carriers launched 108 aircraft to bomb Midway. Swarms of fast, agile Japanese Zeros pounced on the 25 U.S. planes that rose to defend Midway. Only eight of those planes survived, and two would never fly again. Fourteen of the Marine pilots were killed and four were wounded.

Six other Midway planes, TBF Avenger torpedo bombers, set out to attack the Japanese fleet. Each Avenger was manned by a pilot and two gunners. As the planes neared their target, more than 20 Zeros jumped them. All but one Avenger was shot down and all their men were killed. Surprised by the relatively light opposition on Midway, the Japanese leader of the raid ordered a second attack. Back on the Japanese carriers, crewmen had been arming aircraft with torpedoes and armor-piercing bombs for potential attacks on U.S. carriers. Another attack on Midway meant removing the torpedoes and rearming with ordinary bombs.

At almost the same moment, the *Hornet* and the *Enterprise* began to launch their aircraft toward what they believed to be two Japanese carriers, some 25 miles beyond the planes' combat range. The *Hornet*'s 15-plane Torpedo Squadron Eight, first to reach the carriers, flew into an inferno of gunfire from antiaircraft guns and Zeros. The Japanese defenders wiped out the squadron. The only survivor of 30 men was Ensign George H. Gay. His riddled plane cartwheeled into the water with the radioman-gunner dying and Gay wounded. He crawled out and clung to a seat cushion, reluctant to inflate his highly visible yellow life raft. (He was rescued next day by a Navy seaplane.) The doomed TBD Devastator torpedo bombers kept coming—14 from the *Enterprise*, another 12 from the *Yorktown*. All but four were shot down. Some of the airmen who ditched would survive. Two were rescued after 17 days in a life raft. Three, picked up by Japanese destroyers, were interrogated and executed, two by being thrown overboard with weights tied to their feet. Of the 41 carrier-based torpedo bombers that had flown, unescorted by fighters, against the Japanese carriers, only four survived. None of their torpedoes hit a Japanese ship.

The Devastators had not gone down in vain. Lumbering in at low levels, the torpedo planes kept Zeros and antiaircraft crews busy while, far overhead, dive bombers arrived, unnoticed and unopposed by Japanese fighters. Lieutenant Commander Clarence McCluskey, air group commander of the *Enterprise*, had led 33 SBD Dauntless dive bombers to the place where the Japanese fleet was supposed to be and found an empty ocean. His fuel was running out when he spotted a long wake, made by a Japanese destroyer speeding north-northeast after attacking a U.S. submarine. McClusky surmised that the warship was heading toward the carriers and decided to follow it. About ten minutes later, McClusky, with a squadron behind him, dove on the carrier *Kaga*. Another squadron tipped over, aiming at the Akagi. Then 17 SBDs from the *Yorktown* arrived and dove on the *Soryu* as she was turning into the wind to launch planes.

Four bombs hit the *Kaga*, setting off an inferno fueled by the planes on deck. A bomb plunged into the *Akagi's* amidships elevator, which crumpled into the hangar deck. Fires and explosions spread among 60 aircraft, most of them fueled and armed. Two bombs struck the *Soryu*, touching off fires and explosions on the flight and hangar decks. In scarcely five minutes, the three carriers were fatally ablaze and listing.

On board the USS Yorktown, *shortly after she was hit by three Japanese bombs on June 4, 1942. Dense smoke rises from fires in her uptakes, caused by a bomb that punctured them and knocked out her boilers.*

"To Lose Your Ship is to Lose Your Home"

Stanford Linzey and family

I joined the Navy because I wanted to be a Navy musician. I was a young married man and I had a lovely wife at home. I didn't hate anybody. I didn't join the Navy 'cause I was mad at anybody. I joined the Navy to play music, and here I am in a war! I was assigned to USS *Yorktown,* which was the state of the art at that time in aircraft carriers. I'm from Texas, where things are big, but they don't make ships that big! And I thought, my Lord, I'll get lost in that thing. We left Pearl Harbor and we went out to bomb the Marshall and Gilbert Islands and other islands, where the Japanese had come in. Well, as long as you're doing the bombing, there's not much problem.

On the way to Midway, really, a terrible fear gripped my heart, my mind. And I'll never forget lying in my bunk one night and this was a prayer of desperation really, I said, "God, if this is a time I'm going to meet you, OK. All I ask is that You take the fear out of my mind so that I can do the job I'm supposed to do." I'll never forget the day. June the 4th.

Now the Japanese had no idea the American fleet was at Midway. And so our torpedo planes came in first, and it was a horrendous sight. They became sacrificial lambs because they were without cover. So when they attacked the Japanese carriers, the Japanese combat air patrol from overhead, came down and shot 'em all out of the sky. Ours. I think two got away.

At 10:24 on the morning of June 24, the Japanese command had begun to make plans to celebrate the victory at Midway. And that thought lasted for exactly six minutes. For our dive bombers made a blazing inferno out of three aircraft carriers, and they sank. Nimitz says I want that last carrier, and so *Yorktown* went after it. And we found him. The *Hiryu.* We found him, and we bombed him, and we sank it. Their aircraft, however, were in the air, and they followed our aircraft back to the ship. That's how they found us. And that's when we got bombed and torpedoed. We received three bomb hits. Many near misses, but three direct bomb hits. One went down the stack and snuffed out the engines. Now, this is a horrible feeling, you're dead in the water. If torpedoes come now, you're dead, and that's the way it was.

And so, then comes the torpedo attack. We received two torpedo hits and immediately all lights went out. A torpedo is a rumbling, sort of like a terrier shaking a rat. You know the guts are being tore out, but you don't know what's happening. I'll never forget lying on the deck, and when those torpedoes hit and blew, the ship lifted like some great arm had just lifted it up and then dropped it at a 27-degree list. Well, that's the water lapping over the edge of the hangar deck. I made my way to the top side and took a look over, and saw about 2,000 heads bobbing in the water and I'm going to join them. So into the water we go and in those days, when you go over the side, you strip off all your clothes except your skivvies. No shoes, no nothing. And there was oil in the water, probably 6, 8 inches thick. Had there been a fire, we'd have burned to death. There was no fire. And explosions had scared all the sharks away. All we had was warm oily water. And when you get into that muck, you have oil in your hair, in your eyes, in your nose, some got it in their mouths and got sick. Six of our destroyers were picking up men out of the sea. And the six or seven of us, barefooted in soaked skivvies walked to the stern of our destroyer, knelt down and had an open air prayer meeting. It was quite a scene. And nobody was embarrassed and nobody was ashamed.

To lose a ship is to lose your home. I'd been aboard three years. Everything I personally owned was there. My clarinet's probably got barnacles on it down on the bottom of the sea. We only lost 86 men. That's amazing.

One Japanese carrier, the *Hiryu*, still lived. From her deck flew an avenging force of 18 Val dive bombers and six Zero escorts. U.S. fighters got ten of the Vals and a wall of antiaircraft fire from escorts stopped two more. The surviving seven dive bombers flew on, three coming in from astern the *Yorktown*, the others off to starboard. A bomb tore open the flight deck. Red-hot shrapnel touched off fires in the *Yorktown's* hangar deck, where a cool-headed officer switched on the sprinklers and water curtains. A second bomb pierced the flight deck and exploded in the fire room, knocking out five of the six boilers. The carrier which had been twisting evasively at 30 knots, abruptly slowed to six knots. Another bomb hit the No. 1 elevator forward of the island, plunged deep into the ship, and exploded.

The order was passed: "Abandon ship!" While destroyers and cruisers rescued her 2,270 survivors, her own dive bombers, which had landed on the *Enterprise*, joined with planes from that carrier in a sortie to kill the *Hiryu*. They hit her with four bombs that started uncontrollable fires. The last of the four Japanese carriers off Midway was doomed.

The *Yorktown* had been abandoned prematurely. When a belated attempt was made to save her, a Japanese submarine torpedoed her and a destroyer alongside, sinking both.

Besides destroying four Japanese aircraft carriers, U.S. aircraft, in other action during the battle, sank a cruiser and badly damaged another cruiser and two destroyers. All 250 aircraft on the four Japanese carriers were lost, as were many of their pilots, air crewmen, and skilled mechanics. Thus ended the first decisive defeat suffered by the Japanese Navy since 1592. The battle also marked the zenith of Japanese expansion in the Pacific, although the

View from the U.S. Coast Guard cutter Duane *of the* Spencer, *a ship which sank a submarine trying to break into the center of the convoy it was escorting.*

northern phase of the battle was relatively successful. Nimitz had little with which to stop the Japanese move on the Aleutians. Japanese troops made unopposed landings on Kiska and Attu. They would keep their toehold in North America until mid-1943.

Midway was the turning point of the war in the Pacific. There would still be hard-won battles ahead, beginning with the August 1942 amphibious landing of the Marines on Guadalcanal in the Solomons, the first American land offensive of the war. In a long and ferocious defense that included suicidal *banzai* charges, Japanese forces lost more than 25,000 men, including about 9,000 from disease and starvation. And so many American and Japanese ships sunk in the sea around Guadalcanal—48 by some counts—that sailors called the area Ironbottom Sound. (See "The Land War Against Japan.")

U.S. submarines, hampered at first by faulty torpedoes, would also have their turning point, aided by intelligence gleaned through code-breaking. Beginning in 1943, submarines helped to make Japan an island besieged. By sinking merchant ships, U.S. submarines cut Japan off from the oil, minerals, and other resources of her conquests. Late in the war, mine-laying submarines sealed off Japanese ports. Led by the *Tautag*, which sank 25 ships, U.S. submarines sank some 1,300 merchantmen for a total of 5.3 million tons.

THE NAVAL WAR IN THE ATLANTIC

While the historic and epic naval battles in the Pacific grabbed the most attention, the U.S. Navy's operations in the Atlantic proved crucial to winning the war against the Nazis. Among the most important of these was the Navy's ability to halt the destructive power of the German U-boats.

By 1943, new Allied anti-submarine weapons long in production began coming into the battle in decisive numbers. Large numbers of convoy escorts were at sea and fitted with new, highly effective radar; new escort carriers could provide aircraft to close the gap between areas that could be reached by land-based aircraft. And Allied code-breaking efforts were increasingly successful in giving the Allies information on U-boat activity.

After heavy losses in May 1943 Grand Admiral Karl Dönitz, commander-in-chief of the German Navy, withdrew his U-boats from the North Atlantic convoy routes. He acknowledged that Germany had suffered a serious defeat. But he was confident that the withdrawal was only temporary and that German technology would soon provide countermeasures against the Allied advantages, especially radar and the consequent danger of surprise air attacks.

U-boats leaving French ports were regularly located on the surface at night by radar-equipped aircraft. When Dönitz attempted to keep his submarines away from port by refueling and resupplying them with food and torpedoes at sea, Allied code-breaking permitted the rapid eradication of these so-called *milch cow* supply submarines.

AMPHIBIOUS WARFARE

The Navy's first major amphibious operation of the war had come in November 1942 when 108,000 U.S. and British troops landed in Casablanca, Morocco, and Algiers and Oran in Algeria. They were under the command of a general little known to the American public, Dwight D. Eisenhower. Algiers quickly surrendered, but French troops at Oran and in Morocco, surprising the Allied strategists, held out. The Allies were invading territory of the technically neutral country of Vichy France, with which the United States still had diplomatic relations. More than 300 Navy ships and landing craft were involved in what was then the largest amphibious operation in history.

By May 1943 the vaunted German Afrika Korps, caught between Allied pincer movements from the east and west, surrendered, as did the remaining Italian troops in North Africa. Then, using North Africa as a jumping off point, in August 1943 the Allies invaded Sicily and, the following month, Anglo-American forces landed in Italy. Amphibious landings were a key component of Allied successes in the Mediterranean area, and although the British wished to undertake more landings in the Aegean area, they were vetoed by the U.S. leadership as distracting resources from the principal objective, the D-Day invasion.

Lessons the Navy learned here would be applied to all other landings in Europe—and what Eisenhower did here led to his being selected to lead the D-Day forces in 1944.

Anzio was the site, about 35 miles south of Rome, of a large and bloody Allied amphibious landing during the Italian Campaign. The landing was a two-division assault to put pressure on the Gustav Line, the German defenses blocking the advance of Allied forces that had landed at Salerno on September 9, 1943. British Prime Minister Churchill had promoted the landing to hasten the fall of Rome and perhaps even expedite the ending of the European War.

On the night of January 22, 1944, in an initial landing called Operation Shingle, Ranger-led U.S. and British forces landed at a small town on the Tyrrhenian Sea. There was no active opposition to the landing, and prospects for fulfilling the mission of the landing looked promising.

The commander of the invasion troops, U.S. Major General John P. Lucas, should have been

Initial waves of amphibious tractors (LVT) head for the landing beaches on Iwo Jima's southeastern coast, at about 0900 hours on February 19, 1945.

elated. His 36,000 troops and their 3,000 vehicles had landed without casualty and the immediate objective, the Alban Hills, stood only about 20 miles away. There were virtually no German troops between the beach and the hills or beyond them to the ultimate objective: Rome.

The Anzio landing was timed to follow an Allied thrust across the Rapido and Garigliano Rivers. Field Marshal Albert Kesselring sent reserve divisions against the threat to the Gustav Line, leaving the troops landing at Anzio with little opposition. But the attempted river crossing ended in failure and the Germans were able to shift forces to Anzio.

Lucas, overly cautious, delayed an advance inland until he built up more supplies. After a week there were 69,000 U.S. and British troops and their equipment ashore, the beachheads had been secured, and supplies continued to pour ashore. Still, Lucas delayed.

On the day following the landings the Germans had begun intensive air attacks on the troop concentrations. Then they moved up major ground forces to block the invaders and force them back into the sea. Under the pounding of German artillery the Allied troops began a bloody four-month struggle to hold on to the beachhead and a few square miles beyond it.

JUNE, 1944

Although few saw that victory now loomed over the horizon, June 1944 was when World War II began to end. The Navy—with battleship task forces and aircraft carriers, PT boats and landing craft—had island-hopped across the Pacific, putting men ashore in landings on Bougainville, Tarawa, Kwajalein , and, in June 1944 on Saipan.

On June 6, 1944, Operation Neptune, the naval portion of the D-Day invasion, sent 5,300 ships, boats, and amphibious craft across the English Channel to the Normandy coast of France for the largest amphibious landing in history. On June 15, U.S. Marines stormed ashore at Saipan in the Mariana Islands, 1,500 miles east of the Philippines and just as far from the Japanese Home Islands. The "Arsenal of Democracy" had managed to produce enough ships, tanks, aircraft, and guns to equip the brave men who took the war to enemy ground in two almost simultaneous operations.

The D-Day assault, spearheaded by American troops, included British, Canadian, and a Free French force. The Normandy landing was the largest amphibious operation in history. The massive invasion fleet included more than 4,400 ships and landing craft to carry 154,000 troops—50,000 of them the assault troops of D-Day—and 1,500 tanks. About 90 of the ships were manned by U.S. Coast Guardmen, including those who landed troops of the First Division on Omaha Beach. Above the invasion fleet was an aerial armada of 11,000 fighters, bombers, transports, and gliders, an air cover whose enormity matched the historic size of the invasion armada.

U.S. Navy destroyers unexpectedly had to do what the bombers of the Army Air Forces failed to do. The bombers were supposed to shatter

(Next page)
Task Group 38.3 in line as they enter Ulithi anchorage, after strikes against the Japanese in the Philippines (USS Langley, Ticonderoga, Washington, North Carolina, South Dakota, Santa Fe, Biloxi, Mobile, *and* Oakland, *December 1944.*

German shore defenses. Because of bad visibility, the aircraft dropped their bombs miles inland. Risking grounding, destroyers steamed close to shore, acting like artillery as they fired their five-inch guns as supporting fire to the men on the beach. One shot passed through a narrow gun slit, knocking out a German pillbox, another toppled a church spire used by German artillery spotters.

The D-Day landings climaxed the U.S. Navy's role in the European Theater, where amphibious operations had delivered troops during invasions of Sicily, Italy, and southern France.

The Normandy invasion launched the European strategy, which was designed to overcome German forces on the Continent and lead to military defeat followed by political surrender, which came in May 1945. The Saipan landing, an All-American operation, had a more complex purpose. Allied strategists believed that Japan's army would be defeated, but Japan, unlike Germany, would not surrender without a fight-to-the-last-man defense of the Home Islands. An invasion, which could cost a million or more American lives, seemed inevitable.

The taking of Saipan was the first step of a campaign that would end in that invasion. By building air bases there and elsewhere in the Marianas Islands, the United States would be able to strike Japan with a new weapon—the B-29 Superfortress, which was coming off production lines in early 1944. The B-29 could fly from the Marianas, bomb Japanese targets, and return. A massive bombing campaign was needed as a prelude to invasion. And control of the Marianas would block Japan from the resources of Malaya and the Dutch East Indies. At sea, U.S. carrier aircraft hammered what was left of Japan's carrier force, which had been shattered in the Battle of Midway two years before.

In July, U.S. troops continued their campaign in the Marianas, taking Tinian, which would provide U.S. bombers with another base. The same base-building strategy singled out Iwo Jima, a volcanic island about five and a half miles long and two and a half miles wide, some 660 miles from Japan. On its two airfields B-29s flying to and from the Marianas could make emergency landings. The island would also serve as an advance base for P-51 Mustangs and P-47 Thunderbolts, which had shorter ranges than the bombers. From Iwo Jima, the fighters could fly up and escort the B-29s heading for Japan. (See "The Land War With Japan.")

THE BATTLE OF LEYTE GULF

It would be Tinian base that would transform the Pacific endgame. But there was another powerful player in the game of strategy: General Douglas MacArthur, who had been driven from the Philippines at the beginning of the war, but had vowed, "I shall return." His plan, however, clashed with the Navy island-hopping strategy, which in 1944 saw the taking of Formosa as a key step toward Japan. MacArthur prevailed, after personally convincing

Bob Feller,
Hall of Fame Pitcher

"The Heroes Never Return"

I'm from a little town, Van Meter, in Iowa. I joined the Navy, went to Norfolk, went through boot camp, then went on to War College in Newport, Rhode Island. I was assigned to the battleship *Alabama* when it was commissioned in Hampton Roads.

The *Alabama* was a beautiful ship. Our job was to protect the carriers. I was a Chief Petty Officer, and I was the gun captain on the 40 millimeter quad. These were hydroelectric guns. We called them "pom poms." We typically fired when the distance to the target was about 4,000 yards. When you're on the guns and enemy aircraft are coming at you, all you can do is short bombardment. It's very, very noisy, and you can't hear a thing. The only thing you cared about was that the plane splashed into the water before it got to your ship.

We had great anti-aircraft gunners on the *Alabama.* My boys on the guns would keep pouring the ammunition in and we'd keep pumping it out. We believed in what we were doing, we worked at it, and we were well prepared. We practiced at night, blindfolded. You practiced with your eyes closed. Everything became automatic. If something didn't go wrong, nobody got killed.

The *Alabama* was the only ship in the Third Fleet that took to the Pacific that didn't lose a man to enemy action. Our first time out, we headed to Kwajalein, and on to Enewetak, and then the Carolines. We went down and hit New Guinea, came back and took the Marianas, on to the Philippines, and then Japan.

One year, we crossed the Equator 28 times in one year, down around the Carolines, winning back all those islands in the Pacific. The Third Fleet was the most powerful naval armada in the history of the world. If you don't believe me, just ask our opponents. They'll let you know what they thought.

In the Battle of the Philippine Sea, we shot down over 470 Japanese aircraft. Their idea was to fly off their carriers and destroy the American Pacific fleet. They brought their fleet up from the San Bernardino Strait and the plan was to fly over us and hit us with their bombs, dive bombers, kamikazes—whatever—and then go and refuel and rearm over on Tinian or Saipan. Well, our fighters sank several of the Japanese carriers so that the Japanese planes had no place to land when they got back. And the ones that did get back, why, they'd wipe them out on their runways. So that was the end of Japanese naval power.

I played catch aboard ship a lot, at sea, and in port. We had our own baseball team. I got uniforms for 'em. We'd play the battleship *Indiana* or the *Missouri* or the *Iowa.* We had times over there on the beaches when the officers would come and we had some pretty good crowds. It provided some entertainment in the Navy.

Being inducted into the Baseball Hall of Fame is a great honor. Being invited to the White House is a great honor. But to be able to serve the country under the great leadership we had in Franklin Roosevelt and Harry Truman, and with the people we had behind us, back on the farms and in the cities and in the factories, producing what we needed to win the war -- that's the greatest honor.

I'm no hero. The heroes never return. We survivors, we returned. The heroes are still there in the Pacific and the beaches all over Europe.

President Roosevelt of America's responsibility to the Philippines. On October 20, 1944, using two assault forces and some 500 ships, MacArthur landed 202,500 troops on Leyte, the central main island and a strategic link to Mindanao, Mindoro, and Luzon. In a display of bravado highly publicized by still and newsreel cameras, MacArthur waded ashore from a landing craft to personally lead the invasion. (See the chapter, "The Land War With Japan.")

MacArthur, no fan of the U.S. Navy, had made his operation an Army show. But it was the Navy, in the fateful battle of Leyte Gulf, that saved his forces from what might have been a disastrous assault by Japanese carrier-based aircraft. The Japanese Navy, launching Sho-go—the defense of the Philippines—committed, in four naval forces, the war's largest concentration of battleships and heavy cruisers in a single task force, setting the stage for an epic naval battle. The Japanese operation involved four separate forces. Each became the focus of a separate battle—off the island of Samar, off Cape Engano, in the Sibuyan Sea, the island-dotted waters northwest of Leyte, and in the Surigao Strait. When a Japanese force tried to enter Leyte Gulf via the Surigao Strait, U.S. destroyer torpedoes sank one battleship. Behind a screen of P-T boats and destroyers were eight cruisers and six battleships, including Pearl Harbor victims *Maryland*, *West Virginia*, *Tennessee*, *California*, and *Pennsylvania*. Their repairs had included installation of the latest fire-control radar, and they used it in what became the only battle between battleships in the war. In darkness and at a range of 22,400 yards, the *West Virginia* fired a salvo and struck the battleship *Yamashiro*, which was mortally wounded. Another, the *Mogami*, collided with another Japanese warship and was later sunk by aircraft. Confused communications between U.S. naval commands marred the complex, interlocking battles of Leyte Gulf. But when the gunsmoke cleared, all the Japanese task forces had been destroyed and the invasion of the Philippines had been guaranteed by U.S. sea power. The Japanese troops in the jungles of Philippines now had no chance of air support or protection of their supply lines to Japan.

The U.S. invasion force met relatively light resistance to the landings near Tacloban. But in another landing at Ormoc on December 7, Japanese troops in pillboxes and caves fought ferociously, and U.S. ships were attacked by suicide pilots dubbed *kamikazes*—"The only weapon I feared in the war," said Admiral William F. Halsey, the U.S. Third Fleet's otherwise fearless commander. Flying Zero fighters, the *kamikazes* attacked a force of U.S. "jeep" or escort carriers, sinking one and heavily damaging two others. By Christmas 1944 Leyte was declared secured and MacArthur was ready for the next phase of the invasion: the taking of Luzon, held by 250,000 Japanese troops.

However, when the first of 200,000 U.S. troops stormed ashore at Lingayen Gulf in western Luzon, the enemy did not appear in any strength, and U.S. commanders uneasily wondered why. The answer: A new Japanese tactic allowed an uncontested amphibious landing, sparing the defenders a punishing bombardment. Inland, the Americans fought their way through an intricate defense system of caves, tunnels, and pillboxes manned by resolute defenders whose resistance presaged what invaders would face in the Home Islands.

On June 30, 1945, MacArthur declared most of the country was liberated, but the fighting went on. About 65,000 Japanese troops in Luzon's hills held out until the end of the war.

"I HAVE TO DECIDE"

Victory in Europe in May 1945 brought an anticipation of peace in the United States. The Army, 8.3 million strong on VE-Day, was being substantially reduced through demobilization spurred on by Congress. But on VE-Day Japanese soldiers were still fighting and killing Americans in the Philippines and on Okinawa. Japanese *kamikaze* aircraft were still crashing into American warships and transports. Japanese submarines were still going to sea. And the Japanese army's 4 million men, plus untallied millions of civilians, were preparing to die for their Emperor in a final defense of their homeland.

On June 18, Harry S Truman, who had been president for about two months, called a meeting of his military advisers to learn about the strategy for the invasion of Japan. Hovering over the meeting was knowledge of the vicious fighting then raging on Okinawa, which both Truman and the advisers knew to be a prophetic vision of invasion. The American casualty rate on Okinawa was then estimated to be 35 percent. By the time the fighting officially ended on July 2, the final American toll would be 7,613 killed and 31,807 wounded, a total Army-Marine-Navy casualty toll ashore of 39,420. The actual casualty rate would be over 39 percent.

In his diary on June 17, Truman wrote: "I have to decide Japanese strategy—shall we invade Japan proper or shall we bomb and blockade?" He seemed to have been referring to conventional aerial bombardment, but he also had to make a decision about the atomic bomb, which was yet to be tested.

A month later, on July 16, the world's first atomic bomb would be successfully detonated near Alamogordo, New Mexico. And on August 6, Tinian became not a base for an invasion of Japan but a base from which a B-29 named *Enola Gay* would take off to drop an atomic bomb on Hiroshima.

VICTORY
IN EUROPE

★

Carlo D'Este

"We are determined that before the sun sets on this terrible struggle our flag will be recognized throughout the world as a symbol of freedom on the one hand and of overwhelming force on the other."

—GENERAL GEORGE C. MARSHALL

When President Franklin D. Roosevelt appointed General George C. Marshall the new Army chief of staff on September 1, 1939, the United States was not only woefully unprepared for war, but also was arguably a third-rate military power with an army of 189,839 that ranked an inconsequential 17th in the world. The army Marshall inherited lacked modern weapons and its tactics, training, and doctrine were hopelessly inadequate and outdated. Many of its fighting units existed only on paper and most others were critically under-manned.

The U.S. Army of World War II was created virtually from scratch. After conscription was enacted in the summer of 1940, the army consisted primarily of draftees, a small corps of Regular Army personnel, volunteers, and Reserve and National Guard units called to active duty. By 1942, Marshall had completely overhauled the army, streamlined its organization and training, orchestrated the largest peacetime maneuvers ever undertaken, and replaced most of its aging senior leadership with a core of professionals he knew and trusted. But, as Marshall well understood, only minimal preparation could be accomplished in such a short period of time, and no amount of stateside training could compensate for the test of combat on the battlefield that commenced in the autumn of 1942.

THE NORTH AFRICAN CAMPAIGN, 1942–1943

The U.S. Army's baptism of fire began in the Mediterranean in November 1942 with Operation Torch, a joint Allied invasion of French North Africa commanded by (then) Lieutenant General Dwight D. Eisenhower. Torch consisted of three independent operations: the 34,000 U.S. troops of the Western Task Force, commanded by Major General George S. Patton, Jr., seized Casablanca, after landings at Fedala, Safi, and Port Lyautey on the Atlantic side of French Morocco, while the two other task forces—a U.S.

force of 39,000 men commanded by Major General Lloyd R. Fredendall— landed at Oran, and a similar Anglo-American force of 23,000 British and 10,000 U.S. seized Algiers.

Following the Torch landings, an Allied expeditionary force consisting of U.S., British, and French troops moved into Tunisia to block German reinforcement of North Africa, and later to link-up with the British Eighth Army in pursuit of Field Marshal Erwin Rommel's Panzer Armee Afrika, retreating west from Egypt after its defeat at El Alamein.

The roots of the American commitment in the Mediterranean and Northwest Europe date to December 1941 when the United States and Britain agreed to a policy of defeating Germany first, rather than Japan in the Pacific. Marshall, the architect of American strategy, believed that the decisive campaign of the war would be fought in northwest Europe and relentlessly pursued the development of sufficient forces and equipment in the United Kingdom, from which a cross-Channel invasion of France could be mounted at the earliest possible moment.

Soldiers in line at New York port of embarkation.

However, in the summer of 1942 Roosevelt insisted that a suitable role be found for American combat forces before 1943, and heated Anglo-American negotiations resulted in a compromise. In return for an American commitment to military operations in the Mediterranean, the British agreed to a massive build-up of American forces in Britain for a cross-Channel operation in 1943.

The U.S. Army that fought in North Africa in 1942 consisted mostly of minimally trained citizen soldiers facing their first test of combat. They were confident of victory, even cocky, many believing the war would be brief and that they would soon be on their way home. A rude awakening to the reality of what it would take to win the war soon shattered that confidence, and not only raised serious questions over the U.S. Army's training, preparedness and equipment, but about its very survival against a veteran, battle-tested enemy.

The first indication that a rough road lay ahead occurred during the first battles in Tunisia in December 1942, an unequal struggle, won by the Axis, whose ground forces were aided immeasurably by the Luftwaffe, which aggressively disrupted and delayed the Allied advance into western Tunisia. Seriously undermanned with only a single British and French corps, and Fredendall's II Corps, the Allies were compelled to spend the winter of 1942–43 in defensive positions in the mountains of central and southern Tunisia.

On February 14, 1943, the Germans launched a two-pronged offensive designed to split the Allies in two, destroy the untested and undermanned U.S. II Corps, and threaten Allied lines of communication from Algeria. The surprise attack by General Jürgen von Arnim's Fifth Panzer Army crushed major elements of the U.S. 1st Armored Division defending Faid and Sidi Bou Zid, the anchor of the Allied defense east of Kasserine Pass.

Five days later, on February 19, Field Marshal Erwin Rommel's Afrika Korps attacked Kasserine Pass guarded initially by only the 19th Engineer Combat Regiment. The 26th Infantry Regiment of the 1st Division, sent to reinforce the beleaguered engineers, arrived too late to stop the relentless German advance. The bleak landscape of Kasserine became a charnel house of wrecked equipment and the corpses of American GIs. Despite the grim scenes on the battlefield, there was a ray of hope when U.S. troops managed to delay the German advance sufficiently to enable a hastily assembled Anglo-American task force to contain the 10th Panzer Division at Thala, while a similar force stopped the advance of the 21st Panzer Division at Sbiba. Although Rommel won a major tactical victory at Kasserine, it did not lead to the collapse of the Allied positions in Tunisia that he originally envisioned. By February 22, Rommel realized he had lost the strategic initiative and withdrew, leaving in his wake a beaten and dispirited American fighting force.

Although Eisenhower attempted to put on a brave face in his communications to Marshall, the truth was that Kasserine and Sidi Bou Zid had indeed left a bitter legacy. Eisenhower's naval aide wrote in his diary, "The proud and cocky Americans today stand humiliated by one of the greatest

General George C. Marshall
Army Chief of Staff

defeats in our history." Eisenhower, who was as inexperienced in the art of high command as his troops were in the deadly business of combat, wrote somberly to Marshall: "Our people, from the very highest to the very lowest have learned that this is not a child's game." That American morale was at its nadir was epitomized by an entry in the war diary of Company B, 701st Tank Destroyer Battalion, openly questioning U.S. leadership. "We could not help wondering whether the officers directing the American effort knew what they were doing."

II Corps suffered an estimated 6,000 casualties (approximately 300 killed, 3,000 wounded, and 3,000 missing in action) at Kasserine Pass and Sidi Bou Zid, plus massive losses of equipment: 183 tanks, 104 half-tracks, 500 jeeps and trucks, and well over 200 guns. Both battles were a wake-up call. In addition to raw inexperience, not only were U.S. tactics and dispositions woefully unsound, but its combat power was scattered piecemeal over hundreds of miles, with virtually no capability for mutual support. At Sidi Bou Zid some GIs abandoned their positions and equipment and fled to the rear in panic, their commanders helpless to stop them. To make matters worse, American armor and artillery was simply no match for the superior German armor, particularly the deadly Tiger tank. The British regarded the battles as irrefutable evidence that American fighting ability was mostly bravado. Clearly, unless there was an immediate improvement in leadership and training, the long-term effects would be disastrous.

From tragedy often comes redemption, and there was soon unmistakable evidence that Kasserine had imbued the senior American leaders with the necessary determination to reclaim their lost honor. Considerable credit for this was due Major General Ernest Harmon, a veteran cavalry officer whom Eisenhower sent to the front to help reverse the situation. The aggressive Harmon took temporary control of II Corps and brought stability to the rapidly deteriorating front when it was most needed. Eisenhower belatedly dismissed the inept Fredendall and hastily summoned Patton from Morocco to assume command of II Corps on March 6, 1943. Patton brought about a dramatic transformation of U.S. forces by convincing his troops that they were capable of defeating the Germans. In Patton, the U.S. Army in Tunisia now had a warrior like Rommel who had come to fight.

The appointment of British General Sir Harold R. L. G. Alexander to command Allied ground forces in Tunisia brought to the campaign stability it had previously badly lacked. His campaign plan was to unite his ground forces with Eighth Army, which was to breach the Mareth Line and drive into southeastern Tunisia. Eighteenth Army Group, as the combined Allied forces were designated, would then drive Axis forces into northern Tunisia, while the air force and navy prevented the arrival of reinforcements and sealed off any escape by sea.

Although the American commanders in Tunisia had the highest personal regard for Alexander, they bitterly resented the patronizing attitude of the British that questioned American fighting ability. The problem facing American commanders was clear-cut: to improve the performance of U.S.

troops, and in the process convince their skeptical British ally that the fighting qualities of the American soldier were the equal of any in the world. With the removal of Fredendall, the leadership that would accomplish this was now on the scene in the persons of Patton and Omar Bradley, and Harmon, who had taken firm command of the beleaguered 1st Armored in the wake of the disaster at Sidi Bou Zid.

In late March, spearheaded by Major General Terry de la Mesa Allen's 1st Division, II Corps won the first American victory of the war by soundly defeating the veteran German 10th Panzer Division at El Guettar, while William O. Darby's 1st Ranger Battalion bloodied an Italian force occupying key positions to the east of the town. By the standards of World War II this battle was a minor engagement, but for American forces it was a significant victory and a turning point. The lesson for von Arnim and the Axis commanders was equally clear: henceforth the U.S. Army could no longer to be taken lightly as an adversary. An uncompleted letter to his parents found by the body of a young GI killed at El Guettar said it all: "Well, folks, we stopped the best they had."

By early April, General Sir Bernard L. Montgomery's British Eighth Army had cracked the Mareth Line and linked up with the Allied forces in Tunisia. Although von Arnim's Army Group Africa managed to elude entrapment, their ultimate fate was now clear. Arrayed against von Arnim was

(Next page):
Soliders of II Corps on patrol in Tunisia, April 5, 1943.

Near Algiers, Operation Torch troops hit the beach behind an American flag (at left), November 8, 1942.

a massive Allied force consisting of the British First and Eighth Armies, the French corps and the U.S. II Corps. Alexander's mistrust of American fighting ability became crystal clear in his plan for the decisive battle of the campaign. II Corps was relegated to the minor role of protecting the Allied left flank, while the British would make the main effort to corner Army Group Africa in the Cape Bon peninsula.

Major General Omar N. Bradley had replaced Patton (who returned to Morocco to command Seventh Army for the forthcoming invasion of Sicily) as II Corps commander, and he forcefully persuaded Alexander to employ American forces in an independent role of driving to Bizerte in order to block an Axis escape to the west. Hill 609 was a major obstacle to the American advance and Bradley assigned its capture to Major General Charles "Doc" Ryder's 34th Infantry Division, a National Guard unit that had previously been severely criticized by the British as unfit. In one of the bloodiest battles of the campaign, the 34th overcame fierce German resistance and restored their lost honor on the slopes of Hill 609.

As II Corps closed the jaws of the trap by capturing Bizerte and cutting off von Arnim's only escape route, British and French forces completed the operation by forcing Army Group Africa into the plain of Tunis, where von Arnim surrendered on May 12, 1943; some 250,000 survivors became Allied prisoners of war. Alexander cabled Churchill: "All enemy resistance has ceased. We are masters of the North African shores."

The Tunisian campaign was a harsh experience that American commanders were doggedly determined never to repeat: a bloody but necessary testing ground where the U.S. Army came of age. The American leaders were convinced that their soldiers were now the equal of their ally and their enemy. Bradley later wrote, "In Africa we learned to crawl, to walk, then run."

The young men of the 34th Division and the other American units that fought in Tunisia had graduated from the most uncompromising school in the world: combat. GIs who had been never fired a shot in anger were now battle-toughened veterans. As Rick Atkinson has noted in *An Army at Dawn*, four U.S. divisions now had extensive experience of amphibious, mountain, desert, and urban warfare. "They now knew what it was like to be bombed, shelled, and machine-gunned, and to fight on. They provided Eisenhower with a blooded hundred-thousand."

The cost of victory was largely borne by the infantry. Although they eventually made up only 14 percent of the Army strength in the Mediterranean and European theaters, the infantry arm absorbed 70 percent of the casualties. From Torch to Tunis, the U.S. Army suffered over 19,000 casualties, including 2,715 men killed in action, some 9,000 wounded, and another 6,500 missing in action.

With the Allies in complete control of North Africa, a turning point in the war had come. Henceforth they, not Hitler, would dictate the time and place of future engagements. Those GIs who had come there expecting a short war now began to realize that North Africa was but one small step on the long and difficult road to Berlin.

THE SICILY CAMPAIGN

The defeat of Axis forces in North Africa left the Allies divided over future strategy in the Mediterranean. When their leaders met at Casablanca in January 1943 to resolve future strategy, the British came committed to an invasion of Sicily to follow the Tunisian campaign. Marshall opposed further operations in the Mediterranean and argued forcefully for an invasion of Europe in 1943. Eventually a compromise was reached under which the British agreed to renew planning for the cross-Channel invasion, Operation Overlord, but in the meantime, the Allies would exploit their growing strength in the Mediterranean by invading the island of Sicily.

Code-named Operation Husky, the Sicilian operation was commanded by Eisenhower. Alexander was appointed as the ground Commander-in-Chief; the designated invasion commanders were Montgomery, whose British Eighth Army formed the Eastern Task Force, and Patton's U.S. Seventh Army, which constituted the Western Task Force.

Before D-Day at Sicily, the Allied air forces conducted an exceptionally successful air campaign against targets in Sicily, Sardinia, and Italy that left both Axis air forces a shambles, with the Italians all but extinct as a fighting unit and the Luftwaffe severely crippled.

On the night of July 9–10, U.S. airborne and British glider landings seized key targets around Gela and Syracuse as part of a bold pre-invasion night operation, the first of its kind ever attempted. The British glider force encountered dangerously high winds, smoke from the island, and heavy flak both from enemy guns and, unexpectedly, from friendly naval vessels that mistakenly fired upon the aerial armada, with a loss of 147 gliders and the death of 252 British soldiers. The U.S. airborne landings by Colonel James M. Gavin's 505th Parachute Infantry Regiment of the Eighty-Second Airborne Division fared little better, with more than 3,000 paratroopers scattered over a thousand square mile area of southeastern Sicily.

On the morning of July 10, 1943, Eighth Army invaded along a 50-mile front in the southeastern corner of Sicily. Concurrently, Patton's Seventh Army made its primary landings along the south coast at Gela and Scoglitti with the U.S. 1st and 45th Infantry Divisions, while Major General Lucian K. Truscott's heavily reinforced Third Infantry Division assaulted Licata to protect the Seventh Army left flank. The object of the Seventh Army landings was to seize a firm Allied bridgehead in southeastern Sicily and capture the key ports of Syracuse, Licata, and the airfields near Gela, from which Allied aircraft could support the ground forces.

Eighth Army's mission was to drive north toward the port city of Messina, the gateway to Sicily, and the primary Axis logistical lifeline to the Italian mainland across the Strait of Messina. Other than the capture of the airfields near Gela, Patton's only mission was to protect the Eighth Army left flank.

Opposing the Allies was a poorly trained and equipped Italian army of over 300,000 men, and a small German contingent that until June 1943

never consisted of more than a division. Within hours of the invasion the Germans acted to reinforce Sicily by air and sea from mainland Italy with the XIV Panzer Corps.

The Invasion of Sicily, July 10 1943.

The most important of the three American landings was at Gela, where for two days the Big Red One and a small element of Combat Command B of the 2d Armored Division repelled strong counterattacks by panzers and infantry of the Hermann Göring Division and the Italian Livorno Division intent on driving them back into the sea.

On nearby Biazza Ridge, Colonel Gavin led a tiny, impromptu force of his 505th paratroopers and infantry from the 45th Division in a valiant stand against an overwhelmingly superior enemy force of Tiger tanks, artillery, and over 700 panzer grenadiers. Gavin told his men, "We're staying on this goddamned ridge—no matter what happens." His greatly overmatched force managed to repel a grave threat to the beachhead in one of the most heroic small unit actions of the war.

To reinforce the battered defenders of Gela, Patton ordered his reserve in North Africa, the 504th Parachute Infantry Regiment, to parachute into the

Major General George S. Patton, Jr., after the Seventh Army's landing at Gela, on the south coast of Sicily, July 11, 1943.

beachhead the night of July 11. Both at sea and ashore, jittery Allied AA gunners mistakenly fired upon the air armada, shooting down 23 Allied aircraft with a loss of 60 pilots and crewmen, and 81 paratroopers.

By July 12, the two Allied armies were in control of solid bridgeheads, but the British advance on Messina was derailed below Catania by units of the German 1st Parachute Division during a savage five-day battle. The main Axis defensive positions were anchored in the mountains of central Sicily and around the vast obstacle of Mt. Etna, but were as yet incomplete and vulnerable, provided the Allies attacked without delay. Bradley's II Corps was perfectly positioned to strike a killing blow from which the only Axis escape was retreat or surrender. However, Alexander declined to employ II Corps, primarily in the misguided belief that the U.S. Army was still not a reliable fighting force. After Alexander failed to act, a frustrated Patton persuaded him to approve an alternative plan he had devised to employ II Corps in a thrust to Sicily's northern coast, while the remainder of Seventh Army cleared western Sicily. The 3d Division and the 2d Armored Division liberated Palermo on July 22, 1943, where they were greeted by thousands of flag-waving, cheering Sicilians. On July 25, Patton obtained the agreement of both Alexander and Montgomery to seize Messina and end the Sicily campaign.

While the publicity focused on Palermo and the clearing of western Sicily, neither of which had an immediate impact on the outcome of the Sicily campaign, Patton ordered new offensives across rugged north central Sicily by the 1st Division, and along the north coast by the 3d Division. Both divisions encountered very strong resistance as the Germans skillfully carried out a succession of delaying actions by using the mountain terrain to maximum advantage. The Big Red One, reinforced by the 39th Infantry Regiment of the 9th Infantry Division, suffered heavy casualties during a weeklong battle for the hilltop town of Troina. Before he was killed by hostile fire while gallantly helping to repulse a deadly German counterattack near Troina, Private James W. Reese of the 26th Regiment was one of four soldiers in Sicily to be awarded the Medal of Honor for heroism.

Facing entrapment, the Germans accomplished one of the most successful strategic withdrawals in military history by extracting nearly 55,000 troops and over 10,000 vehicles, tanks, and guns from Sicily. When the 3d Division entered the smoking ruins of Messina the morning of August 17, they discovered that the last German had long since departed.

Although the 38-day campaign was beset from the start by controversy and indecision at the top, the U.S. Army acquitted itself with distinction. The outstanding feature of the U.S. Army in Sicily was how quickly it overcame the setbacks of Tunisia and absorbed the lessons necessary to become a first-class fighting force. More than a half million Allied soldiers, sailors, and airmen fought in Sicily in some capacity in what was at the time the largest amphibious operation in history. The wounded and missing totaled 6,544, and 2,440 Americans were killed during a campaign that marked the first occasion of the war in which an American field army had fought as a single entity.

Soldiers of the 1st Division (The Big Red One) enter the hilltop town of Troina, Sicily, August 6, 1943.

In Messina, jubilant Sicilians parade
with soldiers of the 3rd Division,
August 17, 1943.

President Franklin D. Roosevelt pins
medal on Lieutenant W.W. Kellogg
in Sicily, December 8, 1943.

"A NEAR RUN THING"

Operation Overlord was postponed until the late spring of 1944, but the massive Allied force in the Mediterranean could not be left idle in Sicily and North Africa without a new mission. After months of indecision, the Allies acted upon Eisenhower's recommendation that an invasion of Italy follow the fall of Sicily.

The U.S. Fifth Army was organized in North Africa in the spring of 1943 under Lieutenant General Mark W. Clark to plan and execute operations in Italy, and for months had been preparing for Operation Avalanche, an amphibious invasion approximately 20 miles south of Naples, along the Gulf of Salerno, intended to take advantage of the imminent collapse of Italy by gaining the Allies a foothold on the Italian mainland. Clark's Fifth Army would land and link up with Montgomery's Eighth Army driving north after invading Calabria, in the Italian boot. Together, the two armies would continue offensive operations toward Rome under the command of Alexander, whose 15th Army Group would control all Allied ground operations in Italy.

Although the Salerno landings were to be carried out by two corps (the British X Corps and the U.S. VI Corps), the chronic shortage of landing craft reduced the scope of the landings to three divisions (two British and the U.S. 36th Infantry Division), and a small U.S. Ranger and British Commando force.

The German commander in chief in Italy was Field Marshal Albert Kesselring, a superb tactician who skillfully maneuvered his forces against the Allies during what became the longest and bloodiest Allied campaign fought in the West. Kesselring convinced Hitler that German strategy should be to defend south of Rome along Italy's narrowest point, rather than in the Apennines and the Po Valley. Kesselring's aim was to make the Allies pay dearly for every foot of ground in southern Italy. Kesselring had anticipated an Allied landing at Salerno, and the German defenses were every bit as prepared as the Japanese would be at Tarawa two months later. From the outset, the invasion on September 9th became a disaster in the making, beginning with bitter resistance by the 16th Panzer Division, the principal defenders of the beachhead. Despite being outnumbered, the Germans controlled the high ground and the exits from the invasion beaches and quickly established they had every intention of driving the Allies back into the sea. German divisions from as far north as Rome and as far south as Calabria were ordered to Salerno to contest the invasion.

The landings were bitterly resisted and a great many landing craft were hit with the murderous fire of machine guns, artillery, mortars, and anti-aircraft guns. A British survivor called it "terrible carnage." In the U.S. sector, the 36th Infantry Division, a Texas National Guard unit in its first combat, endured a horrendous baptism of fire on the beaches where the first waves were pinned down by machine-gun and mortar fire. An infantry battalion commander sensed panic and indecision and raged at his men to push inland as their only escape from certain death. "Get up, you bastards! Get up and go!" They did.

With timely air and naval support the 36th Division somehow survived D-Day despite the confusion and the vicious German resistance, largely thanks to support by warships that braved deadly artillery fire to maneuver close to shore to deliver direct fire support. "Thank God for the fire of the blue-belly Navy ships," extolled one beachhead commander.

On D+1 badly needed reinforcements began coming ashore, as the 157th and 179th Regiments of the 45th Division Thunderbirds, in floating reserve offshore, joined the fray. Nevertheless, the Fifth Army beachhead became perilous because of a seven-mile gap between the British X Corps and the U.S. VI Corps, which would have to be closed before the Germans were able to exploit it and roll up the Allied flanks. A cable from Eisenhower to the Combined Chiefs of Staff was not reassuring. Avalanche "will be a matter of touch and go for the next few days . . . we are in for some very tough fighting."

When the VI Corps commander, Major General Ernest J. Dawley, reported the grim situation to Clark, the Army commander demanded, "What are you doing about it?" "Nothing," replied Dawley, "I've got no reserves. All I've got is a prayer." A GI exclaimed that, "Only God was protecting our left flank and HE was taking a ten-minute break."

By D+3 the situation on the beaches had become dire as U.S. losses began mounting with disturbing swiftness. Units became isolated from one another and were being chopped to pieces; communications were severed, and the battle became an elemental struggle for survival. A mere 60 men were all that was left of one infantry battalion of the 36th Division at the end of the fight. "Desperate" became a frequently used but scarcely exaggerated word.

Having already committed his slender reserves, Clark had virtually nothing left. He now contemplated the unthinkable: being driven back into the sea, and began making plans to re-embark VI Corps and reland them in the British sector. There remained one thread of hope and Clark seized it. If Fifth Army could hold on long enough for the 82d Airborne Division to respond, there was still a chance to save the beachhead. Across the front came the order: "Hold at all costs!"

Hurried briefings to the paratroopers of the 82d were along the lines of: "The Krauts are kicking the shit out of our boys at Salerno and we're going to jump into the beachhead tonight and rescue them. Put on your parachutes and get on the plane." Like the cavalry of old riding to the rescue, the 3,500 paratroopers of Colonel Reuben H. Tucker's 504th Parachute Infantry Regiment carried out one of the most daring and risky night airborne operations of the war. The 504th successfully parachuted into the beachhead on September 13, and was sent to plug the most dangerous gap along the Sele River. For the first time VI Corps could constitute a reserve. Sheer tenacity by the frontline troops, superb gunnery on the part of the Allied navy and the artillerymen ashore, and close air support, enabled Fifth

Army to hold its ground long enough for additional reinforcements to arrive and for the Germans to exhaust their resources in unsuccessful counterattacks.

When it became apparent that the Allies would hold their beachhead, Kesselring ordered a phased withdrawal from Salerno. By September 17, the Tenth Army was on the move to the north. Naples fell to the Allies on October 1, 1943, thus ending the first phase of the Italian campaign.

The Germans had come close to inflicting a humiliating defeat upon the Allies. More important, Salerno was the validation that Kesselring needed to convince Hitler that his forces could indeed successfully defend central Italy. Had the Allies employed their resources better at Salerno, Kesselring might have drawn a different conclusion, and thus altered the entire course of the war in Italy.

Fifth Army's baptism of fire came at a cost of more than 13,000 casualties. U.S. losses numbered 788 killed, 2,814 wounded, and 1,318 missing. In addition, the U.S. Navy suffered losses of 296 dead, 422 wounded, and 551 missing.

ONE MORE RIVER TO CROSS
THE ITALIAN CAMPAIGN

The Allied high command mistakenly believed that the German defense of Salerno presaged a full-scale retreat to the north and a defense in the Apennines. From Eisenhower on down, the belief prevailed that 15th Army Group would most likely capture Rome by the end of October 1943. Although Allied strategy centered on keeping the Wehrmacht fully committed in Italy so that its veteran divisions could not be shifted to France to help repel the impending cross-Channel invasion, Churchill was emphatic that Rome must fall by the end of 1943.

The mountainous terrain of central Italy was the worst imaginable place to fight a large-scale military campaign, and it became Kesselring's greatest asset. As the Allies advanced north from Salerno, every imaginable obstacle barred their path. The Germans blew up bridges, mined the road and left deadly booby traps everywhere. The terrain, raging rivers, freezing winter weather, wind, mud, and rain all combined to make life hell for every soldier who fought there. Mountains had to be negotiated via mule train by sweating, weary soldiers who had to take over the portage of guns, ammunition, and supplies themselves when the trails became too steep even for mules. When they could muster the energy, GIs, who traditionally disdained their generals, reserved their greatest fury for "General Mud."

What had been anticipated as a relatively brief advance north to capture Rome turned out to be a slow and deadly advance that by the end of December 1943 left the Allies stalemated along the Gustav Line and unable to press beyond the German defenses in and around Cassino. To draw

German forces away from Cassino and hasten the capture of Rome, the Allies elected to launch an end run into the German rear by means of amphibious landings 35 miles southwest of Rome, at the twin resort cities of Anzio and Nettuno.

An attempted breakthrough at the Rapido River by the 36th Division on the night of January 20, 1944 ended in one of the bloodiest failures of the war, and left Fifth Army stalled at the mouth of the Liri Valley, with little prospect for breaking the Gustav Line in the foreseeable future. This came just at the inopportune moment when VI Corps was about to launch the Anzio landings.

Code-named Shingle, the Anzio-Nettuno landings were successfully carried out on January 22, 1944 against scant opposition. Although Kesselring had long expected the Allies to launch an amphibious end run somewhere near Rome, the Shingle landings caught the Germans flat-footed. Despite the surprise, divisions from northern Italy, Germany, Yugoslavia, and France were on the move within hours to Anzio as Kesselring thrust every available unit into the breach to contain the Allied beachhead and block an Allied advance to the Alban Hills. At all costs, the Allies were not to be permitted to establish themselves along this crucial terrain.

Alexander's intention at Anzio was to open the road to Rome by seizing and holding the Alban Hills. Clark, however, was anxious to avoid another debacle on the scale of Avalanche, and neither he nor Major General John P. Lucas, the invasion commander, shared the unwarranted optimism of Alexander and Churchill. Lucas believed that Anzio was an ill-conceived operation that would likely end badly.

The ill-fated Rapido crossing destroyed the questionable premise of the end run to Anzio and an early linkup between VI Corps and the remainder of Fifth Army. Moreover, no one ever did question the perception that the 36,000 troops of the Allied invasion force were enough to seize and hold both the Alban Hills and a logistical lifeline to the port of Anzio. Alexander's belief that they could accomplish both tasks was wholly unrealistic. Clark's instructions to Lucas left him the option of capturing the Alban Hills at his discretion, and he decided that the security of the beachhead was vital before undertaking an advance to enlarge the beachhead.

By the end of D-Day, the Germans had moved 20,000 reinforcements to the vicinity of Anzio, and in the days that followed the German buildup of Colonel Gen Eberhard von Mackensen's Fourteenth Army continued at a relentless pace, eventually reaching 120,000, of which 70,000 were combat troops, supported by large numbers of tanks and artillery, massed in a tight ring across the Anzio beachhead.

At the end of January, Lucas launched an offensive to enlarge the beachhead but it came too late; the Allies now found themselves boxed in. As the lead element of an attack to be launched on January 30 by the 3d Division, Darby's 1st and 3rd Ranger Battalions mounted an operation to capture the town of Cisterna the night of January 29. The rangers were ambushed,

The African-American 92nd Division played a key role in the Italian campaign. Above, members of a mortar company of the 92nd fire on German machine gun nests near Massa, Italy (November 1944); at right, 'doughfoots' of the 92nd Infantry ("Buffalo") Division pursue retreating Germans through the Po valley (May 1945).

trapped, and all but annihilated. Of the 767 rangers who took part in the operation only six returned to Allied lines. The Germans claimed to have taken 639 prisoners, many of whom were publicly marched through the streets of Rome.

Hitler ordered his troops to "lance the abscess south of Rome," and in the early morning hours of February 16 the Germans launched a massive counteroffensive to destroy the Allied beachhead. British and Americans fought a last ditch stand near Anzio. If the Germans broke through, the Allied front would have collapsed with catastrophic consequences. Waves of panzers and infantry hurled themselves upon the Allied defenders in a furious and ultimately futile series of attacks that failed to break the Allied line. A tidal wave of German attackers was cut down by machine-gun fire and the heaviest Allied artillery bombardments of the entire war in the Mediterranean. The battlefield was littered with corpses in scenes reminiscent of Pickett's Charge at Gettysburg. By sheer grit the lines held. Shattered by enormous casualties, the German attacks waned and the beachhead was saved. The British 3d Division, the U.S. 3d and 45th Divisions and Harmon's 1st Armored fought heroically for their very lives under almost indescribable conditions in what has been aptly described as "deafening, mad, screaming, senseless hatred." GIs and British Tommies rose to unheard of levels of fighting performance. Company E of the 2d Battalion, 157th Regiment (45th Division), sent to defend a vital crossroads called the Flyover, bore the brunt of the main German attack. For more than two days Company E somehow fended off wave after

wave of attacks, but with 99 percent losses. Only two returned to Allied lines: an NCO and the intrepid company commander, Captain Felix L. Sparks.

The German counteroffensive marked the turning point of the Anzio campaign. Although he had been given an impossible mission, Lucas was relieved of command and replaced by Major General Lucian Truscott. Instead of one stalemate at Cassino, the Allies now found themselves deadlocked on two widely dispersed fronts. Anzio had turned into a colossal liability for the Allies who were obliged to rush reinforcements from the south to meet the threat of the massive German build-up opposite VI Corps.

Churchill complained, "I thought we were landing a Tiger cat; instead all we have is a stranded whale." During the desperate months of the Anzio beachhead, the Allies lost 7,000 killed, and 36,000 more were wounded or reported as missing in action. Another 44,000 were hospitalized from various nonbattle injuries and sickness.

Wounded soldiers at Anzio. During the five-month campaign, more than 7,000 Allied soldiers were killed and 36,000 wounded or reported missing in action.

In February and March 1944, three offensives failed to capture the town of Cassino, the western anchor of the Gustav Line, over which stood the Abbey of Monte Cassino, one of the holiest shrines of Roman Catholicism. During the bloody First Battle of Cassino, the 34th Division suffered heavy losses in

a valiant but failed attempt to capture the town of Cassino, and the monastery and its heavily defended surrounding heights. PFC Leo J. Powers, a rifleman assigned to the 133rd Infantry Regiment, was awarded the Medal of Honor for single-handedly breaking the backbone of a heavily defended and strategic enemy position on Hill 175 on February 3, 1944. The same day, in a similar act of extraordinary heroism on Hill 175, 2d Lt. Paul F. Riordan, a platoon leader also assigned to the 133rd Infantry Regiment, won the Medal of Honor posthumously. A British historian who commanded a rifle company at Cassino later wrote that the exploits of the 34th Division "must rank with the finest feats of arms carried out by any soldiers during the war."

On both fronts the stalemate continued until late May, when simultaneous Allied offensives on the Cassino front and at Anzio signaled the end of the stalemate. The two fronts linked up the morning of May 25th, and on June 5th the Allies occupied Rome, a short-lived triumph all but forgotten the following morning as the long-delayed cross-Channel invasion of Normandy commenced in France.

During their fighting withdrawal north of Rome the Germans inflicted 34,000 casualties on the pursuing Allies. Alexander believed he could have thrust through the Gothic Line and driven the Germans from Italy during the summer of 1944. Instead, the irretrievable loss of VI Corps and seven veteran divisions detached for Operation Anvil, the invasion of Southern France, left 15th Army Group with a force of only 20 divisions against Kesselring's 22.

The Allies became stalled at the Gothic Line in the Apennines north of Florence, the strongest of a series of defensive barriers designed to slow the Allied advance until the winter weather set in, thereby continuing the war in Italy into 1945. Unrelenting late summer and autumn offensives by the Allied armies cracked but failed to break the Gothic Line. To Clark's bitter disappointment, offensive operations had to be shut down for the winter and did not resume until mid-April 1945.

During the final Allied offensive in Italy, the specially trained 10th Mountain Division won several key positions leading to the Po Valley, and the all-Nisei (American-born Japanese) 442nd Regimental Combat Team, whose soldiers were among the most highly decorated of any unit in the Army, performed brilliantly. The Germans withdrew to the natural defensive barrier of the River Po, which instead became an impassible barrier to their retreat. Some 100,000 German troops were trapped and forced to surrender when the war in Italy officially ended on May 4, 1945.

Between 400,000 and 500,000 troops fought in the Italian campaign as part of the largest Allied multinational force of World War II. Of the 312,000 Allied casualties, 189,000 (60 percent) were sustained by the U.S. Fifth Army. Of 31,886 Allied troops killed in action, 19,475 were American. For 602 days, from Salerno to the foothills of the Alps, the U.S. Army fought some of the bitterest battles of World War II during what has mostly been a forgotten campaign.

THE EUROPEAN THEATER OF OPERATIONS
1944–45

The D-Day landings on the beaches of Normandy on June 6, 1944 were the culmination of what four years previously had been thought of as a virtually unattainable goal. After nearly two years of quarrels, debates, postponements, and growing pressure from Stalin to open a second front, the Combined Chiefs of Staff at the Quebec Conference in August 1943 finally agreed on a firm timetable for Overlord. The operation would be mounted from the United Kingdom in May (later changed to early June) 1944.

Churchill firmly believed Overlord could succeed only with a massive force and meticulous planning, none of which was possible in 1942, or even 1943. He created a Combined Operations Staff to begin preparing for a second front and in October 1941 appointed a dynamic Royal Navy officer, Captain Lord Louis Mountbatten, who was directed: "to prepare for the invasion of Europe, for unless we can go and land and fight Hitler and beat his forces on land, we shall never win this war." In the spring of 1943 this function was transferred to an Anglo-American planning staff.

Beginning in 1944, the Allied buildup throughout the United Kingdom continued on an unprecedented scale. Southern England became the site of the most massive invasion force ever assembled as training for Overlord continued at a frantic pace in order to meet the planned May timetable. Amphibious training exercises took place in Scotland and off the southern coast of England. During Exercise Tiger in April more than 700 American troops drowned off Slapton Sands in Dorset when German E-boats based in Cherbourg attacked their landing craft.

The Overlord planners identified Normandy and the Pas de Calais region of northern France as the only two viable options. The Pas de Calais was the closest point to Britain, provided the most direct route of advance into Germany, and afforded maximum air cover from airfields in southern England. Conversely, it was such an obvious invasion site that the Germans had heavily reinforced its defenses and concentrated the bulk of their troops in France in this region. Normandy, with its lengthy sandy beaches and many excellent port facilities, met every test for a successful amphibious operation and was selected even though it was 100 miles from England

The principal Overlord commanders came from the Mediterranean. Eisenhower was appointed Supreme Commander and Montgomery was given a dual command of both British ground forces (21st Army Group) and of all Allied ground forces until Eisenhower could establish Supreme Headquarters Allied Expeditionary Force (SHEAF) in France and assume overall command after the invasion.

Lieutenant General Omar Bradley was appointed to command the U.S. ground invasion force, designated as First Army. In January 1944 Patton was secretly given command of the Third U.S. Army. Publicly, it was conspicuously revealed he was commanding the First U.S. Army Group. Called by the code-name of Fortitude by the Allied deception planners, Patton's command was an elaborate sham of fictitious units, fake emplacements, rubber and wooden tanks and vehicles, mock radio traffic, and false reports to Berlin by British agents posing as German spies - all created solely to convince the Germans that Patton was to lead the main Allied invasion in the Pas de Calais with an enormous force.

There was no doubt in Berlin that the Allies would open a Second Front by means of a cross-Channel invasion as early as the spring of 1944; and in January Hitler appointed Rommel to take charge of Germany's wholly inadequate defenses in the West. Rommel responded to this challenge in the same manner that had made him a legend in North Africa. Although he had no particular suspicion that Normandy was to be the Allied target, the sector from Caen to the Cotentin Peninsula nevertheless received special attention.

Montgomery devised the Allied invasion plan and the future strategy to be employed during the battle of Normandy. The original Overlord plan was expanded to include the Cotentin peninsula and airborne and glider landings added. The 82d and 101st U.S. Airborne Divisions were to seize the critical approaches to Cherbourg in the Cotentin, while the British 6th Airborne Division carried out a similar mission of protecting the Anglo-Canadian landings.

Montgomery's plan was for the British Second Army to block any attempt by Rommel to defeat the invasion or interfere with Bradley's assault on

"A Rocket Boat"

Right before the war, in 1943, I was playing for the Norfolk Yankee Farm Club. Well, I got drafted—eighteen years old, you know. They were nice enough to let me finish the season because my birthday was in May. I wanted to go in the Navy because they said I might play ball there in Norfolk. But it never happened that way.

I went to boot camp in Bainbridge, Maryland. When I finished boot camp there, I went to Little Creek, Virginia. They came up with this rocket boat, LCSS, and I volunteered for it. Because they were brand new, we couldn't even write home to our parents about what we were doing. It was a 36-footer, with six men and an officer. I used to love the rough water. I really did. I thought it was fun. Hit them waves. You hit a wave, you bounce back about 20 feet. That rocket ship took me to Normandy and Southern France.

Being a kid of 18, I thought Normandy was the 4th of July, I really did. My officer said to me as I was just standing up on board to look at all the pretty colors, "You better get your head down here or it'll be shot off." So I listened to him. I came down.

We went into Omaha Beach—we didn't go into the beach, we only went about 300 yards off shore. We were the first ones there before the Army went in. We had a lot of bombers. I've never seen so many planes in my life come over us! We had the *Nevada* on one side of us. We fired rockets into 'em. We spread out in a v-shape, about 50 yards apart. Then the Army went in. When they ran into machine gun nests, we would fire the rockets in there. I never went on the beach because our officers said, "Don't go on the beach, whatever you do," Even when the beach was secured, we didn't go on it.

I spent 10 days on the water. I was so tired. We lived on this little rocket boat for 10 days. You did the best you could on it. They gave us K-rations to eat and that was it. They used us as a messenger boat. I was very fortunate there because we were on the water a lot. I saw men that drowned. That was a bad sight. We were close to the enemy, but it seems like we didn't lose that many rocket boats. We finally got to go aboard ship and rest, and no sooner had I gotten in my bunk than GQ rings. I said, "I don't care if we get hit or not, I'm not leaving." I was so tired.

I got wounded in Southern France. The second invasion. We were only there that one day. We ran into a machine gun nest, the hotel on the beach. They were shooting at us and one of the bullets just grazed me, but we fired our rockets and knocked the hotel down.

When the war was over, I was happy to get out and go play ball again! I was lucky to get back. I never talked about the war very much. I really didn't. I never talked about being over there. I went to Newark—the Newark Bears—and actually joined them on my birthday in May.

—*Lawrence "Yogi" Berra, Hall of Fame Catcher*

Cherbourg, which would be followed by an offensive into the southern Cotentin and, eventually, operations in Brittany by Patton's Third U.S. Army to secure its ports.

During April and May Allied bombers pounded transportation links in northern France to sever all German ties to Normandy without revealing where the invasion would be launched. Meanwhile Fortitude convinced the German High Command that the primary invasion would occur in the Pas de Calais.

D-Day was set for June 5, 1944, but the weather deteriorated on June 4, as a full-blown storm not only rendered any hope of invading on June 5 impossible but also threatened to wreck the entire invasion timetable. Eisenhower ordered a 24 hour postponement. The SHAEF meteorologists reported a glimmer of hope for June 6; although the weather would remain marginal, visibility would improve and the winds decrease sufficiently to risk launching the invasion. Eisenhower was also aware that there was only one set of alternative dates in July where a full moon and low tides coincided. If the weather was again unfavorable there could be no invasion until 1945. As supreme commander the final decision was solely Eisenhower's, and he made one of the most difficult and fateful decisions in military history when he declared, "O.K., we'll go." There was no turning back.

D-DAY, JUNE 6, 1944

On the morning of June 6, 1944, the Allies carried out the greatest amphibious operation ever mounted when 156,000 troops parachuted from the skies, landed by glider and stormed the beaches of Normandy from the Orne River in the east to the Cotentin Peninsula in the west.

The airborne landings began on the night of 5/6 June when the 82d and 101st Airborne parachuted into the Carentan estuary to support the landings on Utah beach. Although the paratroopers landed scattered over a wide area in small groups, they severely disrupted German attempts to interfere with the Utah landings. To protect the British landings on Sword, Juno, and Gold beaches the British 6th Airborne secured intact the vital Pegasus Bridge, thus denying the Germans the only road link over the Orne between Caen and the sea.

The U.S. assault landings at Utah beach by the 4th Infantry Division achieved total surprise, the least opposition, and the fewest casualties, but on Omaha beach the veteran 1st Infantry Division and the attached 115th and 116th Regiments of the 29th Infantry Division, a National Guard unit in its first combat, ran into fierce resistance. From the steep bluffs overlooking Omaha the German defenders inflicted heavy casualties on confused and badly exposed troops and for the first six hours the Americans held only a few yards of beach. Many GIs died on the beaches, and others never even made it

D-DAY JUNE 6, 1944
YOU ARE ABOUT TO EMBARK UPON THE GREAT CRUSADE TOWARD WHICH WE HAVE STRIVEN THESE MANY MONTHS. THE EYES OF THE WORLD ARE UPON YOU... I HAVE FULL CONFIDENCE IN YOUR COURAGE, DEVOTION TO DUTY AND SKILL IN BATTLE.

GENERAL DWIGHT D. EISENHOWER

that far. The situation remained so perilous that at one point Bradley even briefly considered evacuating the beachhead and switching the follow-up units to Utah beach or the British sector.

Remaining on the exposed beaches was suicidal so the beachhead commanders and their NCOs rallied their troops. In the Big Red One sector the 16th Regiment commander, Colonel George A. Taylor, led his troops in an attack against German machine-gun positions, declaring, "Two kinds of people are staying on this beach, the dead and those about to die. Now let's get the hell out of here." Brigadier General Norman "Dutch" Cota of the 29th Division was one of many that day who deliberately exposed themselves to enemy fire to lead their troops off the beach and overwhelm the German positions entrenched on the bluffs atop Omaha Beach. As a result, others were inspired to act, among them was Private Raymond Howell, Co D, 116th Regiment. After being wounded by shrapnel, he recalled saying to himself, "Bullshit, if I'm going to die to hell with it I'm not going to die here."

Although progress could sometimes be measured in yards and casualties were high, the Americans on Omaha beach succeeded in clawing their way up the steep bluffs overlooking the sea and managed to carve out

(photo next page by Robert Capa)

U.S. Troops wade through water and Nazi gunfire at Omaha beach, D-Day, June 6, 1944.

Allied assault troops relax before a protective chalk cliff overlooking the invasion shore at Normandy, June 6, 1944.

a slender beachhead that withstood furious German resistance.

Through exceptional acts of leadership and gallantry by men of all ranks the Omaha beachhead was secured. One of the most remarkable feats on June 6 was by Lieutenant Colonel James E. Rudder's 2d Ranger Battalion. Under heavy enemy fire, rangers scaled the 100-foot high cliffs of the Pointe du Hoc to spike a battery of 155-mm guns. The rangers were under siege for two days and Rudder's 225-man force was reduced to only 90 combat effectives by the end of the battle.

Many veterans of the Normandy landings carried bitter memories of D-Day. Years later, when asked for his recollections of what it was like, one NCO angrily replied, "I'll tell you what the hell it was like. Water is blue or green, right? Well, the water that day was red with blood, that's what the hell it was like." Bradley should have the last word on the place he called "a nightmare: "Every man who set foot on Omaha Beach that day was a hero."

Despite the crisis at Omaha beach, June 6, 1944, was the most decisive day of the Second World War and marked the beginning of the end of Hitler's Third Reich. Earlier, Rommel had correctly predicted, "The first 24 hours of the invasion will be decisive . . . the fate of Germany depends on the outcome . . . for the Allies, as well as Germany, it will be the longest day."

THE BATTLE FOR NORMANDY

Although the initial landing operations were a stunning success, the strategy devised by Montgomery quickly ran afoul of fanatical resistance by German troops who held Caen and the strategically vital Caen-Falaise plain to the south. Although the German army in Normandy was outgunned, outmanned and often outflanked, Hitler issued "fight to the death" orders and rejected Rommel's plea to withdraw his forces out of range of the deadly Allied naval gunfire. Despite intense pounding from the air and naval gunfire offshore, they fought with a tenacity characteristic of the German army of World War II. The Germans were greatly aided by the close, confined terrain of the *bocage*: thousands of small fields ringed by earthen banks and dense shrubbery, making it impossible to see beyond a single field at a time. Although their reserves seriously dwindled, they stubbornly held Caen and casualties mounted on both sides from a series of bloody battles in June.

Repeated attempts to capture the city resulted not only in heavy British and Canadian losses but also mounting criticism that Montgomery had lost

D-Day, June 6, 1944

The ship dropped anchor at about 3:30. And from that moment on, it was get ready to go aboard the landing craft. And I remember hearing, "Attention on Deck! Attention on Deck! United States Rangers, embarkation stations!" And that was the time that you threw everything on your back and rushed up to the boat deck, started counting your men, checking their equipment, counting them again, checking the equipment again, and then loading into the landing craft assaults, LCAs. The boats were lowered down into the water and we were away, into a sea that was running between 10 and 12 feet. And this is awfully rough for the small boats. So on the 12 miles into the beach, we had an awful lot of men get seasick. But the waves were breaking over us and soon we had to take off our helmets and start baling.

We had three waves. There were five boats of the 2nd Ranger Battalion in front of us in the first wave, then seven boats of the 5th Battalion in the second wave, and I was in the third wave of seven boats. When we made the final turn and started in, somewhere around 500 yards out, the sounds of battle began to reach us—enormous sounds. Artillery bursting. The first thing we saw in the way of actual combat was an LCM, landing craft machine, just to our right front, about 50 yards away, was hit by an artillery shell. And that's pretty close for a shell to be hitting you, or hitting near you, 50 yards, and we realized we were really at war.

It was just like the battle scene in *Saving Private Ryan*. The ramps went down, the machine guns opened up, and those that got out got out alive did so by going over the sides, hiding behind debris. Being Rangers, they didn't hesitate, they came out of the water, rushed across the sand, and took protection behind the seawall or the embankment, but they'd suffered over 50 percent casualties.

The battalion executive officer was the first man off the boat. He went to the left, so I went to the right. And I yelled at my men, "Headquarters over here!" and ran across the beach. Now a lot of people couldn't run across the beach. They were so debilitated from seasickness that they could hardly move. The beach was swept, absolutely swept with rifle and machine gun fire, all coming in from our right hand side. We crossed that beach. We got up to the seawall. It was piled with men, three and four deep, trying to get out of that dreadful rifle and machine gun fire.

I was to follow C Company through a gap in the wire

Major General John Carpenter Raaen, Jr. (Retired)
World War II Ranger

that was blown probably about 75 yards to my left. I started to move my men over when I got tapped by a couple of my men on the elbow. They said, "Cap'n look down there!" And down the beach we could see a man walking, casually, yelling at the troops that were up on the embankment or at the seawall, he was smoking a cigar. I double-timed over to him and when I saw there was a great big star on his collar, I rushed up to him and saluted in the most proper military fashion, "Sir, Captain Raaen, 5th Ranger Battalion." He says, "Raaen? Raaen? You must be Jack Raaen's son." Which was true. He said, "I'm General Cota. What's the situation here?" I said, "Well, Sir, the 5th Ranger Battalion has landed over a 200-yard front extending that way." He said, "Where's the battalion commander?" I said, "He's over there, sir, I'll take you to him." He said, "You will not, you'll stay with your men." And he started away and all the time, he is standing up, artillery fire no more than 20 yards from him landing at the water's edge, and all this rifle and machine gun fire, and there I am forced to stand up with him. And he turned around and looked at the men, he said, "You men are Rangers, I know you won't let me down." And with that, he was off.

I got opposite the hole in the wire. I watched C Company go through, still under that dreadful machine gun fire, but there was a grassfire on the bluffs that blocked the visibility of the German troops on the hill. Many of them had actually been burned out of their positions and forced to retreat. So we had relatively little resistance. I actually climbed the seawall, crossed the road, went through the wire. And that's where I usually stop talking about the fight... Me, I was just following along. I didn't have to do any fighting. All I had to do was duck when the artillery came in.

control of the campaign. By the end of June the two sides were locked in a protracted stalemate.

In the U.S. sector First Army was similarly stalled in the mud and dense bocage north of St Lô. The most important objective in western Normandy was to capture the port city of Cherbourg, which was vital to satisfying the enormous logistical needs of the Allied expeditionary force. Before Cherbourg fell on June 27, the Germans managed to destroy its harbor facilities, and it was weeks before the port began to function anywhere near its intended capacity. Another key objective was the important crossroads town of St. Lô. Before it finally fell to the 29th Division on July 18, St. Lô was one of the bloodiest and costliest battles fought by the infantry. One young officer described it as "a boiling cauldron that no man entered without dread or emerged from unmarked."

BREAKING THE STALEMATE

In an attempt to break the impasse around Caen, on July 18 the British launched Operation Goodwood, a massive tank attack to break the German grip on Caen by employing heavy bombers to blast a path through which three armored divisions could gain access to the Caen-Falaise plains. Some

Medics helping an injured soldier in France.

LSTs landing vehicles and cargo on the beaches of Normandy, June 1944

4,500 Allied aircraft bombarded German positions and nearly a quarter of a million rounds of naval and ground artillery fire pounded the battlefield into a cauldron of smoke, dust, and destruction unprecedented in the history of ground combat.

The aerial and artillery bombardments failed to knock out all of the dreaded 88-mm anti-tank guns and panzers situated in several hamlets astride the British route of advance. These guns took such a heavy toll of British tanks that the offensive failed to break the stalemate.

Among the German casualties was Rommel, who was gravely wounded on July 17 when British fighters attacked his staff car. The Desert Fox had fought his final battle and several months later was forced to commit suicide in the aftermath of the abortive putsch against Hitler on July 20.

THE ALLIED BREAKOUT

Although Goodwood had failed, a similar American operation in the west, Operation Cobra, initiated by Bradley, broke the stalemate, but not without a heavy price. On July 25 there was a virtual repeat of the Goodwood bombardment as wave after wave of U.S. Ninth Air Force fighter-bombers attacked the target area, followed by 1,500 heavies of the Eighth Air Force that disgorged 3,400 tons of bombs. Tragically, however, some of the bombs struck the 30th Division and a unit of the 9th Division, killing 111 and wounding 490. Among the dead was the highest ranking officer killed in Europe, Lieutenant General Lesley J. McNair, Commander of Army Ground Forces, who, against Bradley's advice, had gone to the front to observe the bombing.

Despite its dreadful beginning, Cobra precipitated a breakout by First Army and by Patton's Third Army at Avranches on August 1. Incredibly, the Germans still continued to believe the Fortitude hoax, and most of their Fifteenth Army remained in the Pas de Calais awaiting what was thought to be the main invasion by Patton's fictitious army group.

The real plan, however, was to secretly move Third Army to France in early July. Patton's original mission was to liberate Brittany, but the unexpected success of Cobra resulted in a major shift in Allied strategy. Operations in Brittany were scaled back while the greater part of Third Army drove eastward toward the Seine. This significant decision was made just as Hitler, against the advice of his generals, ordered a powerful armored counterstroke against First Army at Mortain, to cut off and isolate all American forces that had advanced beyond Avranches. The German attack failed disastrously, primarily as the result of a heroic stand by the 120th Infantry Regiment (30th Division) at Hill 317. The 2d Battalion lost 300 men killed and wounded and won a presidential unit citation. The corps commander, J. Lawton Collins, praised it as, "one of the outstanding small-unit actions of World War II."

Hitler's failed gamble exposed the German army in Normandy to entrapment. With British and Canadian forces driving south from Caen and Patton's XV Corps north, the Germans were squeezed into a pocket between Argentan and Falaise. However, Bradley elected not to close what has come to be known as the Falaise Gap, thus spawning one of the campaign's lingering controversies and the myth that the Allies squandered an opportunity of epic proportions by permitting the majority of the surviving German Army in Normandy to escape.

Argentan, August 20, 1944.

While fierce battles were being fought in the Falaise Gap, the remainder of Third Army, spearheaded by the 79th Division and the 5th Armored Division, sliced across southern Normandy with little opposition. At Mantes, the 79th Division gained a crossing over the Seine. Both First and Third Armies blocked any further German escape across the River Seine. When German resistance collapsed east of the Caen-Falaise plain, the First Canadian Army and Lieutenant General Sir Miles Dempsey's Second British Army began

similar drives to the Seine. Except for mopping up operations, the battle of Normandy ended in an Allied triumph when the aptly named Corridor of Death was closed at Chambois on August 19.

The German Army Group B absorbed terrible punishment in the final days of the campaign. Some 10,000 perished attempting to escape through the last open escape route between Trun and Chambois. An estimated 50,000 more were taken prisoner and vast quantities of materiel were destroyed. Though it later proved impossible to make an accurate accounting of how many Germans escaped, the figure is estimated to be about 20,000.

THE ALLIED DRIVE ON GERMANY

The original Allied plan to pause and regroup at the Seine was hastily scrapped in favor of pursuit operations designed to crush the German army before it could defend the borders of the Reich. This decision led to the contentious broad front vs. narrow front question that pitted Eisenhower and Montgomery against each another.

In late August and early September, British, Canadian, and American armies swept into Belgium and across France during the most fluid period of World War II in the Western Front. As the Canadian First Army began

Crowds of French patriots line the Champs Elysées to view Allied tanks and halftracks, after the liberation of Paris on August 25, 1944.

(Next page) American soldiers in the victory parade down the Champs Elysées, August 29, 1944

clearing the Pas de Calais and the heavily defended Scheldt estuary around Antwerp, Third Army had swept east into Lorraine and spearheads of the British Second Army and the U.S. First Army slashed their way into southern Belgium.

Eisenhower took command of Allied ground forces from Montgomery on September 1, 1944, and thereafter directed the land battle. Eisenhower's post-Normandy strategy called for a broad advance by the Allied armies into Germany, and despite strong British protests he rejected outright Montgomery's plan for what the British general had termed a single, "full-blooded" thrust toward the Ruhr industrial complex.

On September 3, the British liberated Brussels, but in one of the worst blunders of the war neither Montgomery nor Dempsey ordered the capture of the vital Scheldt estuary, which temporarily remained in German hands—preventing the opening of the great port of Antwerp. The weeks

Blood Brothers

For U.S. Senators Bob Dole and Daniel Inouye, Pearl Harbor remains a vivid memory. "We thought we were being protected by these two oceans, and so suddenly that myth was exploded," said Dole. "I remember exactly where I was on that Sunday—the University of Kansas in our fraternity house. It changed our lives."

On December 7, 1941, Inouye was preparing to go to church when the radio blared information of the attack on nearby Pearl Harbor. Going into the street with his father, he saw three Japanese aircraft fly overhead. "They were gray in color, pearl gray, with red round dots. And I knew my world had come to an end," he said. Inouye raised his fist in the air and cursed the planes overhead.

A Red Cross first aid instructor, Inouye went to help injured civilians. "I had never seen dead people other than those I saw on December 7th, but to see them sprawled all over the place was quite a shock."

Dole grew up in rural Russell County, Kansas, and was a premedical student at the University of Kansas in 1942 when he enlisted in the U.S. Army. "They were losing a lot of second lieutenants," said Dole. "We had what they called Officer Candidate School in Fort Benning, Georgia. I decided that was a good idea and 90 days later, or thereabouts, I was a second lieutenant." By 1945, he was with the 10th Mountain Division fighting in the hills of Italy.

Only about a mile from Dole in Italy was another second lieutenant with the Army's 442nd Regimental Combat Team, the famed "Go For Broke" regiment. Daniel Inouye

had risen through the ranks to become an officer and he displayed fierce determination to prove that Japanese-Americans were first and foremost Americans.

After Pearl Harbor, the United States declared that Americans of Japanese ancestry were considered 4C—the Selective Service Commission designation for enemy alien. "We could not be drafted, nor could we volunteer," Inouye said. "In late 1942, we appealed to the government and the president, and they approved our petition. In early 1943, they opened the doors and we volunteered. They wanted about 1,800 from Hawaii, and about 10,000 volunteered—representing about 85 percent of the eligible young men of Japanese ancestry.

"We had to demonstrate to our fellow Americans and to the government that they had made a mistake when they considered us to be disloyal and not good citizens," Inouye said. "And we fully realized at the very outset that to demonstrate this would mean shedding of blood, but we were prepared for that."

Dole and Inouye were both severely wounded in combat only days apart and met while recovering from their injuries. They later served as friends, but on different sides of the aisle, in the U.S. Senate.

Dole was wounded April 14, 1945, as he was trying to rescue an injured radioman. Crawling out of the protection of

Bob Dole, former U. S. Senator, and presidential candidate

that followed saw a return to the sort of painfully slow, bloody warfare fought in Normandy as German units heeded Hitler's mandate to fight to the bitter end to prevent the port of Antwerp from becoming an Allied staging area for the final battle for Germany.

The acrimonious debates over strategy in the late summer and early autumn of 1944 were largely a reflection of the fact that the Allied campaign was now more logistical than tactical. The insatiable supply needs of the increasing numbers of Allied divisions and support troops dictated what could be accomplished on the battlefield. The downside of the great victory in Normandy was that the Allies had outrun their supplies, most of which were still positioned more than 400 miles to the rear. At the front there were increasing shortages, particularly of fuel, to fully support both American and Anglo-Canadian operations simultaneously. To the annoyance of Bradley and Patton, Third Army came to a halt in early September from

(Next page)
Parachutes open overhead as waves of paratroops land in Holland during operations by the 1st Allied Airborne Army, September 1944.

Daniel Inouye, U. S. Senator

his foxhole, Dole stayed low to reach the man. "I was dragging him back to the foxhole and suddenly I felt this sting on my right shoulder," he said. "My hands were over my head and I couldn't move my arms. I thought I'd lost my arms. I couldn't move them. It turned out I had a broken neck."

Dole lay there for nine hours before he was finally taken to an evacuation hospital. He was later transported to the Winter General Army Hospital in Topeka, Kansas, where he continued his painful recovery, and then later to Percy Jones Army Medical Center in Battle Creek, Michigan.

"Bob Dole was wounded on a hill about a mile away from mine," said Inouye. "I could see that hill on April 14, 1945. I was wounded on April 21, 1945."

Inouye was leading his platoon in an attack against a hill well defended by one of the last Italian units still in the war when he was shot through the stomach. "The only thing that I felt was a massive punch. It was bleeding slightly, and I felt that it did not in any way obstruct my movements, so I told the fellows let's keep on going."

Inouye was again wounded in the battle He was about to throw a hand grenade when his right arm was shattered at the elbow by a rifle grenade. "It was obvious that my arm was gone because it was just hanging and blood was squirting out," he recalled. "I took the grenade from my right

hand because the muscles just constricted, and I threw it. Somebody must have been looking after me, because it was very accurate. I continued going up to go for the second machine gun nest and then I got hit in the leg and began rolling down the hill. I kept telling my platoon, 'Keep on going!' We wiped out three machine gun nests and we took the hill. One casualty, me." In 2001, Inouye received the Medal of Honor for his actions that day.

Inouye spent 20 months in Army hospitals after losing his right arm. Dole's right shoulder was shattered and he was paralyzed from the neck down for a time, but a series of corrective surgeries and his personal courage restored his movement, except for his right hand.

"I think I looked like a scarecrow," said Dole "I couldn't walk. It took about 11 months before I could walk. You go through this period, 'why me? Why did this happen to me?' And you feel sorry for yourself, at least I did, I confess. But then you get over that and you figure I'm lucky, I'm here."

Fate had brought Dole and Inouye close in Italy, and fate brought them together at Percy Jones Army Medical Center in Michigan.

"By strange coincidence, we ended up in the same hospital," said Inouye. "And we became close buddies. There was another fellow, Philip Hart. So three of us were in the same hospital, same type of injuries."

"Hart took care of us and he later turned up in the Senate, too." Dole said. Lieutenant Colonel Philip Hart was wounded during the 1944 D-Day assault on Utah Beach in Normandy. Later, he was elected to the Senate in 1958 and served until his death on December 26, 1976. Today, the Hart Senate Office Building is named in his honor.

lack of fuel when Eisenhower allocated priority to Montgomery, a decision predicated on the fact that the advances of 21st Army Group to secure bridgeheads over the Rhine in Holland were of a higher priority.

THE LANDINGS IN SOUTHERN FRANCE

On August 15, the Allies landed the U.S. VI Corps (the primary element of the U.S. Seventh Army), a small force of French commandos and an airborne landing by a U.S. airborne task force along the French Riviera in Operation Dragoon (formerly called Anvil). Another of the controversial military operations of the war, the strategic necessity for the Allied landings in southern France has been debated ever since. Its many critics were adamant it was never a viable operation of war and that events in Normandy had by mid-August rendered it unnecessary. Eisenhower vehemently disagreed and insisted the Allies still required additional ports, particularly Marseilles, and that the second invasion force would protect the right flank of the broad Allied advance toward Germany. Eisenhower later noted, "I firmly believed that the greatest concentration of troops should be effected on the great stretch between Switzerland and the North Sea, whence we would most quickly break into the heart of Germany . . ."

OPERATION MARKET-GARDEN

By September 5, 1944, First Army had driven into eastern Belgium and crossed the Meuse to capture Namur, and had units in the Duchy of Luxembourg. By September 11th Seventh Army and the French First Army had driven up the Rhone Valley against only token opposition and linked up with Third Army.

As their armies advanced ever closer to Germany, the Allies began finalizing plans for the largest airborne operation of the war to seize key bridges over the River Waal at Nijmegen, the Rhine at Arnhem, the Maas at Grave, and the rivers and canals around Eindhoven. This would be followed by a ground thrust to relieve the airborne by the British Second Army from the Belgian-Netherlands border area.

The airborne operation by the First Allied Airborne Army was code-named "Market." "Garden" was the ground operation in which the XXX British Corps was to thrust north along a narrow corridor opened by the airborne. Once in control of the vital bridge along the lower Rhine at Arnhem, the remainder of Second Army was to turn the German flank and rapidly assault the Ruhr. By means of this surprise assault through the so-called back door to Germany, Montgomery hoped to hasten the collapse of the Third Reich and end the war in 1944.

The British 1st Airborne Division was assigned the mission of seizing Arnhem and the Rhine bridge, while the 82d and 101st Airborne Divisions were to be dropped near Nijmegen and Grave respectively. Despite warnings that the British landing zones were too far away from Arnhem Bridge, the planning for Market-Garden went full-steam ahead despite the stubborn refusal of the air commanders to drop the paratroopers or land the glider

As the Allies began their march across the Rhine, the German army blew up several famous bridges; but the Luddendorff bridge in the small town of Remagen, south of Bonn, somehow defied the efforts of the German engineers to destroy it. When the U.S. 9th Armored Division found the bridge standing they did not wait for orders but secured a bridgehead, and within 24 hours 8,000 men had crossed. Five divisions as well as hundreds of tanks and armored vehicles followed. Traffic was so heavy on the weakened bridge, however, that it crumbled only days later.

troops closer in the mistaken belief that German ack-ack ringing Arnhem made the operation too dangerous for their aircraft.

On September 17th, the Allies carried out the largest airborne and glider operation ever mounted. Although the landings initially went well, Allied intelligence had failed to heed reports from the Dutch underground that the German II SS Panzer Corps (consisting of elements of two panzer divisions) was bivouacked near Arnhem. Lieutenant Colonel John Frost's 2d Parachute Battalion was the only unit to reach the bridge, where it was cut off from the remainder of the 1st Airborne but fought off heavy German attacks for four days before being overwhelmed and its survivors compelled to surrender.

The success of Market-Garden hinged on the ability of XXX Corps to rapidly relieve the lightly armed airborne troops at each of the bridges along their route of march. Mammoth traffic congestion and German resistance along the only road to Nijmegen and Arnhem (nicknamed "Hell's Highway") delayed the British ground advance by crucial hours and although XXX Corps linked up with the 101st Airborne at Eindhoven on September 18, the 82d U.S. and 1st British Airborne Divisions remained unrelieved and engaged in savage battles for survival.

By September 25 it was clear that the operation had failed and a rescue attempt was made to save what remained of the British 1st Airborne and a

Polish airborne brigade. Of the 10,300 men who had landed at Arnhem on September 17, 1,400 had been killed, more than 6,000 were POWs, and the division was no longer a viable fighting unit.

What had begun with high optimism ended tragically. Although the heroic stand of Frost's paratroopers at Arnhem Bridge was one of the legendary episodes of World War II, Operation Market-Garden itself was an abject failure. The Allies had failed to establish their objective of a bridgehead north of the Rhine in what has been dubbed "a bridge too far."

THE AUTUMN STALEMATE

Although the Allied armies had advanced to the borders of the Third Reich by early autumn, the resiliency of the Wehrmacht and the advent of bad weather left the Allies virtually immobilized in the mud, snow and the harsh terrain of the outer Ruhr and in the Ardennes Forest. American attempts to crack the Siegfried Line and gain access to the heartland of Germany met with failure across the entire Allied front, from Schmidt and the Roer River in the north, to the Moselle in the south, where Patton's Third Army was mired in Lorraine. The fortress city of Metz held out throughout October against the siege warfare that Patton detested.

That Bridge at Remagen

I got permission to finish the baseball season before I went in the service. But boy the minute the baseball season was over, I was in the Army and I wound up in the 14th Armored Division as a combat engineer. And that was a nice way of having units to do all the dirty work that other people didn't want to do.

Well, we wound up in the Battle of the Bulge. And we were surrounded by the Germans. And I think one of the interesting things is that you didn't know if the guy next to you was American or German, because they had our uniforms, they had our dog tags, and they spoke our language fluently. But the one thing that they didn't know very much about is our game of baseball, so a password between the Americans was: Who played the Keystone sack for the Dodgers? And unless you know that the second baseman was the Keystone, and the Dodgers were the Brooklyn Dodgers, they were automatically shot.

I think one of the big things is that we had a cause that was greater than the Germans had. That we were fighting for freedom. We were fighting the Germans in Europe rather than have to fight them over here. So that here's a baseball player that all I want to do is get the war over and get back to the game I love, and it didn't happen over night. There were a lot of trials and tribulations that happened. And I think the differential, too, is that we were proud to be American. That we believed in our country. . . we were bound and determined that we were gonna win and we did.

You know there were months that we didn't get to change our clothes. Didn't get to take a shower. The food was horrible, and it was HORRIBLY cold! You know, I lived in Buffalo, New York so that was cold. But that winter in Germany was terribly, terribly cold. And we used to sleep with our boots on, with our clothes on. If your socks were wet, they stayed wet. And why we didn't get frostbitten, I'll never know.

We were supposed to stop at the Rhine River, but we had an opportunity to take the Remagen Bridge. There was just a handful of people protecting it, and they had wired it with detonation to blow the bridge. But the explosives didn't go off. So we took over the bridge. And we established a bridgehead about three miles on the other side. And even Eisenhower didn't know that we had that bridge.

It was a railroad bridge and we were trying to get treadway over it to get tanks and vehicles across it. And we actually added so much weight to that bridge that it fell of its own accord. We were standing on the east side of the bridge, and all of a sudden, it sounded like rifle shots, the rivets coming out of that bridge, and this is when the bridge fell, literally collapsed.

We lost a lot of people. We lost a lot of officers, that's how come I got a battlefield commission. And so we did something that the Germans couldn't do—destroy that bridge at Remagen. But the big thing about it is that we got enough people across there that it probably shortened the war.

I'll never forget that when I did come back, I was pitching and I thought, hey, what a great way to make a living. If I don't do well, nobody's gonna shoot me. And that I could take a shower after the game was over, which we couldn't do in Europe.

It was a great experience. I think it was the greatest education I got toward my endeavor in life. The military taught me so many things about perseverance, about determination, about stick-to-itiveness. I think it taught me a lot. There was no situation that happened on the baseball field that I didn't experience in the military. And I think that's maybe why we're the nation that we are. We've been through rough times including now and we're veterans of dealing with adversity. And I think that's why America is so great.

Warren Spahn
Hall of Fame Pitcher

Advancing through the Rhone Valley from the French Riviera, Lieutenant General Jacob L. Devers's Sixth Army Group (the U.S. Seventh Army and the French First Army) managed to drive through the Vosges Mountains before they too were stalled at the at the west bank of the Rhine.

The 761st Tank Battalion was the first African-American tank unit to see action in northwest Europe and earned the respect of the numerous units they supported during 183 days of combat, beginning on October 31, 1944, with the 26th Infantry Division near Metz, and ending on May 6, 1945, with the 71st Infantry Division on the Enn River near Steyhr, Austria. Along the way, the 761st also supported the 79th, 87th, 95th, and 103d Infantry Divisions, and the 17th Airborne Division, and action in the Third, Seventh, and Ninth Army sectors. In January 1997, Staff Sergeant Ruben Rivers, who was killed in action on November 19th, 1944, near Guebling, France, was posthumously awarded the Medal of Honor—one of seven black soldiers to fight in World War II so recognized by President Clinton.

The most brutal battles of all were fought in the frigid, dense Huertgen Forest, which lay astride the route to the Roer dams. In November 1944, in a series of battles reminiscent of the worst combat of the First World War, the U.S. First Army commander, Lieutenant General Courtney Hodges, who had succeeded Bradley, flung one division after another into the bloody cauldron of the Huertgen. Although the U.S. First and Ninth Armies suffered 57,000 combat losses and 70,000 more to the ravages of the elements, the Germans remained in control of the vital Roer dams.

THE BATTLE OF THE BULGE

Hitler elected to gamble the fate of Germany on a last-ditch attempt to split Eisenhower's armies by a sudden, lightning blitzkrieg thrust through the Ardennes Forest, naively believing his armies could drive clear to Antwerp and compel the Allies to sue for peace. Although his ground commanders strongly opposed Hitler's counteroffensive, their protests fell upon deaf ears. Under the cover of the bitterest winter weather in years, 30 divisions (consisting of an estimated half-million German troops), supported by more than 1,400 tanks and 2,000 guns, were secretly moved into the thick forests of the rugged Schnee Eifel on the eastern fringes of the Ardennes.

The Allies did not expect a major offensive in the Ardennes, and this belief, combined with German audacity, the harsh winter weather, and faulty intelligence enabled the Germans to catch the Allies flat-footed on December 16th, 1944, when two German panzer armies launched the main attack against the most lightly defended sector of the U.S. First Army. The thinly held lines of the untested U.S. 106th Division were quickly overrun by a vastly superior German force.

The key to German success was to advance rapidly and for their panzer spearheads to secure bridgeheads west of the Meuse River before the Allies could react. At first the juggernaut appeared unstoppable, but in some of the most gallant individual and small unit actions of the war, weary American fighting men gained time for reinforcements to arrive by either holding their positions or slowing the German advance by precious hours. Places named Saint Vith (held for nearly a week by the 7th Armored Division and an ad hoc collection of U.S. units), Elsenborn Ridge, Houffalize, and Bastogne became immortalized in American military history.

The other vital element for German success was to control Bastogne, through which all major roads in the Ardennes passed. The 101st Airborne held Bastogne and although surrounded, its acting commander, Brigadier General Anthony McAuliffe, responded to a German surrender ultimatum with the now famous one-word reply: "Nuts!"

Eisenhower ordered Patton to turn Third Army 90 degrees and attack toward Bastogne, which it did in only three days, in exceptionally difficult conditions, and in the worst winter weather in a half-century. In one of the great feats of military history, Third Army, aided by a welcome break in the weather that permitted Allied air support, broke the siege of the beleaguered town on December 26th with the 4th Armored Division. Although heavy fighting continued well into the new year of 1945, the Battle of the Bulge (so-named for the "bulge" created by the deep German penetration into Allied lines) was effectively won by Christmas when the German spearheads stalled east of the Meuse River for lack of fuel and ammunition.

In retrospect, Hitler's desperate gamble had virtually no chance of success, despite achieving surprise. The paucity of German resources combined with the gallantry of American troops proved fatal to Hitler's ambition to somehow attain, if not victory, at least a draw with the Allies and a voice in the terms of Germany's surrender.

(Next page)
Bodies of U.S. officer and soldiers massacred by Nazis after capture near Malmedy, Belgium, December 11, 1944

American soldiers of the 289ᵗʰ Infantry Regiment march along a snow-covered road on their way to cut off the Saint Vith-Houffalize road in Belgium, January 24, 1945.

A panoramic view of the city of Nijmegen, Holland, and the Nijmegen Bridge over the Waal (Rhine) River in the background. The city was hit by German and Allied bombardment and shelling, Sepember 28, 1944.

The Battle of the Bulge, notes historian Charles B. MacDonald, was the "greatest pitched battle ever fought by American arms." The 600,000 Americans who participated constituted "more than three times the number that fought on both sides at Gettysburg." American casualties totaled 81,000, approximately 19,000 of whom were killed and another 15,000 taken prisoner. German losses, estimated at over 100,000, were irreplaceable.

THE INVASION OF GERMANY

Eisenhower continued to advance his armies across a broad front to the Rhine. In what constituted the largest force ever assembled, nearly 4,000,000 U.S., British, and Canadian troops of three army groups, seven field armies, 21 corps and 73 divisions were poised to launch the final offensive to end the war. By V-E Day these numbers would grow to 4.5 million men and 91 divisions, while the Red Army drive on Berlin had over two million troops, 6,000 tanks, and 16,000 aircraft in action on the Eastern Front.

The Rhine was unexpectedly breached on March 7, when the U.S. 9th Armored Division captured a railway bridge at Remagen intact. Taking

America's Most Decorated Soldier

In the snow and cold of France on January 26, 1945, a twenty-one-year-old Army lieutenant named Audie Murphy was in command of B Company, 1st Battalion, 15th Infantry Regiment, 3rd Division, and already was a battlefield legend. In 1944, he had won a Silver Star and the Distinguished Service Cross for valor.

Murphy and his men were in the Alsace region of France, where the Germans were trying a new offensive to push back the Allies. Murphy's assignment on this brutally cold day was to hold his position when the Germans came. They came all right, two companies and a half-dozen tanks, bearing down on Murphy's under-manned unit. German artillery fire exploded around him, killing and maiming his men. Murphy leaped aboard a burning American tank, grabbed a machine gun and began firing in a frenzy. Smoke obscured his position, but he could see his enemy perfectly well. All the while, he directed American artillery fire over a radio line. He turned his fire on a dozen Germans in a ditch 50 yards away. He would later say that he "stacked them up like cordwood."

Single-handedly, Audie Murphy repulsed the German attack. For his bravery, he would receive the Medal of Honor, one of 37 medals he would receive by war's end, making him the most-decorated soldier in the nation's history.

Audie Leon Murphy was born into a Texas sharecropping family on June 20, 1924. The Murphys, descendants of Irish immigrants who left their native land during the potato famine of the 19th century, were poor and numerous. And Audie, known by his middle name until he joined the Army, was the family's seventh child. More would follow, until Emmet and Josie Bell Murphy were the parents of nine children, not counting three others who had died in infancy.

Audie Murphy's formal education stopped after fifth grade. But Murphy was learning a skill in the Texas countryside that would define the course of his adult life. He was a natural marksman. Armed with a shotgun or a .22 caliber rifle, Murphy shot rabbits, squirrels and other small, fast-moving targets with deadly precision.

Emmett Murphy disappeared one day—although he would turn up here and there until he died in 1976—and Josie Bell, worn out by life, died in 1941, an old woman at age 49. Audie was 16 and already on his own.

Lieutenant Audie Leon Murphy, U.S. Army

Immediately after the Japanese attack on Pearl Harbor on December 7, 1941, the 17-year-old Murphy presented himself to recruiters for the armed services. He was turned down: He was too young and too small, just over five feet, five inches and weighing just 112 pounds, according to Don Graham's fine biography, *No Name on the Bullet*. Finally, though, on June 30, 1942, Audie Murphy joined the Army.

Murphy hit the beaches of Sicily on July 10, 1943, and quickly saw the gruesome, terrifying realities of war for the first time. He proved himself to be a natural soldier, and won several medals, including the Bronze Star, during the Italian campaign.

On August 15, Murphy and the 3rd Division landed in southern France. The invasion was only a few hours old when Murphy and two other soldiers quietly crawled toward a German gun emplacement. The two other soldiers were spotted and killed, but Murphy continued forward. He killed two Germans and then began firing on a machine-gun nest. A friend of his, Lattie Tipton, joined him. When the Germans waved a white flag, Tipton rose, and was shot dead. Murphy went berserk. Throwing grenades and firing his machine gun, he attacked the position and killed every German he saw, winning the Distinguished Service Cross for his effort. Several weeks later, he won the Silver Star when he came to the aid of trapped comrades, once again eliminating a German position single-handedly.

By war's end, Audie Murphy was credited with killing 240 enemy soldiers. After his picture ran on the cover of *Life* magazine in July, 1945, he was not only the most-decorated soldier in American history, he was a celebrity. His fame led to a career in Hollywood, where he starred in a film version of his military exploits, *To Hell and Back*, and in such films as *The Quiet American* and *Red Badge of Courage*, as well as many westerns.

He died in a plane crash in 1971, at the age of 46. He is buried in Arlington National Cemetery. —*Terry Golway*

advantage of this extraordinary opportunity, the 9th Armored established a bridgehead east of the Rhine. By the end of March some 300,000 German troops were trapped in the rapidly closing Ruhr pocket.

With the Allies on the Rhine, only about 300 miles from Berlin, and the Russians astride the Oder River, a mere 30 miles east of the German capital, the question of Berlin became of paramount importance. Earlier, Eisenhower had expressly stated that Berlin was an Allied objective, but in light of the Yalta agreements, he changed his mind and unilaterally announced that the city was no longer of military consequence. Eisenhower formalized his intentions in a message to Stalin on March 28. The Combined Chiefs of Staff were split on the issue but never overruled Eisenhower, thus tacitly validating his controversial directive. Churchill vehemently protested that Allied failure to take Berlin will "raise grave and formidable difficulties in the future," but Roosevelt, who was gravely ill and in the last days of his life, endorsed Eisenhower's decision to avoid Berlin and instead halt at the Elbe River, 100 miles to the west. Although the U.S. Ninth Army already had established bridgeheads over the Elbe and was capable of driving into Berlin before the Russians, Eisenhower turned down the plan.

On April 25, 1945, Americans and Russians met at the Elbe, when a patrol of the 2d Battalion, 273rd Regiment (69th Division) made contact with a small Russian force near the town of Strehla.

Aerial view of the Reichschancellory in Berlin, damaged by Allied bombing, July 1945.

Liberated prisoners in the Mauthausen concentration camp near Linz, Austria, welcome Cavalrymen of the 11th Armored Division, May 6, 1945. The banner across the wall was made by Spanish Loyalist prisoners.

During April 1945 the death knell of the Third Reich sounded as the rampaging Allied armies began mopping up pockets of resistance from the central plains of Germany to the Alps, capturing tens of thousands of prisoners and drawing the noose ever tighter. In mid-April the Red Army began a three-week siege of Berlin. In one of the bloodiest battles fought by the Red Army, German troops responded to Hitler's order to fight to the death by inflicting more than 300,000 Russian casualties. The once great city of Berlin was reduced to smoking rubble, and on May 2 the Germans surrendered their capital.

Hitler committed suicide the night of April 30, and his body was burned in a funeral pyre outside his Berlin bunker that would have done justice to Wagner's *Götterdammerung*. To the bitter end the German madman who had unleashed the worst conflagration in history entertained delusions that somehow he could still snatch victory from the jaws of defeat.

By early May, Third Army had driven into Austria and Czechoslovakia, but Patton's troops were forbidden to enter the Czech capital of Prague even though they could easily have done so well before the Red Army liberated the city on May 9. On May 4, Eisenhower made another controversial decision by prohibiting any advance by Third Army beyond the prewar border near Pilsen on grounds that Czechoslovakia was to become part of Russia's so-called "sphere of influence" agreed earlier at Yalta, and on the (erroneous) premise that the Red Army would liberate Prague before Patton could.

With the liberation of the Bergen-Belsen concentration camp by the British, Buchenwald and Dachau by units of Patton's Third Army, and Mauthausen in Austria by the 11th Armored Division, the world learned for the first time the full extent of the gruesome atrocities perpetrated by the Nazis.

On V-E Day, May 8, 1945, the war formally ended when Germany surrendered unconditionally in Reims, France, after Eisenhower rejected an earlier attempt to negotiate a separate surrender only to the Western Allies. Europe was devastated, and the staggering cost of World War II in Europe and the Mediterranean were legacies of the worst conflagration in the history of mankind. Civilian and military deaths have been estimated as high as 50 million dead. Germany lost some 4.6 million dead, and untold thousands (perhaps several million) of German POWs disappeared into Soviet slave labor camps and were never seen again.

American battle casualties for the entire war were 201,367 killed (160,045 of them in Europe and the Mediterranean) and exceeded the combined losses of both sides of the Civil War. In 2001 there were still 78,000 MIAs from World War II still unaccounted for.

In his final report as chief of staff, Marshall issued a powerful and prophetic warning:

> We have tried since the birth of our nation to promote our love of peace by a display of weakness. This course has failed us utterly.

THE LAND WAR
WITH JAPAN

★

Allan R. Millett

"... Uncommon valor was a common virtue."
—ADMIRAL C.W. NIMITZ,
MARCH 16, 1945,
IN A COMMUNIQUE ABOUT IWO JIMA

THE ORIGINS OF WAR WITH JAPAN

Having followed European models of industrialization and modernization since the 1870s, the political and military leaders of Imperial Japan decided that their nation's cultural and economic greatness depended upon creating an Asian empire. Many Japanese did not trust the Europeans to concede Japan's right to have an empire or to demand equitable trading relations. The first thrust of Japanese imperialism came against the two weakest targets, Imperial China and Czarist Russia, and in two wars (1895, 1904–1905) Japan annexed Formosa, made Korea a protectorate, and made itself the dominant foreign power in Manchuria. This phase of Japanese imperialism enjoyed the support of Great Britain by treaties in 1902 and 1905 and by the United States through executive agreements in 1905 and 1908. Great Britain judged Japan a firm ally against Russia and, less menacingly, Germany and the United States. The United States sought to enter Japanese markets, to restrict Asian immigration, and to guarantee the security of the Philippines, annexed in 1899 but directed toward independence after 1916.

The first Japanese empire expanded dramatically, then partially collapsed during World War I and its aftermath. Japan's supporters became its betrayers—in Japanese eyes. When the Japanese armed forces occupied Germany's China and Pacific colonies and then took portions of Russia's Maritime and Siberian provinces "under protection" from the Bolshevik revolutionaries, Great Britain and the United States led the effort to force Japan to surrender its new conquests in Asia to weak Chinese and Russian governments. Japan also accepted a League of Nations–supervised trusteeship over Saipan and Tinian in the Marianas Islands group and the Caroline Islands, including Palau, rather than an outright annexation. The Anglo-American "conspiracy," as the Japanese viewed it, continued in the Washington Conference treaties of 1922, which ended the Anglo-Japanese alliance, guaranteed China's independence and the security of the European-American colonies in Asia, while placing various limits on the battle fleets of Great Britain, the

United States, Japan, Italy, and France. Facing a postwar economic crisis, Japan could not afford to alienate the other powers. The Japanese government, under the control of civilian politicians and economic leaders, accepted conditions for future collaboration with the West that struck the Japanese ultra-nationalists as humiliating appeasement, and a blueprint for economic disaster.

The collapse of the world economy after 1929 and the rise of fascism in Europe gave the Japanese neo-imperialists and ultra-nationalists, including Emperor Hirohito, a new opportunity to remake Japan as an expansionist power. Their goal was to eliminate all European and American colonies in Asia and to strip China of Western influence. The new governing coalition in Tokyo—the military leadership and leading industrialists—also wanted to stamp out Communism in China before it infected the Japanese urban-industrial masses. Emboldened by Western political demoralization, Japan first tested the new international environment by driving the Chinese administrators and armies from Manchuria and establishing the rules for foreign participation in Manchuria's economy. Russians of every political persuasion were unwelcome, although some diehard Czarist Russians remained in the new puppet state, Manchukuo, ruled by Henry Puyi, the last Qing emperor of China. The Japanese leaders of the Kwantung Army not only eliminated any rivals in southern Manchuria, but, exceeding their instructions from Tokyo, occupied all of the country up to its border with the Soviet Union, 1931–1933. Japan regarded with contempt the symbolic condemnation of its "aggression" by the League of Nations. It also abrogated all the Washington and London naval treaties.

Now fully under the control of ultra-nationalist imperialists, the Japanese government consolidated its expanded Asian domain by joining Nazi Germany in an anti-Communist alliance in 1936 and then attacking China proper in July 1937. Japan justified "the China Incident" by arguing that the Chinese Nationalists and Communists, in league with the Soviet Union, threatened Manchukuo with guerrilla warfare. The charge was true, but only a minor irritation to the Kwantung army. The invasion of China had a single determining cause: to place food, raw materials, and millions of cheap laborers safely under Japanese control. By 1939, Japanese troops held China's major coastal cities and had advanced up the great valleys of the Yellow and Yangtze Rivers. Japanese bombers ranged farther inland to attack the remnants of the Chinese Nationalist army, largely destroyed in fighting around Shanghai and Nanjing, as they fled to the new capital at Chungking. Under the halting leadership of Generalismo Chiang Kai-shek and sturdier direction of Madame Chiang (Soong Mei-ling), the Nationalist government could purchase war supplies abroad as long as it had money or received private loans, but it received no official military aid until after the United States established the Lend-Lease program in March 1941. It did profit from indirect Russian support of the Chinese Communist armies in hiding in 1938–1939 in remote northwest China. In 1939 the Japanese army tested the Russian armies along the border of

Mongolia and suffered embarrassing defeats. The Japanese army generals thus lost some of their taste for more northern campaigns, which boded ill for southern China and southeast Asia.

The Germans created the next geopolitical advantage for Japan by defeating the Allies in France in 1940 and invading the Soviet Union in 1941. Japan forced the Vichy government of France to consent to the occupation of Indochina, accomplished in stages in 1940 and 1941. The Japanese movement into Southeast Asia plugged up one route of supplies to Nationalist China and put Japanese air, naval, and ground forces within striking distance of Malaya, the Dutch East Indies, and the Philippines, all part of a region labeled the South Seas Resource Area. Japanese economic anxiety soared when the United States attempted to force Japan from China and to renew its pledge not to attack European colonies through a series of economic sanctions. The United States in 1940 regulated exports to Japan by government licensing (a slow process) and then placed an embargo on scrap iron, steel, aviation gasoline, and other petroleum products.

After the Japanese moved into strategic bases in southern Indochina in July 1941, the United States froze Japanese assets and extended the embargo to almost all forms of oil products. American loans and direct military aid to China increased during the same period. To improve its military posture against Japan, the Roosevelt administration shifted much of the Pacific Fleet to the unfinished base at Pearl Harbor, Oahu, Hawaiian Islands in 1940–1941 and called the army of the Commonwealth of the Philippines to active duty in 1941. The United States planned to stiffen its western Pacific

A baby wails in the wreckage of Shanghai's South Station after a Japanese bombing, August 1937.

forces with bombers, submarines, and ground forces heavy with artillery, tanks, and antiaircraft artillery in late 1941 and early 1942.

The Japanese leadership believed that it faced a time of both peril and opportunity—another chance to use a European war to remake the borders of Asia and the Pacific. The modern Japanese Empire could finally be self-sustaining and immune from Western economic coercion and cultural arrogance. Since Japan and the Soviet Union had signed a neutrality treaty of mutual advantage in April 1941, the United States became the only likely opponent to a campaign to take the Allies' rich colonies of Southeast Asia, with the Philippines the geographic cork in the raw materials bottle. For its part the United States hoped to negotiate a graduated Japanese withdrawal from China and to preserve the Asian colonies as resource areas for the Allied war against Nazi Germany. Since the United States faced a likely war against Germany as Great Britain's reluctant ally—as the Japanese reasoned—the Americans would accept the second Japanese empire rather than weaken their war effort in Europe. The Americans, they were sure, had no stomach for an Asia-Pacific war.

THE ALLIED OBJECTIVES IN ASIA

The American land campaigns in the war with Japan reflected an essential strategic truth for the United States: the unconditional surrender of Japan required the overwhelming use of Allied air and naval forces to destroy the Japanese navy and air forces. The defeat would isolate the Home Islands from all natural resources and raw materials. If a complete economic blockade and strategic bombing did not destroy the Japanese will to fight, then the captured air and naval bases would become the foundation for an invasion of the Home Islands. Ground defended and assaulted had no meaning for the Americans except for its utility in the great air-naval offensive that began in August 1942, and ended three years later when the Emperor Hirohito surrendered his battered nation. The only partial strategic deviation from the American way of war against Japan was the liberation of the Philippines, 1944–1945, the redemption of a prewar pledge to grant independence to the Filipinos in 1946.

The other members of the Allied coalition would have welcomed a greater land force commitment to the Asia-Pacific war, but American political and military leaders knew that the Allies had different war aims. Great Britain wanted to recapture Burma and Malaya, while France sought a return to Indochina and the Netherlands to the Dutch East Indies. Australia and New Zealand wanted the Japanese driven off the Malay Barrier, the doorstep to "down under." The Soviet Union only awaited the right moment to renounce its neutrality pact with Japan and to take back its privileged position in Manchuria and Korea, lost in 1905. The Chinese of every political persuasion—with the exception of a small pro-Japanese faction—would have welcomed an American army to drive away the hated invaders of 1937.

Generalissimo Chiang Kai-Shek

(Previous page)
American troops of the 160th Infantry Regiment rush ashore from a landing boat during amphibious training at Guadalcanal, March 1, 1944.

With the exception of its sentimental attachment to China and some real, if limited, strategic advantages to an alliance with the Chinese Nationalist government, headed by Generalissimo Chiang Kai-shek, the United States avoided campaigns on the Asian mainland, which it regarded as of minimal relevance to Japan's defeat. With its commitment to a major European offensive against Nazi Germany and its role as the Allies' "Arsenal of Democracy," the United States could hardly afford to create an expeditionary force of U.S. ground troops comparable to its army (68 divisions) that confronted the Wehrmacht. Instead, the U.S. Army sent 21 divisions, and several separate regiments to fight the Japanese, along with a U.S. Army Air Forces (USAAF) tactical air force of 70,000 aircraft. The U.S. Marine Corps contributed six divisions and four aircraft wings. Had the Japanese massed their army and army aviation against the U.S. armed forces alone, they would have outnumbered the American armed forces 2:1. Growing U.S. air and naval superiority, secure by mid-1944, made the Imperial ground forces of limited strategic relevance, whatever the skill and suicidal tenacity of the Japanese soldiers.

The Asia-Pacific Theater, however, imposed hardships on all ground forces that only the Allies could eventually overcome. The terrain was often mountainous and road-poor; island ports and harbors had not been developed to support an industrialized, consumer-oriented ground force like the U.S. Army and Marine divisions. The logistical coin-of-the-realm became beaching ships, tanker ships with fuel hoses, earth-moving engineering equipment, rough terrain vehicles, and pre-packaged ammunition and supplies adequately protected from water and sand. The rain forests of Burma and the South Pacific produced tropical diseases in unidentifiable abundance and encouraged wound infections and psychological breakdowns among American troops that exceeded those in the European Theater. Losses from disease and rates of not-returned-to-duty wounded were the worst in the history of U.S. armed forces. American deaths included victims of snake bites as well as tiger and shark attacks. Even with a reduced need for gasoline and lubricants for vehicles, American ground forces required 4.5 tons of materiel per deployed soldier and one ton of supplies a month thereafter to keep that soldier in action.

Against this strategic-logistical background, the experience of the Army and Marine divisions and their supporting air wings can be divided by time and place into four major Asia-Pacific sub-theaters and campaigns: mainland Asia, specifically India-Burma-China; the South Pacific; the Central Pacific, and the Western Pacific, including the Philippines.

MAINLAND ASIA

Until the last 14 months of the Asia-Pacific war, the Japanese armed forces held the strategic initiative in the Asian mainland theater. Although about half of Chinese territory and population remained beyond Japanese occupation, the United States could not turn China into a strategic asset. The British hardly thought the effort sensible. In fact the American war effort reflected two competing strategic visions. One vision, advocated by General Joseph W. Stilwell, stressed the reform of the Chinese Nationalist army for limited ground offensives against the Japanese, a plan that would prevent the redeployment of Japanese divisions to the Pacific and the encouragement of American-supported Chinese partisans, including the two Communist armies in the field in northern China. The other vision stressed an air campaign by the USAAF China-based Fourteenth Air Force, commanded by the legendary Major General Claire Chennault, a special confidant of Chiang Kai-shek. Chennault saw his air forces as essential to a Chinese ground offensive, but he and his USAAF superiors also saw China as a great air base for heavy bombers, especially the new B-29, that would attack the Home Islands.

The essential problem of either the Stilwell or the Chennault strategic concept—attractive to Franklin Roosevelt but less so to the Joint Chiefs of Staff (JCS)—was logistical. The Japanese conquest of Burma (December 1941–April 1942) cut off the 700-mile "Burma Road," actually a network of dirt tracks, the only land route to China. The key to supporting an Allied war effort in China became building a new road from Ledo in the province of Assam, India to a juncture with the Burma Road, 230 miles distant. The only alternative, one taken in late 1942, was to fly supplies over the mountains of "the Hump," a spur of the Himalayas. A trip of 500 air miles, the "Hump" route cost the USAAF more than 1,000 air crewmen and almost 600 aircraft to deliver 650,000 tons of supplies, but by January 1944 the force of 650 USAAF transports could carry 15,000 tons a month to China. Both Stilwell and Chennault wanted the Ledo-Burma road opened and relied on four American-sponsored forces to drive the Japanese from northern Burma: a U.S. Army regimental combat team led by Brigadier General Frank D. Merrill (officially the 5307th Composite Unit or unofficially "Merrill's Marauders"); a USAAF special operations wing of 209 transports and fighter-bombers known as the 1st Air Commando; a partisan army of 5,000 Karen and Kachin hill tribesmen lead by OSS Detachment 101; and six American-supplied and trained Chinese divisions. In a grueling mountain campaign (January 1944–1945) these forces drove two Japanese divisions away from the north Burma road network. The campaign, however, ruined "Merrill's Marauders," which began the campaign with 3,500 soldiers and left the war with 200 effectives after the battle for Myitkyina (March 1944). Stilwell formed a new brigade of two infantry regiments (MARS Force), which joined two Chinese divisions for the remainder of the campaign. Stilwell's campaign profited from British operations to the south by the Anglo-Indian-African Fourteenth Army and the five-brigade Long Range Penetration Group against the Japanese Fifteenth Army of eight divisions. Despite the Army's best efforts and those of a Navy and Marine-commanded Chinese guerrilla army, the Japanese did not surrender much of China and also managed to release divisions to defend the Home Islands and its island approaches. A Japanese offensive in January 1944 forced Chennault's Fourteenth Air Force and the independent Twentieth Air Force of B-29s from their forward bases and convinced the USAAF to redeploy the B-29s to other bases. China became a "might have been" in the war with Japan.

THE WAR FOR THE SOUTH PACIFIC

The campaigns in the South Pacific began with the futile defense of the Philippines (December 1941–May 1942) and ended with the surrender of isolated Japanese garrisons, sick and driven to cannibalism, in August 1945. At issue were the American air, ground, and naval forces in the Philippines, the support of those forces through Australia and the Allied island bases to the east, and, eventually, the Japanese base structure centered on Rabaul, Cape Britain Island. Before the Allies began offensive operations along the Malay Barrier in August 1942, the Combined Chiefs of Staff approved an awkward division of command: the Southwest Pacific Theater (General Douglas MacArthur) and the South Pacific Theater (Admirals Robert L. Ghormley and William F. Halsey). The real force behind Allied strategy was Admiral Ernest J. King, Chief of Naval Operations, the only American officer of equal strategic vision to MacArthur. The forces under American direction included Australian, New Zealand, and Dutch units of all services as well as Melanesian and Polynesian special operations units.

None of the American contingency plans of the interwar period—Plan ORANGE and the RAINBOW variants of 1940–1941—foresaw operations along the Malay Barrier. Japanese base development in the Central Pacific Mandate islands and the invasion of the Philippines suddenly rewrote American concepts of a war against Japan. The Japanese navy closed the door to the Central Pacific route to the Philippines by destroying the battle line of the U.S. Pacific Fleet at Pearl Harbor (December 7, 1941) and capturing Guam (December 10, 1941) and Wake Island (December 8–23, 1941) in concurrent amphibious operations. The two islands, naval stations, and air bases, were defended by small garrisons of Marines and sailors. Of the two, the Wake Island detachment (units of the 1st Defense Battalion and Marine Fighter Squadron 211) fought off the Japanese naval expeditionary force until it finally lost all its aircraft. Its heavy shore and antiaircraft batteries, vulnerable to bombs and shells, soon ran low on guns, ammunition, and able-bodied Marines. The base commander also had responsibility for the lives of 1,146 civilian construction workers, who outnumbered the military garrison of 517 sailors and Marines. With no naval relief force willing to engage the Japanese fleet, the Wake Island garrison, less 52 military and 70 civilian dead, surrendered. The heroism of the Wake defenders helped rally American public opinion as well as expose the closure of the Central Pacific. The Marines killed 700 Japanese invaders, sank two destroyers and damaged seven other vessels, as well as shooting down several dozen aircraft.

The defense of the Philippines (actually the island of Luzon) drew both Japanese and American forces to the Malay Barrier. Although the Army and Navy were reluctant to send reinforcements to a lost cause, President Roosevelt and other political leaders insisted that the Asiatic Fleet (Admiral Thomas C. Hart) and U.S. Army Forces Far East (General MacArthur) be supported as long as possible. Any Japanese force delayed in the Philippines might buy time for Allied reinforcements to reach Malaya and the Dutch East Indies. Thus the U.S. armed forces opened a major supply line from Hawaii, California, and the Panama Canal to Australia, 5,000 miles distant. To protect the maritime and air line of communications, American forces occupied Samoa, the Tongas, the Fijis, and the French-governed New Hebrides and New Caledonia. To threaten this new Allied defense line, Japanese forces from the Central Pacific mandates moved south to occupy

U.S. Marines rest in the field on Guadalcanal, circa August-December 1942. Most of these Marines are armed with M1903 bolt-action rifles and carry M1905 bayonets and USMC 1941 type packs. Two men high on the hill at right wear mortar vests and one in center has a World War I type grenade vest.

the Bismarck Archipelago, the north coast of New Guinea, and the Solomon Islands, an area under Australian and British administration. Against weak resistance the Japanese captured Rabaul (January 1942) and Bougainville, Northern Solomons (March 1942), the twin naval and air bastions for future operations to the south. In the meantime, to the west the Japanese Fourteenth Army and the Imperial Japanese Army's (IJA) 45th Air Group had joined with the 3rd Fleet and 11th Air Fleet to eliminate the American military presence in the Philippines.

The first campaign for the Philippines demonstrated the decisive air-naval character of the Asia-Pacific war and the superiority of well-trained, well-armed forces in land battles, even if inferior in numbers. The Japanese in this case were the teachers and victors. On December 8th Japanese air units from Formosa destroyed about half of the 150 first-line bombers and fighters of the USAAF's Far East Air Force. Japanese air strikes damaged the facilities at Clark Field, Iba Field, the Subic Bay naval base, and the Cavite naval station. Most of the surviving aircraft and ships redeployed south to Mindanao and the Dutch East Indies in a forlorn hope of forming effective Allied naval and air task force to check the Japanese. Futile bomber and submarine attacks on the Imperial Japanese Navy invasion forces demonstrated Japanese air and naval superiority. Any resistance thus depended on MacArthur's Luzon ground forces, consisting of American regulars of the USAAF, the Philippine Division, and coast artillery and antiaircraft battalions (about 32,000 officers and men); the regulars of the Philippine Scouts, American-officered, eight regiments of infantry, artillery, and cavalry, another force of 12,000 dependable soldiers; the 4th Marine Regiment, 1,600 regulars redeployed from Shanghai to reinforce the Marine defense battalion at Manila Bay; and nine of the 12 divisions of the Philippine Army, an ill-trained, ill-equipped native militia of 100,000, led by American and Filipino reserve officers and stiffened by four regiments of the Philippine Constabulary. The Japanese invasion force, two reinforced divisions, was half the size of the Luzon defense force, but it was an integrated force of trained infantry, artillery, and armor, operating with air and artillery superiority and capable of multiple amphibious landings.

The Japanese won the Philippines by occupying Luzon in a four-phase campaign: landings at northern and southern Luzon beach sites, the encirclement of Manila, the grinding attritional warfare on the Bataan peninsula and Corregidor island, and the rapid defeat and disarmament of American-Filipino forces in the Visayans and Mindanao. MacArthur made two critical decisions that reduced the chances that USAAF could prolong its resistance: (1) to fight a campaign of maneuver against the

African-American soldiers of the 93rd Infantry Division on patrol in the jungle on Bougainville Island, May 1, 1944.

Japanese; (2) and then to abandon Manila for the Bataan peninsula (the original concept) without adequate time to transfer food, medical supplies, and ammunition to the Bataan redoubt. Without the air and naval superiority that allowed resupply and reinforcements, however, the Philippines were doomed. After several diversionary landings in far northern Luzon and south of Manila, most of the 14th Army landed at Lingayen Gulf, about 100 miles north of Manila. After four days of ineffective defense, MacArthur reverted to the Bataan plan and declared Manila an open city. On January 2–6 the northern and southern wings of MacArthur's battered army joined north of Manila and occupied the Bataan positions where the combined force of 80,000 soldiers and 26,000 civilians dug in to face Homma's smaller but better army. Food and medical shortages combined to weaken the Bataan force, commanded by Lieutenant General Jonathan M. Wainwright. Daily caloric intake shrank from 2,000 to 1,000, far below the requirement for combat soldiers; starvation multiplied the spread of malaria and other tropical diseases. The Fourteenth Army's reduced progress came as much from personnel shortages and illness as from the Filipino-American defenders, who could not long endure Japanese bombs and shells or stop tank-infantry assaults. On March 12th, Roosevelt ordered MacArthur to flee to Australia to take command of the American forces there. MacArthur made a better live, heroic commander, rallying the demoralized Australians

The start of the bloody "Death March" of American prisoners of war in 1942 after their surrender on Bataan to the Japanese.

and angry Americans, than a dead martyr or humiliated POW, especially since Roosevelt saw no reason to advance a Republican general's deification. The Bataan force surrendered on April 8, and Wainwright capitulated the battered Corregidor defenders on May 6. Most of the remaining forces to the south gave up by mid-June, but throughout the Philippines, American and Filipino veterans took to the mountains with their arms to begin a guerrilla war against the Japanese.

Although he could not fulfill his pledge "to return" to the Philippines for two long years, MacArthur, supported by Admiral King, proposed to the JCS in June 1942 that the United States (with Australian and New Zealander forces) take the offensive in New Guinea and the Solomons with the ultimate objective of retaking Rabaul and menacing the IJN's major base to the north, Truk. The JCS was inclined to strike back, already authorizing carrier raids as far west as Tokyo itself. Moreover, the Japanese had shown renewed aggressiveness. In May 1942, the Japanese Northern Fleet consisting of 19 combatant vessels sailed toward the Aleutians, Alaska (at the time like Hawaii, a U.S. territory). On June 2–6, Japanese carrier aircraft bombed the U.S. forward air and naval base at Dutch Harbor. A landing force occupied Kiska and Attu Islands to use them for later reconnaissance operations. Neither a U.S. Navy task force of 19 cruisers and destroyers nor land-based USAAF bombers could check the Japanese operation, but their presence discouraged a larger raid on Adak, the key Alaskan base. An oceanic world away, other Japanese forces moved south into northeastern New Guinea and into the Southern Solomons (Tulagi and Guadalcanal) to establish air and naval bases for further operations against Australia and the Allied logistical sea routes to the United States. The Japanese planned next to capture Port Moresby on New Guinea's south coast, the only surviving Allied enclave. The main thrust, however, was another Combined Fleet (Admiral Isoroku Yamamoto) operation against the U.S. Pacific Fleet (Admiral Chester W. Nimitz) based in Hawaii.

At the high tide of victory, the Imperial Japanese Navy sailed into twin defeats (Coral Sea and Midway), characterized by strategic bravura and tactical timidity, defeats handed it by the U.S. Navy carrier force. The naval setbacks encouraged Roosevelt, the JCS, and MacArthur to launch a campaign of opportunism and attrition along two axis, New Guinea–New Britain under MacArthur and the Solomons under USN command. The goal was airbase denial and operational occupation with Rabaul as the final objective. The critical element in the campaign, Operation Cartwheel, was the effectiveness of land-based air, which for the Allies meant USAAF, USN, USMC, Australian, and New Zealander fighter and bomber squadrons, a force of 500 combat aircraft that grew to more than 1,000 by early 1943. The Pacific Fleet could also deploy as many as three carriers to the theater. The Allied ground forces in Cartwheel eventually numbered eight U.S. Army divisions, three Marine divisions, seven Australian divisions, and a New Zealand brigade group, plus assorted independent regiments and special operations groups. The Australian land forces made up two-thirds of

MacArthur's army; the South Pacific Theater forces were roughly half Army, half Marine Corps. In operational terms both sides had to cope with the jungle and its diseases. The Japanese advantages were naval night-fighting ability, dogged infantry, and the excellence of their air force, both planes and pilots. The Allied advantages when exploited were ground force firepower (especially artillery), carrier and land-based aviation, logistics, intelligence, and willingness to take risks.

The air-ground campaign began with the 1st Marine Division's landings on Guadalcanal and Tulagi (August 7, 1942) and an Australian counteroffensive from Port Moresby against the Japanese base of Kokoda (August-December 1942). The battle for Guadalcanal, which eventually involved two Army and two Marine divisions and the Japanese Seventeenth Army of equal size, centered on control of Henderson Field and the U.S. Navy's ability, achieved at great cost by November, to stop the Japanese air and naval bombardment of the airfield and to bring in more troops and supplies. The ground forces first checked four Japanese army attacks on the enclave, then began an offensive to the west that drove 13,000 surviving Japanese soldiers from the island. The Japanese army lost 23,000 men dead in battle and to disease, the American ground forces about 2,000 deaths. Japanese aviation squadrons lost about 600 pilots, the Americans one-third that number. Guadalcanal and its environs were in Allied hands in January 1943.

In addition to ensuring air superiority over the land battlefields and reinforcing carrier aviation operations against the Japanese fleet, American land-based air raids of all the services reduced Japanese army reinforcements to its beleaguered expeditions to Guadalcanal and New Guinea. Operating from Henderson Field and a new strip on Guadalcanal, USMC, USN, and USAAF fighter-bombers, operating under the direction of the 1st Marine Aircraft Wing (Brigadier General Roy S. Geiger), struck transports and barges wherever and whenever found—in daylight hours. The single greatest success followed the naval battles of November 12–14, 1942. On November 15, American aircraft surprised an undefended Japanese reinforcing convoy and destroyed 13 transports, 6,000 soldiers, and tons of precious supplies. An aerial task force of USAAF-RAAF light bombers and fighter-bombers scored a similar success in the Battle of the Bismarck Sea (March 2–3, 1943). Allied pilots sank 12 of 16 Japanese transports headed to New Guinea, preventing all but 1,000 of 6,000 Japanese soldiers from reaching the front and destroying ammunition and critical supplies. (See the section, "Victory in the Air.")

The New Guinea offensive, less naval than the Solomons, started with the horrific Allied struggle to take the Buna-Gona enclave on the north shore, a grueling battle that used up the U.S. 32d Infantry Division and two more infantry regiments as well as four Australian brigade groups before the final Japanese collapse on January 2, 1943. The campaign cost the Allies more than 10,000 casualties, the majority Australians. The Japanese losses were comparable, but almost all of them deaths. MacArthur, however, now had an opportunity to move north along New Guinea's coast under the umbrella

of USAAF aircraft, which attacked Japanese air-fields and bases with devastating effects. The theater ground forces moved from objective to objective, carried by the Seventh Fleet's amphibious forces and by the Fifth Air Force's transports, which conducted one major regimental parachute drop and many resupply drops. In March 1943, the JCS approved a MacArthur-King-Nimitz plan to occupy all of the Solomons, hop-scotch up New Guinea's north coast, and jump the straits to Cape Britain Island and drive on to Rabaul. With special task forces built from two U.S. divisions and five Australian divisions, MacArthur's army attacked the Japanese bases of Lae, Salamaua, and Finschafen (August-November 1943), bypassing several other base areas. The final capture of the Huon Peninsula gave the Allies the opportunity to land on Cape Britain Island, accomplished by the 1st Marine Division in December 1943. The Marines and the follow-on 40th Infantry Division cleared half the island and turned the final siege of Rabaul over to two Australian divisions, who eventually accepted the surrender of 90,000 starved survivors in 1945.

MacArthur, in fact, had lost interest in Cartwheel. His strategic vision had now shifted to the Philippines, and his American ground force, the U.S. Sixth Army (Lieutenant General Walter Krueger), moved relentlessly westward along New Guinea's north coast . The objectives of the Sixth Army took it far from Rabaul: Madang, the Admiralty Islands, Sarmi, Biak Island, Noemfour Island, and the Vogelkop peninsula. For most of 1944 the Southwest Pacific ground forces fought two wars, the U.S. Sixth Army taking MacArthur back to the Philippines and the Australian divisions completing the encirclement of Rabaul. The American forces—principally the 1st Cavalry, the 32d Infantry, the 24th Infantry, the 41st Infantry, and the 6th Infantry Divisions—now enjoyed sure air and naval superiority and logistical security. When the American forces reached the Vogelkop peninsula, in July 1944, they were clearly ready to meet the Japanese army to westward.

The South Pacific Theater ground forces drove northwest through the central Solomons toward Bougainville, site of three important Japanese air bases and eastern outpost of Rabaul. The Japanese became reluctant to commit their air and naval forces to a "forlorn hope" delaying action, but IJA soldiers proved they were willing to give their lives dearly on island after island. The key objective in the central Solomons, New Georgia Island, proved to be no pushover with 5,500 American casualties to defeat a comparable defense force. The assault force, built around the 43d Infantry Division and a Marine task force of Raiders and Defense Battalion artillery,

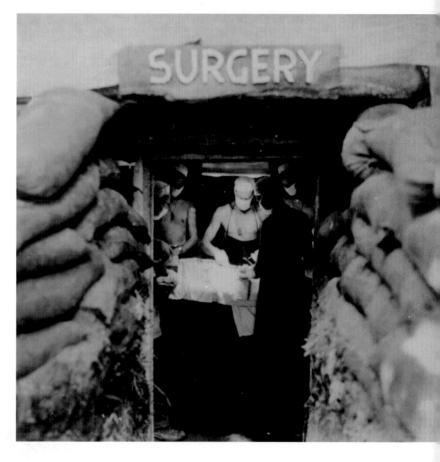

In an underground surgery room behind the front lines on Bougainville, an Army doctor operates on a soldier wounded by a Japanese sniper, December 13, 1943.

(Opposite page) Columns of troop-packed LCIs trail in the wake of a Coast Guard-manned LST en route for the invasion of Cape Sansapor, New Guinea, in 1944. The deck of the LST is closely packed with motorized fighting equipment.

ran into an entrenched Japanese defense force of two army regiments and two Special Landing Force (Marine) regiments, about 15,000 effectives. From February until September 1943 the U.S. XXIV Corps battered away at the Japanese with Munda airfield as the key objective. The American infantry had great difficulty in identifying Japanese bunkers in the jungle; only massive artillery and tank fire opened the defenses. Close air support also helped. New Georgia proved, however, that American ground forces could still fight without much distinction and win.

The campaign for the northern Solomons completed the isolation of Rabaul. After completing the summer 1943 operations at New Georgia, Rendova, and other islands, Admiral Halsey ordered the I Marine Amphibious Corps to attack Bougainville on November 1, 1943, with the Army's XIV Corps to exploit the landing of the 3rd Marine Division. As directed, the Marines established a beachhead in the west-center of the island and beat back Japanese counterattacks until the Army's Americal Division and 37th Infantry Division could land and drive south against the Japanese bases. In the meantime, U.S. Navy aviators and surface forces ravaged Japanese naval efforts to halt the invasion. The XIV Corps fought its way south through the rain forests, January-March 1944, against Japanese counterattacks and suicidal defenses. The XIV Corps' edge was its 18 heavy

U.S. infantrymen, with tank support, mopping up the resistance on Bougainville in March 1944.

artillery battalions and plentiful USAAF close air support. In March 1944, the Japanese force of two under-strength divisions attempted to halt the American advance with local attacks without success. The XIV Corps advance stopped when the Japanese airfields came within artillery range. In October 1944, four Australian brigades began a campaign to secure the island, taking 2,000 casualties to reduce the remaining garrison from 31,000 to 13,000 by the time of the surrender in 1945. Most of the Japanese died of disease. When the Australian forces on Cape Britain Island and Bougainville were given the option of joining MacArthur in the Philippines, General Thomas A. Blamey, Australian army commander, ordered the sieges to continue.

The South Pacific campaign faded away in early 1944 because all the belligerents saw no profit in continuing a war in a region that had no intrinsic merit except as a killing ground. MacArthur's Southwest Pacific forces headed for the Philippines, taking with them most of the Army and USAAF units commanded by Halsey. Admiral Nimitz redeployed his Navy and Marine Corps forces (except the 1st Marine Division) to Hawaii or bases where they could prepare for a new campaign. The Japanese military leaders declared Rabaul irrelevant. The essential strategic line ran from the Home Islands through the Marianas (Saipan, Guam, Tinian) and the Philippines to the Dutch East Indies. The Allies agreed. In August 1943, Roosevelt and Churchill approved a drive across the Central Pacific toward the Home Islands. This was the campaign the U.S. Navy always wanted, and in early 1944 it would have the carriers, battleships, and cruisers that would make the grand naval expedition possible.

THE CENTRAL PACIFIC CAMPAIGN

The Central Pacific Campaign (November 1943–August 1944) sealed the fate of the Japanese Empire because the American victory placed B-29 bombers and the Pacific Fleet submarine force in easy reach of the Home Islands and the Japanese sea lanes to the raw materials of the Greater East Asia Co-Prosperity Sphere. Moreover, the campaign virtually ended the threat of the Japanese carrier force, its experienced pilots killed in the Battle of the Philippine Sea. For the Central Pacific ground forces the campaign meant amphibious assaults of the most demanding sort. Unlike the many landings in the South Pacific, where Japanese waterline defenses were limited or absent, the Central Pacific landings had to be made into the teeth of dense, prepared beach defense systems on the small atoll islands or against well-sited field artillery, mortars, and antitank guns on the bigger islands of the Marianas. Marines and soldiers learned how impregnable bunkers of palm logs, concrete, and sand could be, and the Navy faced coastal guns and automatic cannon made in Japan to European standards or stripped from the British defenses of Hong Kong and Singapore. The air attacks and naval gunfire before and during the ship-to-shore movement needed not just a greater volume of bombs and shells, but far more precise target acquisition and fire adjustment (meaning spotters on the frontlines) as well as coordination with the assault infantry teams, armed with flame throwers and demolitions. American infantry and Marines had faced some of these problems in the South Pacific but only on an occasional basis. From the Japanese perspective, as their navy's ability to wreck the U.S. Pacific Fleet declined, and the army assumed the burden of killing as many Americans as possible so that the demoralized stateside public would pressure Roosevelt to seek a negotiated peace.

The Pacific Fleet task forces and small Army and Marine landing forces had tested the Japanese oceanic outpost system in 1942–1943 with limited effectiveness. The Navy mounted carrier raids into the Marshalls, and a sub-

marine-based Marine raider battalion destroyed a Japanese station on Makin Island, the Gilbert Islands (August 1942). In a larger prelude the U.S. 7th Infantry Division recaptured Attu in the Aleutians (May 1943) in a bitterly contested amphibious assault. The Japanese abandoned Kiska when an Allied attack was imminent (July 1943) Japanese air and naval attacks could not discourage the naval amphibious forces, well-protected by escort carriers and older bombardment warships. This pattern of employment freed the fast carrier task forces and their new battleships and cruisers for wide-ranging operations against the Combined Fleet without endangering the naval amphibious forces.

The campaign began with an expedition into the Gilbert island group, at the southeastern corner of Micronesia, the 1,000 islands spread over 2,000

miles of ocean in the Central Pacific. Two Gilberts atolls, Tarawa and Makin, had become Japanese bases for air and naval reconnaissance units, which made them reasonable objectives. The atolls had one large island—for Tarawa, Betio, and for Makin, Butaritari—that served as the key Japanese defense position. The Butaritari garrison numbered but 800 soldiers, but Betio, bristling with fortifications with coastal artillery, had a defense force of 4,800 Japanese naval infantry. The Japanese did not contest the Fifth Fleet's movement to the objective area, although an IJN submarine later sunk an escort carrier off Makin. The amphibious landings, however, revealed worrisome defects (November 20–23, 1943). At Butaritari an Army regimental team of the 27th Infantry Division showed major problems in command and tactics. The 2nd Marine Division suffered more than 1,000 dead and 2,300 wounded; the essential truth was that naval gunfire and navy fighter-bombers could not yet destroy enough enemy gun positions to make a landing easy. A reef and unpredictable tide put too much pressure on the one small amphibian tractor battalion; unde-

(Photographs on this and next page)

The taking of Tarawa, an atoll in the Gilbert Islands about 12 miles wide and 18 miles long, was one of the bloodiest battles in the history of the Marine Corps. The landings began on November 20, 1943, when amphibious craft, including amtracs—amphibious tracked vehicles with little armor—carried Marines across three and a half miles of choppy seas under fire from the Navy's guns. Smoke and coral dust raised by the heavy bombardment obscured the command ship's view of the landing craft fleet. Fire was halted for 30 minutes to allow the smoke to clear. This allowed the Japanese regroup and brace for the assault.

The landing craft came in at extremely low tide, and some of the craft had to stop and unload the Marines half a mile from shore. They began wading ashore in reddening surf, where many died. Others, trapped in barbed wire strung in shallow water, were cut down by murderous fire. Survivors of the landing huddled on the beach, hemmed in by surf and a coconut log seawall about four feet high. They expected a nighttime banzai charge that luckily did not come.

At 6:15 the next morning more Marines came ashore, wading into the same merciless fire that had cut down their comrades. The Marines managed to get tanks and howitzers ashore and, using flamethrowers, TNT charges, and grenades, they breached the shore defenses and fought their way inland, where defenses were thin. By the fourth day, Tarawa was in American hands, at a great cost. Total American casualties were 1,027 dead and some 3,300 wounded. Almost the entire 4,836-man garrison of defenders was wiped out. Only 17 wounded Japanese and 129 Korean laborers survived.

stroyed guns ravaged landing craft along the reef, amtracs in the lagoon, and those Marines of reinforcing battalions that had to wade ashore through 300 yards of beaten zone. The survivors had to root out the Japanese with grenades, demolitions, flamethrowers, and tankfire, a slow and very dangerous process. Some senior commanders and the press wondered if the nation (let alone the Marines) would accept similar bloodbaths in larger landings and bigger battles.

The subsequent campaign to penetrate the Marshall Islands showed how quickly the American amphibious forces—from Navy admiral to Marine private—could improve their operational effectiveness. In the capture of the three major islands of Kwajalein atoll (February 1944), the Navy's air and shore bombardment forces used methodical, planned, and protracted fire support, including special spotting teams, to reduce the Japanese defenses. Marine artillery batteries took positions on small, unoccupied islands to provide more observed and adjusted fires. The 4th Marine Division employed twice as many amtracs as those available at Tarawa. The Navy used swimming demolition experts (the UDTs) to breach reefs. Amtracs with guns and flame throwers joined the tank force in bunker-busting. The U.S. 7th Infantry Division showed that it had learned to fight the Japanese on Attu. Japanese deaths (8,000 plus) outnumbered American deaths 27:1. Admiral Nimitz immediately decided to jump 1,000 miles to Eniwetok atoll, captured by one Army regiment and a Marine regiment on February 18-23, 1944. Japanese dead numbered 3,400, Americans 348. Even if the assault on the Marianas, moved up 20 weeks, proved more difficult, the senior naval officers (Admirals Nimitz and Raymond A. Spruance) and the soul of the Fleet Marine Force, Lieutenant General Holland M. Smith, USMC, believed that the Japanese could no longer make any landing a serious risk.

Air and naval forces reduced the Japanese defenders the landing forces had to face. Although long range reconnaissance aircraft and B-24 bombers of the Seventh Air Force (Central Pacific) and Fifth and Thirteenth Air Force (Southwest Pacific) continued operations against Japanese objectives, the U.S. Navy's submarines provided increased weight to the interdiction of seaborne reinforcements. A submarine sank a large troop transport off Truk (February 1944), and two submarines sank three transports off southern Mindanao (April 1944), thus stopping two divisions headed to face MacArthur's army. The campaign for the Marianas included the commitment of seven submarines (two lost) to stopping Japanese reinforcements. Between January-June 1944, USN submarines sank 11 transports and supply ships destined for the Marianas, eliminating a division's worth of troops and arms from the defense force. In July 1944 submarines destroyed ships carrying 28 of 40 tanks bound for Iwo Jima, plus scarce construction materials and ordnance.

The campaign for the Marianas (Saipan, Tinian, and Guam) began with an amphibious landing and ground operations (June 15–July 9, 1944) to seize the key Japanese position, Saipan. About 3,600 miles from Hawaii and only 1,200 from Japan, Saipan, 14 miles long and six miles wide, was no

coral atoll. Its volcanic mountains, thick forests, caves, gullies, and open sugar fields protected a Japanese garrison of 31,000, one reinforced army division and a naval group armed with 231 artillery pieces, 44 tanks, and hundreds of entrenched heavy machine guns and mortars. The American landing force, V Amphibious Corps, included the veteran 2nd and 4th Marine Divisions and the untested 27th Infantry Division. The fire support naval task forces numbered 88 vessels from escort carriers and old battleships to gunboats. The entire expeditionary landing force, supplied with additional amtrac and artillery battalions, mustered 127,000 Marines, soldiers, and sailors, embarked on more than 100 amphibious ships.

From the initial four-regiment Marine landing to the last firefights at Marpi Point, made more horrific by Japanese civilian suicides and family murders, the Americans faced an enemy of murderous cunning. Japanese artillery saturated the landing beaches; counterattacks of manic ferocity fell on vulnerable American units from unexpected directions and times; the cave-bunker defenses defied all but close infantry assault. A frustrated Holland Smith relieved the Army division commander, but his departure did not improve the 27th Division's halting performance. The Marine division commanders, hardened by combat service in both World Wars, could defy Smith and did so on issues of operational tempo. A final banzai attack that overran four Army battalions and two Marine artillery battalions became a famous

(Previous page)
American medics treat casualties at an American portable surgical unit during the 36th Division drive on Pinwe, Burma, November 12, 1944.

Marines with a pack howitzer in battle with the Japanese at Tarawa.

battle that destroyed the Japanese force and ended organized resistance. Two days later, the Americans reached the northern tip of Saipan in a mopping-up operation, and Holland Smith declared Saipan secure. Still, this Japanese resistance provided another example of how many casualties fanatics—even walking wounded and civilians—could inflict. Of the entire Japanese defense force, only 736 became prisoners. The Americans suffered 3,500 dead or missing and 13,000 wounded. Saipan became a new benchmark in "the war without mercy."

Although the Saipan campaign and the Battle of the Philippine Sea disrupted Nimitz's overly-optimistic schedule, the conquests of Guam (July 21–August 10, 1944) and Tinian (July 24–August 1, 1944) reflected the diminished Japanese strength in the Marianas. The Japanese 29th Division and its attached units (18,500) exhausted itself trying to pin the 3rd Marine Division and 1st Provisional Brigade to the landing beaches on Guam's western coast. Major General Roy S. Geiger, USMC, the III Amphibious Corps commander, showed exceptional skill as a joint commander by committing the U.S. 77th Infantry Division and giving it an important role in the exploitation operations that followed the last banzai attack of July 25–26. Major General Andrew D. Bruce's division of overage draftees proved very good infantrymen, driving north beside the 3rd Marine Division. With the early capture of Orote airfield and Agana harbor, the Americans held the key objectives on July 26. The campaign ended with almost all of the Japanese garrison dead and the Americans reduced by 2,124 dead and 5,800 other casualties. Again the United States had demonstrated its invincibility.

The capture of Tinian by the 2d and 4th Marine Divisions became a deadly clinic on destroying a Japanese garrison of 8,000 at a cost of 328 dead and 1,571 wounded. A landing that surprised the Japanese in terms of time and place started the Marines with the initiative, exploited through massive artillery and naval gunfire support. The Marines brought six artillery battalions ashore, supplemented by four Army battalions on Tinian and 13 battalions firing from Saipan. The Japanese assisted the Marines by launching two hopeless banzai charges.

Even though Japanese survivors roamed Saipan and Guam for years, the Marianas soon became forward operating bases for the B-29s of the USAAF Twentieth Air Force (Tinian and Saipan) and the Pacific Fleet submarine force (Guam). A future of economic strangulation and blazing cities became Japan's fate.

THE WESTERN PACIFIC CAMPAIGN

The decision to take the Marianas created a new crisis for American strategists, for MacArthur wanted most of the forces in the Pacific committed to the liberation of the Philippines. He profited from a division of opinion in the U.S. Navy; Admiral King wanted to invade Formosa while Admiral Nimitz preferred an advance through Iwo Jima to Okinawa, potential bases for an intensified bombing campaign and the invasion of the Home Islands. Nimitz pointed out that his submarines did not need the Philippines as a base area; they were already ravaging the Japanese merchant marine throughout the western Pacific. Knowing Roosevelt would not halt MacArthur in an election year and acknowledging the Army's large role in providing ground divisions and tactical aircraft to the Pacific War, the JCS in March 1944 approved the two-axis advance, which meant that MacArthur would soon return to the Philippines. Roosevelt himself journeyed to Honolulu in July 1944 to bless both the MacArthur and the Nimitz plans. MacArthur's optimism ran amok. He cancelled an invasion of Mindanao and ordered a maximum effort to capture Leyte, a promising site for air bases and a jumping off spot for Luzon.

The Philippine campaign began with a Third Fleet and III Amphibious Corps operation to eliminate the Palau island group as a Japanese outer defense system protecting Mindanao. Although MacArthur decided to bypass Mindanao, Nimitz ordered the 1st Marine Division to take Peleliu and the 81st Infantry Division to capture Anguar, two volcanic wastelands defended by 12,000 Japanese. In one month (September 15–October 15, 1944) the Americans rooted out or sealed up Japanese defenders committed to cave warfare without counterattacks or retreats. It took six days of naval gunfire, two infantry regiments, a tank battalion, and four artillery battalions to destroy Anguar's garrison of 1,400 in three days ashore. Peleliu's defenders, however, ruined the elite 1st Marine Division, new to Central Pacific warfare, in the first week's fighting on the island. Two Army regiments finished the cave-by-cave battle in another 10 days. The Palau campaign, one of the clearly avoidable Pacific battles, cost the Marines 6,400 casualties and the Army 3,278 dead and wounded.

Although MacArthur proposed a strike directly on Luzon, the JCS approved only a more cautious advance to Leyte. The united Seventh and Third Fleets should have given the U.S. Navy ample superiority over the Combined Fleet. Even though bereft of carrier aviation, the Japanese surface forces, lurking in bases in the Dutch East Indies, Indochina, and Formosa, still remained a serious threat. Moreover, the Japanese naval land-based aviation force now included a "special attack force" of kamikaze suicide planes. The Japanese air threat gave extra value to the rapid capture of two airfields on Leyte. On October 20, 1944, the U.S. Sixth Army put four divisions ashore on Leyte's eastern shore near the airfields. The Sixth Army faced stiffening Japanese resistance that did not diminish with the catastrophic defeat of the IJN in the related battles of the San Bernadino Strait, Cape Engaño, and Surigao Strait (October 24–29, 1944). Against his better judgment but under orders, General Tomoyuki Yamashita reinforced the 35th Army (six divisions) until the Japanese ground forces numbered 65,000. The U.S. Sixth Army ashore increased to six divisions. With little operational deftness, General Walter Krueger closed the straits of Samar to enemy reenforcements as his worn divisions clawed their way across Leyte's central mountain range until the Japanese defense force finally fled or died on December 31.

MacArthur's optimistic campaign schedule changed after Leyte because his naval commanders wanted more USAAF fighter cover before they sailed for Luzon. On December 15th, Army infantry and engineers occupied Mindoro and put two major airfields into operation. MacArthur also received the support of five Marine fighter-bomber and light bomber squadrons for his Luzon campaign. Yamashita intended to prolong his defense of Luzon by creating three ad hoc army corps whose mission was to delay the Americans with as many casualties as possible. He expected no reinforcements, no naval aid except kamikaze attacks, and no tactical air support. He did not intend to fight for Manila, but a mixed force of IJN sailors and army engineers violated this plan at a cost of 30,000 Japanese and 100,000 Filipino lives. On January 9, 1945, General Krueger landed four fresh, veteran Sixth Army divisions (6th, 37th, 40th and 43rd Infantry Divisions) in Lingayen Gulf and marched on Manila. Lieutenant General Robert Eichelberger's new U.S. Eighth Army entered the encirclement with the 11th Airborne Division and 38th Infantry Division, and the rehabilitated 1st Cavalry Division became the spearhead of the Manila-bound corps. It was not until March 4, however, that the city, ruined and an open-

(Previous page)
Two Coast Guard-manned LSTs open their jaws in the surf on Leyte Island, as soldiers strip down and build sandbag piers out to the ramps to speed up unloading operations.

General Douglas MacArthur wades ashore during initial landings at Leyte, Philippine Islands, October 1944.

air cemetery, fell. Aided by thousands of Filipino guerrillas, MacArthur's soldiers fought their way into the Luzon mountains to seize reservoirs, liberate towns, and recapture military bases. The Japanese sold their lives dearly. Although probably 200,000 Japanese died on Luzon, Yamashita's army killed and wounded 44,000 Americans. The revered Japanese commander still had 50,000 soldiers in the field when his Emperor surrendered. Convicted of war crimes for atrocities in Manila, Yamashita went to the gallows because of his generalship.

With MacArthur stalled in his return to Luzon, Admiral Nimitz with King's reluctant approval planned a more direct drive on the Home Islands through Iwo Jima and Okinawa. For landing forces the CINCPAC had all six divisions of the Fleet Marine Force,

Iwo Jima during the pre-invasion bombardment, 17 February 1945, looking north with Mount Suribachi in the foreground.

plus Marine heavy corps troops, and the 27th, 96th, 7th, and 77th Infantry Divisions, all but one veterans of earlier campaigns. Iwo Jima became the first objective because it had proven an air defense nuisance to the B-29s headed for Japan; as an American base it became a much-used emergency landing strip, radar station, and fighter base.

The invasion plan for Iwo Jima called for a landing on February 19 and the seizing of two objectives: an airfield directly inland and 550-foot Mount Suribachi, the main bastion at the extreme southern tip of the island. By the second day the Marines advancing on Mount Suribachi had advanced only 200 yards. Then, on the morning of February 23, Marines reached the top and raised a small American flag. That afternoon, when the slopes were cleared of Japanese defenders, a larger flag was sent ashore from a Navy ship. Five Marines and a Navy hospital corpsman raised the flag on a piece of Japanese pipe. Photographer Joe Rosenthal of the Associated Press made the photograph that won him the Pulitzer Prize and became the most famous photo of the war. Three of the flag raisers died before the bloody fight for Iwo Jima ended on March 16.

The Iwo defense force of 22,000, commanded by Lieutenant General Tadamichi Kuribayashi, brought the cave defense system to a new level of deadliness on the volcanic wasteland; few Marines of the 3rd, 4th, and 5th Marine Divisions ever saw a Japanese, although they saw many stricken comrades, 6,140 dead and about 18,000 wounded. From start to finish (February 19–March 26, 1945) the Japanese shelled and raked with machine-gun fire every inch of Iwo within range; 700 Marines died for every square mile of

The American flag flies atop Mt. Suribachi, Iwo Jima; this small flag was soon replaced with a much larger one, as documented in the famous photograph by AP photographer Joe Rosenthal. (See page 129)

Soldiers dig in to the southeast edge of Motoyama Airfield #1, covering the beach area from Mt. Suribachi to the east boat basin, Iwo Jima.

"Iwo"

I went in the Marine Corps in 1943 when I was 19 years old. Iwo was my only battle, thank God. We just called it Iwo instead of Iwo Jima. Iwo wasn't that big of an island: only five and a half miles long, and two and a half miles at the widest part. We were told it was going to be a three to five day battle. That was it. We weren't going to lose anybody. We had 'em completely surrounded by cruisers and battleships. Thirteen thousand Japs—they were all crippled and hungry and had no water. They were in bad shape. It wasn't that way. I don't know where our intelligence came from. They sure goofed up on that one.

We landed on a nice calm day—February 19. Sunny. The sea was not rough. The island was being shelled by battleships, cruisers, destroyers, everything you could think of. All the bombing and all the shelling did not help us. The enemy were all in caves. Nothing was above ground. I never saw a building on Iwo. There were no civilians. It was just a battlefield. That's all it was. We were told there were only going to be about 13,000 Japanese on the island. Instead, we encountered 21,000 Japanese men in good physical condition.

Amtracs were supposed to take us in about 600 yards. They had three terraces, about 25 feet or so high and we were digging into that volcanic ash—that's why they call it the black sands of Iwo Jima. It was real loose, like going into some kind of quicksand or something. We struggled to get up the terraces. We carried about 75 pounds of equipment on our backs, including the grenades and the extra ammunition, food, one change of clothing, a poncho, blanket, a shirt, stuff like that. We wore those packs just about all the time because if you left them, you'd be out of food, water, everything else. So we pretty well fought with our packs on just about all the time.

My captain was hit within 15 minutes. And I lost my platoon sergeant that afternoon. We had quite a number of casualties. We fought all those pillboxes along the shoreline all the way up to the northern part of the island. When we got across the island, we got into heavy firefights. Iwo was close fighting, but you didn't see anybody. That's what worried us. You very seldom saw a Jap on the island. And we stayed on front lines just about all the time. Those Japs would let us get pretty close and then they'd open up with everything they had, and most of the time we couldn't tell where the fire was coming from.

On February 23 we were advancing toward the north, and all of a sudden we heard all the ships start blowing their sirens and everybody started shooting up in the air behind us. People were screaming and we didn't know what it was. At first we thought it was a banzai charge. Scared the devil out of us! Finally somebody says, "Jay, look up there. There's the American flag." We were so happy! It still gets me. We said, "Well, we ought to be finished with this battle in a couple of days since we got Surabachi," not knowing we hadn't even started to fight yet. We hadn't met the main line of resistance that the Japanese had put up for us.

I never saw one Jap give up. Of course, we couldn't surrender to the Japs—they'd kill you anyway. But we begged 'em to give up. We had interpreters come up with these microphones once in the battle and it blasted these caves where we knew Japs were in, and we'd tell 'em we got a flamethrower tank out here. We got flamethrowers on our backs, we're gonna burn 'em if they don't come out. And they wouldn't come out. They'd fight you to the death. And that's what was scary.

I was on there for 36 days. We lost right at 7,000 men killed and we had over 19,000 wounded. One man out of every three was either killed or wounded.

My lieutenant is the only officer we brought back in my company. My captain was hit the first day. His replacement got hit about two days later with a mortar shell. Third Marine platoon leader got hit the day they raised the flag. We lost the 1st Marine platoon leader in Death Valley. Everybody else was killed or wounded. No sergeants. All sergeants were wounded or killed. Our company was run by PFCs and privates at the end of the battle. We went through our officers real fast. They didn't have a chance.

I guess like most veterans, I didn't talk about the war when I got home. My father asked, "How come you don't talk about Iwo?" I said, "Daddy, if I tell you what happened on Iwo, you'd call me a doggone liar. You can't imagine what went on in that battle." I imagine all battles are like that. But that was the only battle I was ever in. I said, "You talk about nightmares, the way people got killed, and slaughtered. You can't believe it."

—Jay J. Rebstock Jr., U.S. Marine

(Previous page)
A formidable task force carves out a beachhead on Okinawa, about 350 miles from the Japanese mainland. Landing craft of all kinds blacken the sea out to the horizon, where battlewagons, cruisers and destroyers have massed.
April 13, 1945

A soldier of the 1ˢᵗ Marine Division draws a bead on a Japanese sniper with his tommy-gun as his companion ducks for cover. The division is working to take Wana Ridge before the town of Shuri, on Okinawa, in 1945.

ground taken. For their part the Marines blasted Japanese caves with tanks, flamethrowers, and demolitions; engineers sealed cave after cave, tunnel after tunnel like insect exterminators. Infantry companies that came ashore with over 200 Marines left with fewer than 20 of their original members. One company had nine different commanders; one of its platoons had 12 different commanders, two of them privates. Twenty-seven Marines and sailors won Medals of Honor, 14 posthumously. As Admiral Nimitz later observed, "uncommon valor was a common virtue." The greatest comfort was that 24,761 aircrewmen on 2,251 B-29s made successful emergency landings on Iwo Jima.

The campaign for Okinawa (April 1–June 21, 1945) simply repeated the horrors of Iwo Jima on a larger scale with the added wretchedness of being fought among a civilian population of almost 500,000, a third of whom died. The other awful novelty was the effectiveness of the kamikaze attacks on the Fifth Fleet. The scheme adopted by General Mitsuru Ushijima's 32d Army (100,000 troops in three divisions and three brigades) was to defend only the most favorable terrain. With the exception of two northern defense zones, the battle for Okinawa was fought over the southern third of the island, the site of the airfields and harbors. Under the control of the U.S. Tenth Army

Okinawa: The Stench of Death

The almost continuous downpour that started on 21 May turned Wana Draw into a sea of mud and water that resembled a lake. Tanks bogged down and even amtracs could not negotiate the morass. Living conditions on the front lines were pitiful. . . Food, water, and ammunition were scarce. Foxholes had to be bailed out constantly. The men's clothing, shoes, feet, and bodies remained constantly wet. Sleep was nearly impossible. The mental and physical strain took a mounting toll on the Marines.

Making an almost impossible situation worse were the deteriorating bodies of Marines and Japanese that lay just outside the foxholes where they had fallen during the five days of ferocious fighting that preceded Company K's arrival on Half Moon. Each day's fighting saw the number of corpses increase. Flies multiplied, and amoebic dysentery broke out. The men of Company K, together with the rest of the 1st Marine Division would live and fight in that hell for ten days.

After digging in the gun. . . and preparing ammo for future use, I had my first opportunity to look around our position. It was the most ghastly corner of hell I had ever witnessed. As far as I could see, an area that previously had been a low grassy valley with a picturesque stream meandering through it was a muddy, repulsive, open sore on the land. The place was choked with the putrefaction of death, decay, and destruction. In a shallow defilade to our right, between my gun pit and the railroad, lay about twenty dead Marines, each on a stretcher and covered to his ankles with a poncho—a commonplace, albeit tragic, scene to every veteran. Those bodies had been placed there to await transport to the rear for burial. At least those dead were covered from the torrents of rain that had made them miserable in life and from the swarms of flies that sought to hasten their decay. But as I looked about, I saw that other Marine dead couldn't be tended properly. The whole area was pocked with shell craters and churned up by explosions. Every crater was half full of water, and many of them held a Marine corpse. The bodies lay pathetically just as they had been killed, half submerged in muck and water, rusting weapons still in hand. Swarms of big flies hovered about them.

The mud was knee deep in some places, probably deeper in others if one dared venture there. For several feet around every corpse, maggots crawled about in the muck and then were washed away by the runoff of the rain. There wasn't a tree or bush left. . . The rain poured down on us as evening approached. The scene was nothing but mud; shell fire; flooded craters with their silent, pathetic, rotting occupants; knocked-out tanks and amtracs; and discarded equipment – utter desolation.

The stench of death was overpowering. The only way I could bear the monstrous horror of it all was to look upward away from the earthly reality surrounding us, watch the leaden gray clouds go skudding over, and repeat over and over to myself that the situation was unreal—just a nightmare—that I would soon awake and find myself somewhere else. But the ever-present smell of death saturated my nostrils. It was there with every breath I took.

I existed from moment to moment, sometimes thinking death would have been preferable. We were in the depths of the abyss, the ultimate horror of war. . .Men struggled and fought and bled in an environment so degrading I believed we had been flung into hell's own cesspool.

From With the Old Breed, *a memoir about the terrifying nature of the land war in the Pacific, by E.B. Sledge, who was a 19-year-old U.S. Marine (First Division). He later was a college professor of biology. Military historian, John Keegan, called the book "one of the most arresting documents in war literature."*

(Lieutenant General Simon B. Buckner), the III Marine Amphibious Corps (1st and 6th Marine Divisions) and the Army XXIV Corps (Major General John R. Hodge) of four divisions landed without serious opposition, cleared the northern island, and replayed World War I trench warfare for 70 days of sustained battle. About 700 Americans died (averaged-out) for each day of battle, and the final accounting for the Tenth Army was 7,000 dead (among them General Buckner) and 33,000 wounded, plus a disturbing sick and "battle fatigue" count of 26,000. In addition, more than 5,000 Americans died at sea. Only 7,000 defenders eventually surrendered. Casualties on both sides came primarily from shells, mortars, hand grenades, and machine guns. Close air support and artillery barrages simply drove the Japanese deeper into their reverse slope tunnel systems from which they emerged to blast their attackers. Okinawa even had World War I mud.

At left, General Douglas MacArthur signs as Supreme Allied Commander during formal surrender ceremonies on the USS Missouri *in Tokyo Bay, September 2, 1945. Behind General MacArthur are Lieutenant General Jonathan Wainwright and Lieutenant General A. E. Percival. At right, Japanese surrender signatories arrive to participate in the ceremony.*

Even though the western Pacific victories cut off Japan from its raw material and food sources in Asia and the Dutch East Indies, the ground war of 1944–1945 convinced American political and military leaders that a final invasion of the Home Islands—Operation Downfall—should be avoided at all costs. This calculus included the agreement at the Teheran Conference (November 1943) that the Soviet Union would enter the war with Japan ninety days after Germany's surrender. It also justified firebombing Japanese cities, unrestricted submarine warfare, and the total destruction of the Japanese air forces. The use of two nuclear bombs in August 1945 simply reflected an American conviction that an immediate peace at any cost had become preferable to a ground war that had become unbearable for both belligerents.

Victory
in the Air

Thomas Childers

". . . you really grew very close to the people you flew with, almost more than brothers, because you shared a common danger all the time. So it really hurt a lot when you lost a person. But we didn't say much about it, and everybody made believe it didn't matter too much. But it did matter. You just sort of made believe they went on leave and you didn't see them anymore."

—DON LOPEZ, FIGHTER PILOT

NOVEMBER 5, 1944

In the predawn stillness a distant motor whines, coughs, turns over. Above the eastern horizon a sliver of pale light cuts the darkness, shimmering off a maze of tapered wings and props and Plexiglas. Another engine whirs and catches, then another and another. Within seconds the air pulses with a deep, pounding rumble that builds into a thunderous roar. One by one the planes lumber from their hardstands and pivot onto the perimeter track, forming a long, serpentine procession that lurches in fits and starts toward the main runway. Lined up in position, shuddering with barely harnessed energy, they wait. The noise of the assembled aircraft is deafening. The aluminum walls, the instruments, and the belts of ammunition rattle and shake, and the damp air is thick with the smell of aviation fuel. At last a green flare hisses overhead, and the lead plane thunders down the tarmac, strains for an agonizing moment under its load of fuel and munitions, and lifts off into the haze. It is hardly away before the next in line follows in its wake, then the next, and the next, until the morning sky is filled with silver planes climbing high through the clouds.

The planes rise higher and higher, sliding cautiously into place as the formation assembles. The men inside—the pilots, navigators, bombardiers, engineers, radio operators, and gunners—have been awake for hours. They have crawled out of bunks in Nissen huts or tents scattered around the base, collected their flight gear—their parachutes, Mae Wests, their oxygen masks—gone to chow, and attended briefings on the target for the day, the route in and out, anticipated enemy action, known flak areas, procedures for escape and evasion if shot down. Now, after hours of preparation, they are on their way, and throughout the formation, there is the certain knowledge that some of them will not be coming back.

On this morning three squadrons of four-engine bombers, B-24 Liberators from the 466th Bomb Group of Second Air Division of the American Eighth Air Force, are bound for a target in southwestern Germany. Within an hour they will rendezvous with two other groups of Liberators from the

B-17 Flying Fortresses fly high above the Bavarian Alps, headed for rail targets near Munich.

(Next page)
A group of TBM Avenger torpedo bombers searching for the Japanese in the Pacific. Avengers sought out enemy ships and sank them with torpedos, or carried bombs to attack land and sea targets. An Avenger *piloted by former President George Bush was shot down in 1944 on a bombing raid over ChiChi Jima.*

467th and 458th to form the 96th Combat wing. It is one of several mammoth formations, together numbering more than 1,000 aircraft, which will crowd the skies over southeastern England. Some will be B-17 Flying Fortresses from the First and Third Air Divisions of the Eighth; others will be twin-engine medium bombers, B-26 Marauders of the Ninth Air Force, headed for objectives in German-occupied Europe.

As the bombers make their way across the English Channel or out over the North Sea, scores of fighters—long-range P-51 Mustangs and bottle-nosed P-47 Thunderbolts—scramble from their forward bases in France. "Little friends," the bomber crews call them. They are a welcome sight at the rendezvous point. Some will escort the bombers all the way to their targets deep inside the Third Reich; others will peel away to conduct sweeps across northwestern Europe, searching for enemy movement on the ground or in the air.

Meanwhile, even as the lead elements depart the coast of England, the clouds above southern Italy are speckled with aircraft. Five hundred Liberators and Fortresses of the American Fifteenth Air Force, escorted by over 300 P-38 Lightnings and P-51s, are streaming from their fields near Foggia, Italy, toward the Alps and targets in Austria. Some will veer eastward across the Adriatic to Balkan objectives near Mitrovica and Podgorica in Yugoslavia. Meanwhile, fleets of medium bombers, twin-engine B-25 Mitchells from the Twelfth Air Force, drone northward, following the Apennines to attack targets as far north as Brenner, and fighter squadrons, flying close air support of Allied troops, roar over German positions from Rimini to Livorno on the Mediterranean.

On the other side of the world, the planes already have returned from their raids. Fighters from the U.S. Fourteenth Air Force in China have pounded storage facilities around Mang-shih and Chefang in eastern Burma. B-24s from the Far Eastern Air Force attacked airfields and barge traffic in the central Philippines, and A-20 light bombers struck Japanese positions near Sarmi in New Guinea. From their field in Kharagpur in Bengal, B-29 Superfortresses of the Twentieth Bomber Command have raided the Japanese naval base at Singapore, while other Superfortresses, launched from Tinian in the Marianas, attacked air fields on Iwo Jima in the Bonin

Islands. Flocks of blue F6F Hellcats and Corsairs, flying from carriers of the U.S. Third Fleet in the Philippine Sea, are back on their decks, having struck Japanese installations near Manila. Now, in the darkness, mechanics and armorers swarm over the planes, repairing the damage, checking electrical systems, loading munitions, and filling tanks with aviation fuel. It is November 5, 1944, and there will be another mission tomorrow.

FIRST STEPS TO VICTORY

Three years earlier, on the eve of America's entry into the Second World War, undertakings of such geographic scope, of such monumental scale and power, would have seemed pure fantasy. Established in 1926, the U.S. Army Air Corps (AAC) was a tiny organization staffed by professional military men and operating with a modest fleet of aircraft, almost all stationed within the continental United States. Through the 1930s, its mission was to protect American shores from potential enemies, and its responsibilities were limited to a range of 300—beyond that was the province of the U.S. Navy.

When war broke out in Europe in September 1939, the AAC consisted of fewer than 25,000 men and far fewer combat aircraft. The sudden fall of France in the summer of 1940 and the very real prospect of a German invasion of Great Britain at last jolted the United States into action, prompting the nation's first peacetime draft and plans for an ambitious expansion of America's military capabilities. In May 1940, President Franklin D. Roosevelt issued a dramatic call for the production of 50,000 aircraft a year, an utterly fantastic number even to the most ambitious air planners.

The crew of a Navy SB2C Hell Diver, the Navy's last dive bomber, await their turn to make an always-dangerous carrier landing.

Several months later, in early 1941, the Ford Motor Company began construction of a cavernous plant at Willow Grove near Detroit to mass produce B-24 heavy bombers.

The Japanese attack on Pearl Harbor on December 7, 1941, and Hitler's declaration of war on the United States four days later hurled the country into a global conflict for which it was woefully ill-prepared. Yet, in 1942 the American military—and the economy on which it was based—began a radical transformation. Young men poured into the Army Air Corps (officially renamed U.S. Army Air Forces or AAF in June 1941), filling the newly established training programs for pilots, navigators, bombardiers, radio operators, engineers, and gunners. From coast to coast new bases were scraped out of the landscape and old ones vastly expanded. From the shop floors of factories, aircraft of every description and function poured forth in a volume that was little short of stunning. By November 1944, the AAF commanded a force of over two million troops, comprising 31 percent of all Army personnel, and at its peak strength in the spring of 1945, deployed 26 very heavy bombardment groups, 72.5 heavy bombardment groups, 28.5 medium and light bombardment groups, 71 fighter groups, 32 troop carrier groups, and 13 reconnaissance groups. Over half were serving overseas, stationed on bases that stretched from the Caribbean to Iceland, Greenland, England, Italy, North Africa, India, China, Australia, and a string of islands that arced across the Pacific from the frigid Aleutians in the north to the tropical jungles of the Solomons. Under the leadership of General Henry "Hap" Arnold, it was the most powerful air force on earth.

Formations of B-25s wing their way to rail targets in northern Italy

AIR POWER EMERGES

The expansion of American naval aviation was also both swift and spectacular, spurred by dramatic events in Asia and the Pacific. When Vice Admiral Nagumo Chuichi launched his carrier-based planes against the American installations at Pearl Harbor in Hawaii, Imperial Japan possessed, by almost every measure, a decisive advantage in naval aviation. Under the leadership of Admiral Yamamoto Isoroku in the 1930s, the Japanese Navy had undertaken an ambitious program of aircraft carrier development, and in 1941 possessed nine carriers and 1,400 naval aircraft. At the controls of these aircraft was a large, well-trained cadre of experienced pilots, their skills honed in combat over China.

Against this, the U.S. Navy would muster a smaller carrier force, aircraft

"More than Brothers"

I had always wanted to be a fighter pilot from when I was a kid. I got my first flight when I was 7 in an open cockpit bi-plane. I used to scrounge rides out in Floyd Bennett Field in Brooklyn and I read all the pulp magazines about World War I fighter pilots. And I really wanted to do that. I wanted to fly.

I joined the Army Air Force right at the beginning of World War II, a few months after Pearl Harbor. I became a fighter pilot and served in China under General Chennault in the 14th Air Force. I was in the 23rd Fighter Group, which was formed directly from the "Flying Tigers," an American volunteer group.

The Flying Tigers were disbanded on July 4th, 1942, and the 23rd Fighter Group was formed from them. That was a regular Army Air Force outfit. Their record was really tremendous. They were credited with, I think, 299 aircraft destroyed, with the loss of only eight in the air. Chennault had devised tactics that worked very well against the Zeroes and the light Japanese airplanes.

On December the 10th, 1943, the Japanese conducted a daytime raid. Our squadron took off, and everybody climbed to 25,000 feet thinking that's where they'd be. But the bombers came in at less than 1,000 feet. They really bombed the heck out of our field. Two days later, on December the 12th, they came in again, but we only had 12 airplanes that would fly then. I was flying the #2 man in the 3rd flight. The CO ordered the first two flights to stay down low because he knew they'd do the same thing again. My flight would go up high to cover in case there were fighters. So we took off and we were climbing up to about

Don Lopez, Fighter Pilot
Deputy Director, Smithsonian Institution National Air and Space Museum

15,000 feet and I heard the others engaging the bombers. All the sudden, my leader yelled, "Zeroes!" They weren't really Zeroes, they were Oscars, which is an Army version, but we called 'em all Zeroes. I dropped my belly tank, which you do before you go into aerial fight and rolled over and started to dive, and there were about 35 or 40 Oscars below us. They didn't fly formation like we did, they flew something we called the "squirrel cage." They all were jumping around, but they never seemed to run into each other, so I guess they knew what they were doing.

In the distance, I saw a P-40 being chased by an Oscar. I was way out of range, but I got a big lead and fired my tracers over that way hoping he'd see it and break off, which he did, and he turned toward me, which wasn't part of my plan. And so we were making a head-on pass at each other. I was diving slightly, and he was climbing slightly, but when we got within range, we both started shooting. I could see his guns, they sort of wink as you're looking at 'em, and I could see my bullets hitting on the front of his plane. And at the very last second, before we hit engine to engine, he made a very sharp break to the right. And my wing hit his wing and knocked off most of the propeller arc, and I lost about 2 or 3 feet off my left wing. I straightened out again and he went spinning down into the haze. I didn't see what happened to him, but I found out later they found his airplane on the ground.

I was flying in a big circle trying to find some other airplane to lead me back home. Then I spotted my leader's plane. He had a big pair of dice painted on the tail, so I saw it and joined up with him and he did a double-take because I could get in closer in formation now with that much less of a wing on that side. We went in and landed, and everything was fine.

In combat, you share an unspoken promise to risk your life to save your fellow pilots, and they would do the same for you. Consequently, you really grew very close to the people you flew with, almost more than brothers, because you shared a common danger all the time. So it really hurt a lot when you lost a person. But we didn't say much about it, and everybody made believe it didn't matter too much. But it did matter. You just sort of made believe they went on leave and you didn't see them anymore.

I flew 101 missions. I shot down five enemy aircraft, making me a flying Ace. I did what I had to do in my time and I was very glad to be a part of it. I wouldn't have missed it for the world.

that would soon be obsolescent, untested pilots, and a fledgling sense of how to deploy its own air power. The learning curve was steep. Chief of Naval Operations Admiral Ernest J. King, who before the war had commanded the aircraft carrier *Lexington* and had served as Chief of the Naval Bureau of Aeronautics, was a forceful advocate of naval aviation and was determined to create a large fast carrier force capable of projecting American power across thousands of miles of ocean. Its mission would be multifold: to secure lines of communication and supply; to support Marine and Army campaigns in the Southwest and Central Pacific; and to destroy the Japanese Navy's vaunted aerial forces. It was a daunting task.

Three events in the spring and early summer of 1942 offered a preview of the role air power would play in naval operations in the Pacific. On April 18, 16 B-25s were launched from the deck of the USS *Hornet*, some 600 miles from the Home Islands of Japan. Led by Lieutenant Colonel James (Jimmy) Doolittle, the AAF crews were specially trained for short takeoffs (medium bombers were not intended to fly off aircraft carriers), and were bound for Tokyo. The bombers dropped their small bomb loads on the Japanese capital and other cities and then, running out of fuel, landed or crashed in China or in the ocean. The Doolittle raid did little physical damage but the psychological impact was profound, revealing to the Japanese leadership that the Home Islands were vulnerable and providing a tremendous boost to American morale at a time when there was precious little good news.

An Army B-25 takes off from the deck of the USS Hornet *on its way to take part in the first U.S. air raid on Japan, April 18, 1942.*

Less than a month later, on May 7–8, Japanese and American naval forces collided in the Coral Sea. In an engagement that stretched across hundreds of miles of ocean and sent one Japanese and one American carrier to the bottom, none of the opposing ships came within sight of one another. For the first time, a naval battle had been fought entirely with carrier-based aircraft. That encounter prompted the Japanese to scrub their planned landing on the south coast of New Guinea, but it was not a decisive blow to the Imperial Navy. The dramatic Battle of Midway was. On June 4, two great carrier forces clashed in the waters off Midway Island. In a furious air battle, dive bombers from Rear Admiral Raymond A. Spruance's *Enterprise*, *Yorktown*, and *Hornet* sank all four of Nagumo's heavy carriers, se-

B-25s lined up for takeoff on the USS Hornet, *April 18, 1942*

Aircraft carrier crew members watch as a Navy F6F Hellcat fighter awaits the dropping of the checkered flag, the signal for takeoff on a mission against the Japanese in the Pacific.

The catapult officer of the USS Enterprise clambers up the side of a flaming F6F fighter to rescue the pilot, after a raid on Makin Island in November 1943.

Navy dive bombers during the Battle of Midway, June 4–6, 1942. A burning Japanese ship is visible at center.

curing Hawaii, halting the Japanese advance in the Pacific and fundamentally altering the critical balance of carrier forces.

Thereafter, the disparity in production of ships and aircraft increased dramatically. By January 1943, American air power in Asia and the Pacific virtually tripled that of Japan. In the fall of that year, six new *Essex*-class carriers, each carrying almost 100 aircraft, arrived in the Pacific Theater. Joining them were a half dozen light *Independence*-class flattops—converted cruisers that were just as fast and could carry about 50 aircraft each. Numerous smaller escort carriers—"jeeps" or "baby carriers"—followed in large numbers. These versatile ships provided air support for amphibious operations, hunted submarines, and transported troops and aircraft.

The widening gap in forces was not a result of industrial production alone. By 1943 a new generation of American fighter aircraft appeared in the Pacific which proved more than a match for the Japanese Zero. Joining the Dauntless dive bomber as a staple of the Navy's arsenal, the versatile F6F Hellcat would become the star of the American carrier fleet, and the Corsair, at first shore-based, would become the favorite of Marine pilots.

Organized into powerful task forces, the carriers roamed the Central and Southwest Pacific in 1943–44, launching hundreds of planes against Japanese installations and in support of Marine and Army operations. When the final push for the Japanese Home Islands began after the fall of Okinawa in the summer of 1945, the American Third Fleet was able to marshal a force of 26 fast carriers, 64 escort carriers, and 14,000 combat aircraft.

STRATEGIC BOMBING IN EUROPE

Although the AAF would be called upon to perform many missions during the Second World War, the concept of strategic bombing occupied center stage in the American approach to air power. During the First World War, the vast and grisly carnage had been confined largely to the front, to the soldiers, fortresses, and trenches strung along No-Man's Land or to the sailors and their ships at sea. Airplanes had been used for the most part either in reconnaissance or in support of ground operations. None of the combatants had been able to mount a sustained campaign of strategic bombing aimed at destroying the industrial power of its enemies. The use of air power to demolish an enemy's manufacturing base, its energy sources, its communications network, its system of transportation, and ultimately its capacity and will to make war, was a radically new departure for military planners, and it fundamentally altered the nature of warfare in the modern age.

The war in the air was an utterly new experience for everyone involved, from the men who formulated the doctrine of strategic bombing to the young crewmen who executed it to those hiding beneath the bombs. There were no historical precedents, no guidelines for the planners or the crews and no preparation for those in the target cities. No one, either on the ground or in the planes overhead, was prepared for what the air war meant. A plan of

strategic bombing involved attacking obvious military targets, but those targets were now defined more broadly and tended to be located in heavily populated areas. Civilians lived in these target cities, so civilians, both planners and crews understood, would now inevitably become casualties of war in mass numbers. More than any other form of combat, the air war would capture, in all its horrors and complexity, the moral ambiguity of modern war.

At the outset of war in Europe, many feared that Hitler would unleash a colossal air offensive against civilian targets, and German raids on London and other British cities in the dark summer of 1940 at first seemed to confirm those fears. But the Luftwaffe was neither equipped—it developed no long-range, heavy bombers—nor trained for such a mission, and in the face

Bombers of the Eighth Air Force strike the Focke-Wulf plant in Marienburg, Germany. (1943)

of ferocious resistance by the RAF's Fighter Command, could not sustain its assault. In fact, Germany's air doctrine remained closely tied to its army's land operations throughout the war. Among the major powers, only Great Britain and the United States adopted a broad view of air power that placed strategic bombing at its center. In Britain, a commitment to strategic bombing evolved during the pre-war years and was viewed as an attractive alternative to a large, land-based army, and in Winston Churchill, who became prime minister in May 1940, the Royal Air Force's Bomber Command found a passionate advocate.

Across the Atlantic, Franklin Roosevelt echoed Churchill's enthusiasm. During the 1930s, the doctrine of high altitude precision bombing had emerged from the Army Air Corps Tactical School in Montgomery, Alabama. That doctrine was based on the premise that a massive fleet of four-engine bombers—B-17 Flying Fortresses and later B-24 Liberators—equipped with technologically advanced aiming devices and flying at altitudes above effective enemy fire could identify and destroy carefully selected military and industrial targets. It also offered a politically acceptable prospect of American involvement in a European war without heavy casualties, and found expression in the AWPD-1 (Air War Plans Department) statement of American air power drawn up in mid-1941.

The plan called for a general air strategy that would not only "provide for the close and direct air support of the surface forces in the invasion of the continent and for major land campaigns thereafter" but also would "conduct a sustained and unremitting air offensive against Germany and Italy to destroy their will and their capability to continue the war." Indeed, air planners actually held out the prospect that this air offensive might "make an invasion of Europe unnecessary." After Pearl Harbor, AWPD-42 replaced the pre-war plan, with renewed emphasis on "establishing complete air ascendancy over the enemy as a prelude to close support operations," but the United States, like Great Britain, entered the conflict with a commitment to the concept of strategic bombing.

The RAF would be the first to test the theory. During 1940, RAF Bomber Command attempted daylight bombing of the Ruhr and other military/industrial targets on a very limited scale. Daylight operations were quickly abandoned, however, when it became brutally obvious that the aircraft, mostly two-engine medium bombers with limited range and bomb loads, were incapable of defending themselves against enemy fighters. Losses were extremely high, and the damage inflicted on the targets minimal.

One solution was to fly by night, a step taken by the Germans during the Battle of Britain in 1940. But navigational problems—on the frequent moonless or overcast nights the crews simply couldn't find the targets—coupled with primitive aiming devices, suggested that the theory of strategic bombing had exceeded the RAF's ability to execute it. By spring 1942, improvements in navigational technology and the introduction of new four-engine bombers, especially the mammoth Lancaster, made it possible to send a large bomber force along the same route, a great improvement over

"War is a Terrible Thing"

I was a sophomore in college at Dakota Wesleyan University out in South Dakota. Pearl Harbor came in December of '41. Well, to be honest with you, I didn't know where Pearl Harbor was. Just a few short days later, I and nine other Dakota Wesleyan students went to Omaha. We all wanted to be pilots. There was no Air Force then. There was the Army Air Corps and the Navy Air Corps.

We've heard a lot about the Flying Fortresses, the B-17s. They operated primarily out of England. The B-24s were largely based in Italy, and that's where I flew all 35 of my missions.

You then would taxi out and take off usually about one-minute intervals. And I can tell you those B-24s loaded with bombs, with thousands of gallons of high octane gasoline, with 10 men, with our metal flak protecting suits, ammunition, machine guns, all the rest, they would barely get off by the time you got to the end of the runway. You'd just skim treetops until you finally got enough momentum where you could start flying.

Anybody who tells you that they flew combat bomber missions in World War II without any fear has to be crazy. Everybody was afraid. When those anti-aircraft shells started to explode right off your wing, and you saw a plane with 10 young men in it that you'd had breakfast with just a short time before, laughing and talking and betting as whether the Yankees were going to beat the Cardinals and all that sort of thing, and then you see that plane take a direct hit, you can even see the people in the plane next to you through the small windows we had. You see those people take a direct hit and the plane catches fire and blows up, falls in pieces 25,000 feet to the ground, no parachutes, you never forget that. And at first you have a great feeling of terror. Maybe the next shell is going to hit the plane you're in. You never forget that.

We were bombing the Skota Ammunition Works in Pilson, Czechoslovakia one day. We got hit over the target. Lost two engines and we were forced to drop out of formation. We were trying to go home when a third engine, under the strain of having to pull the plane, went out on us. So we're now down to one engine. We come to the Isle of Vis in the Adriatic Sea, and my navigator said, "Let me tell you there's a short runway on the Isle of Vis. It's only 2,200 feet long, and we need 5,000 feet as you know. But it's all there is. Do you think you can land this plane on that runway?" I said, "Well, we have no recourse. We can't ditch in the water here, there's too much, the waves are

too high. It's a stormy windy day." And it was in cold weather. And I said, "We'd freeze to death before they ever got to us. So let's take a run at it. Well, as you turn on the final approach, coming into that runway on the Isle of Vez, it looks even shorter. You have to hit right on the end of the runway, and then get on the brakes with all your worth and ride those brakes all the way down to the end of the runway.

George McGovern, Bomber Pilot former United States Senator, and 1972 Presidential candidate

Well, as luck would have it, I hit the end of that runway within four or five feet of the end of the runway. The co-pilot and I both jumped on the brakes. They skidded all the way down to that end of the runway. We stopped short — I don't think more than eight or ten feet from the end of that runway. There was a hill at the end of the runway, where you could see the carcasses of planes that had over-shot the runway — and then trying to go around again had plowed into the hill. Anyway, we walked away from that landing. I should say we danced away from it, with a leap of joy, and for that I won the Distinguished Flying Cross.

Well, war is a terrible thing. Nobody likes war. Certainly not the participants. There may be people who theoretically like it who've never tasted war, but I don't know anybody that's ever participated in a war who thinks it's a pleasant experience. It's the most inhumane thing that men do to each other. But as a young man, I believed that Hitler was a madman. I still do. I thought the United States had no other recourse except to go after him, and I still think that. After all these years, I'm proud of my participation in the Second World War.

I don't think we ought to forget that war. Hundreds of thousands of young Americans died in that war. Several times that many were crippled or weakened emotionally or psychologically. So I don't think we ought to forget those sacrifices. But there's no question my experience in World War II has made me cautious about committing our forces overseas. The old British conservative, Edmund Burke, once said, "A conscientious man would be cautious how he deals in blood." That's the way I feel.

the earlier freelance approach. Now under the command of British Air Vice-Marshal Arthur Harris, Bomber Command also made a significant shift in targeting: rail yards and factories might be aiming points, but targets for future operations were to be Germany's large industrial cities. The first indication of Harris's intentions came on May 30, 1942, when he sent every available aircraft—1,000 planes—to bomb the Rhineland city of Cologne.

As the RAF embarked on a strategy of nighttime area bombing during the summer of 1942, the Americans arrived in the European Theater of Operations (ETO) with their own approach to strategic bombing. The unit initially charged with executing American bombing policy was the Eighth Air Force, commanded by General Carl Spaatz, and Eighth Bomber Command, led by Lieutenant General Ira Eaker. Both were avid champions of strategic bombing, but neither was convinced by Harris's nighttime area raids, which indiscriminately killed many civilians without, they believed, delivering a decisive blow to German industrial targets. They were confident that American B-17s and B-24s, flying in tight formations high above effective anti-aircraft fire and bristling with fifty-caliber machine guns, could defend themselves against German flak and fighters. They also believed that they could identify key industrial and military bottlenecks and, using the Norden bombsight, destroy them.

The buildup of an American strategic presence in England was slow. During its first year of operations in Europe, the Eighth Air Force remained underequipped and understaffed. Planes and crews were so scarce that three months after the RAF mounted its thousand-plane raid on Cologne, the Eighth was able to dispatch fewer than 20 aircraft on the first American attack on German-occupied Europe. That mission, a raid on Rouen in western France, came on August 17, 1942, but by the close of the year, Eaker still had fewer than 100 operational heavy bombers at his disposal.

American plans for the strategic bombing of Hitler's Europe also suffered from shifts in Allied priorities. Just as the Eighth was beginning to develop a reasonable complement of forces, three of its bomber groups and three fighter groups were diverted to the Mediterranean in support of Operation Torch, the Allied invasion of North Africa in November 1942. Throughout that campaign, American P-40s and P-38s flew close air support for British and American ground forces, C-47 troop carriers dropped airborne units, and Jimmy Doolittle, now a general and also an ardent exponent of daylight precision bombing, led the newly formed Twelfth Air Force's bombers on missions against Axis installations and shipping in the Mediterranean area.

Meanwhile, the Americans found themselves under mounting pressure from the British to abandon daylight bombing and to join the RAF in its nighttime raids. Harris remained deeply skeptical about daylight bombing and about the American emphasis on attacking industrial bottlenecks—ball bearing factories or oil depots, for example—which he derided as "panacea bombing." Churchill was also distinctly unimpressed by the American effort from England and let his allies know it.

In an effort to defend American doctrine at the Casablanca Conference in January 1943, Eaker coined the term "Round-the-Clock Bombing." The formulation implied a coordinated plan of attack—the Americans would hit key targets during the day, the RAF would go over at night. Churchill was particularly taken with the phrase, and the Casablanca Directive from the Anglo-American Combined Chiefs of Staff ordered the two air commanders to embark on the systematic demolition of a range of German target systems as essential preliminaries to an invasion of Europe: submarine yards and bases, the German aircraft industry, oil facilities, ball bearing and synthetic rubber factories, and military transportation facilities. "Your primary aim," the directive stated, "will be the progressive destruction and displacement of the German military, industrial and economic system, and the undermining of the morale of the German people to a point where their capacity for armed resistance is fatally weakened...."

Yet, despite the apparent unity, genuine coordination remained something of a mirage; rather than "a Combined Bomber Offensive" there were two distinct, parallel efforts. Harris routinely ignored pressure to send his planes against the priority targets and instead continued to press them against large urban centers. These attacks occasionally overlapped with

Ambulances stand ready on the field as formations appear in the east.

A flight of P-51 Mustang fighters. The legendary P-51, with a powerful British-made Merlin engine, became one of the deadliest fighters to engage Axis air forces during World War II.

American raids but were rarely coordinated. The apogee of Harris's labors came in a four-month-long assault on Berlin between November 1943 and March 1944. The city was relentlessly bombed, but the Nazi government continued to function, the factories continued to produce, and Bomber Command lost 1,000 aircraft. By spring 1944, Harris had largely failed in his repeated promises to break Germany through saturation bombing, and his losses in the Battle of Berlin and in the calamitous Nuremberg raid of March 30, 1944, when Bomber Command lost more than 100 planes in a single night, cost him a great deal of his credibility with both Churchill and Allied military planners who were preparing for the invasion of northwestern Europe (Operation Overlord).

For their part, the Americans in mid-1943 believed that they were at last in a position to begin a sustained bombing offensive in Europe. The opening salvo was fired not from England but from Africa. On August 1, 1943, the Ninth Air Force, reinforced by two B-24 groups from the Eighth and operating from a desert base near Bengazi in Libya, dispatched 176 Liberators on Operation Tidalwave, a daring raid on the sprawling oil complex at Ploesti in Romania. If all went well, it would be a round trip of 2,700 miles. Despite both losing the lead and deputy lead aircraft shortly after takeoff and a serious navigational error en route, 164 Liberators reached Ploesti, roaring over the refineries at smokestack level. Those who survived the inferno of antiaircraft fire over the target and turned for home found hordes of German fighters waiting for them. Damage assessment reports suggested that the refineries suffered a serious—if not crippling—blow, but 54 bombers had been lost and more than 500 airmen were dead or missing. Five Medals of Honor were awarded to airmen on that raid, three posthumously, the most for a single air action in the Second World War.

Just over two weeks later, the Eighth Air Force flew its first major raid deep into the Third Reich, an ambitious two-pronged attack against the Messerschmitt aircraft factory at Regensburg and the ball bearing plants at Schweinfurt. Flying without fighter escort, two large formations of B-17s fought their way through wave after wave of German fighters to unload their bombs on the objectives. The targeted factories suffered some significant damage, and in Washington General Henry "Hap" Arnold proclaimed the raid a victory for daylight bombing. Back in England, the crews were not so sure; 60 bombers, with their 10 men crews, had gone down in one grisly afternoon.

After a lull to regroup, the Eighth resumed its daylight raids into Germany, absorbing terrible punishment in the process. On October 14, the bombers returned for a second raid on Schweinfurt. Another 60 planes were shot down on that day—"black Thursday," the crews dubbed it. During one week of bombing in mid-October, 148 heavy bombers were shot down. In all, 730 heavies were lost between June and the end of the year. It was the nadir of American air operations in Europe.

Despite these appalling losses, American leaders believed that improvements in formation flying, an increase in aircraft and crews, and the development of long-range fighter escorts would ultimately prove the feasibility of daylight bombing. By January 1944 aircraft and crews were pouring into the European commands, not only to the Eighth and Ninth in England, but to the Fifteenth Air Force, which was activated in November 1943. Flying from a complex of bases near Foggia in Italy, the Fifteenth would expand the range of the bomber offensive, reaching targets in eastern Germany and in the Balkans as well. Arnold also shuffled his commanders in the European theater. Doolittle assumed leadership of the Eighth; Eaker took charge of the AAF in the Mediterranean, and Spaatz became the commander of all U.S. air forces in Europe.

Among the aircraft arriving in Europe in late 1943 was the P-51 Mustang. An American fighter refitted with a British Merlin Rolls-Royce engine, the Mustang proved to be exactly the high-performance, long-range fighter the American commanders so badly needed. The new Mustangs were ready when the Eighth resumed its attacks on Germany early in January 1944, and Doolittle quickly introduced a new operational policy for Eighth Fighter Command. Although the fighters would still fly escort, they were no longer required to stay with the bombers but could seek out and pursue enemy aircraft. Their mission was to destroy the German Luftwaffe wherever they found it. The bomber crews weren't thrilled, but the fighter pilots loved it.

During the last week in February, both the Eighth and Fifteenth mounted monster raids against aircraft production facilities at Braunschweig, Halberstadt, Gotha, Leipzig, Regensburg, and Steyr and the ball bearing industry at Schweinfurt. Losses for what came to be called "Big Week" were high: 137 bombers from the Eighth and 89 from the Fifteenth, but the raids dealt a devastating blow to German air power. Not only did production plants sustain serious damage, the Luftwaffe lost more than 600 fighters. In the following month, American bombers attacked Berlin for the first time, escorted by P-51s all the way to the target. By spring swarms of Mustangs were accompanying ever-larger bomber formations into Germany, routing the Luftwaffe, both in the air and on the ground. For the first time it was possible to maintain the sort of relentless assault that AAF planners had envisioned.

With his air forces brimming with new aircraft, new crews, and long-range fighter support, Spaatz believed that he had isolated the great bottleneck of the German war industry—the one strategic industrial sector that, if destroyed by bombing, would cripple the German war machine and deliver victory to the Allies, perhaps without an invasion of Europe. That target was oil. Supported by Harris, Spaatz made an appeal to General Eisenhower, now in charge of the preparations for Overlord, to marshal all Allied power against German oil production in one massive campaign. Both Harris and Spaatz believed that their forces could defeat Germany before any land campaign was launched in 1944, if only they were given the resources to do so.

In March, Eisenhower chose instead to direct the Allied air forces to focus their efforts on establishing air superiority for the coming invasion and on destroying key transportation centers in France and western Germany in preparation for the Allied advance after D-Day. Harris and Spaatz were disappointed, convinced that a terrible error had been made, but between March and June 1944 the Allied Air Forces were able to establish the air superiority essential for a successful cross-Channel invasion. They relentlessly bombed railway yards, bridges, and other approaches to the planned Normandy beachheads. On D-Day and in subsequent operations in northwestern Europe, the Thunderbolts and Mustangs of the Ninth flew in tactical support of ground operations; Troop Carrier Command dropped paratroopers and towed gliders both in

Just as aircrews painted nose art on their planes, armament personnel sometimes painted bombs with personal greetings to the Führer.

Normandy and later in Operation Market-Garden; and even the heavies were occasionally employed in support of tactical objectives.

The objective of strategic bombing—destroying the capacity of the enemy to make war—implied a relentless attack against key priority targets, returning to hit them again and again. Following the invasion of France in June 1944, the AAF, joined by the RAF, was at last able to execute just such a sustained assault against German oil, staging raids of five, six, seven hundred planes against synthetic fuel complexes and other related targets. More raids were possible now as well, in part because the AAF increasingly used radar to identify targets beneath the clouds. The AAF was still committed to daylight precision attacks against industrial and transportation targets, but bombing with radar was less accurate. Ironically, the apex of German war production came that summer, amid the intensified bombing. Thereafter, German industrial output plunged precipitously in every category—aircraft, tanks, ball bearings, and, of course, oil. By the close of 1944, the German military machine was quite literally running out of gas.

What did the strategic bombing of Germany accomplish? Was it successful? The independent U.S. Strategic Bombing Survey (USSBS), commissioned by President Roosevelt in 1944, concluded that the impact of strategic bombing was powerful but perhaps not so profound as its champions in the Allied air staffs claimed. To understand the apparent paradox raised by the USSBS—that as bombing increased between 1942 and mid-1944, so, too, did German war production—it is important to examine the way in which the Nazi economy was organized and developed. In spite of an ambitious program of rearmament in the 1930s, Nazi Germany had not undertaken the necessary economic steps to prepare for a major European war. Even after the German invasion of the Soviet Union in June 1941 and the American entry into the war in December, the Nazi regime was reluctant—and structurally unable—to organize its economy for a prolonged conflict. It was really only in 1943, with Albert Speer in charge of a newly created Ministry of Armaments and Munitions, that the Germans were gradually able to set consistent industrial priorities and pursue them with some degree of order.

Speer's efforts to remove the considerable slack in the German economy began to bear fruit in late 1943, just as the Allied air offensive intensified, and reached their peak the following summer. While not able to prevent this expansion of the arms industry, Allied strategic bombing tied down more than one million Germans in air defense and repair work, forced a time-consuming and difficult dispersal of industry, and also placed a ceiling on German war production, which would have been considerably higher without the constant pressure of the air campaign. With Germany's considerable economic skills and the resources of all occupied Europe to draw on, Speer would have enjoyed, as British historian Richard Overy concludes, "the same economic freedom as that enjoyed by the United States to plan, build and operate the war economy without interruption and as near to the economic optimum as possible." Bombing made that impossible, and in doing so made a major contribution to the defeat of Nazi Germany.

A terrible price was paid in the process. Approximately 500,000 Germans perished in the target cities, many in ghastly firestorms such as those created in the bombings of Hamburg, Darmstadt, and Dresden. RAF Bomber Command lost 55,000 men. Of the roughly 40,000 Americans killed in air operations during the war, 26,000 were from the American Eighth Air Force alone—more than died in the entire U.S. Marine Corps in the Second World War. Another 18,000 were wounded, and 21,000 more were shot down and became prisoners of war. More than 30,000 Americans died in the air assault on Hitler's Germany, the Eighth Air Force suffering the highest casualty rate of any of the U.S. armed forces.

THE AIR WAR AGAINST JAPAN

In Asia and the Pacific the application of air power followed a different course and was not, until late in the war, oriented toward the sort of strategic bombing campaign that characterized the conflict in Europe. The air resources of the AAF and the Navy would be divided between three theater commands. General Douglas MacArthur led Allied forces in the Southwest Pacific, an area that stretched from Australia, the Solomons, New Guinea, the islands of the Bismarck Archipelago, and the Philippines, to the Dutch East Indies. Admiral Chester Nimitz, in charge of the Pacific Fleet, also became Commander-in-Chief of the North, Central, and South Pacific Theaters, while a British and American command, under Vice-Admiral Louis Mountbatten, exercised operational control over Burma and the rest of southeast Asia (the China-Burma-India or CBI Theater).

Nimitz believed an offensive across the island chains of the central Pacific—the Gilberts, the Marshalls, the Carolines, and finally the Marianas—offered the most favorable and direct route to Japan. Spearheaded by Navy and Marine forces, the conquest of the Marianas, or possibly Formosa, would bring American bombers, especially the very long-range B-29s that would become available in 1944, within striking distance of the Japanese Home Islands. Not surprisingly, MacArthur favored a drive from his base in Australia along the northern coast of New Guinea as a prelude to a return to the Philippines. Although Major General Claire Chennault, leader of the legendary "Flying Tigers" and commander of the Fourteenth Air Force in China, argued for a major air offensive from the Asian mainland, Washington was unwilling to commit large resources to the CBI Theater. In the end, a strategic compromise was reached: American forces would advance along two axes, from the southwest and across the Central Pacific. Each would seize islands, scratch an airfield out of the jungle or volcanic atoll, then leap forward, drawing closer and closer to the Japanese Home Islands.

The importance of forward air bases was driven home in March 1943,

A young P-51 pilot of the 357th Fighter Group

(Previous page)
A ground crewman, working on American P-40 Tomahawk fighter planes painted with the shark-face emblem of the legendary Flying Tigers, waves at a returning B-24 Liberator at a flying field in China, ca. 1942.

when Major General George C. Kenney, MacArthur's air commander (Fifth Air Force), used B-17s, low-flying B-25 Mitchells, and AAF dive bombers to devastate a Japanese troop convoy sailing from Rabaul to New Guinea. The Battle of Bismarck Sea was the first time shore-based aircraft had destroyed a Japanese fleet without the support of naval forces. Shortly thereafter, P-38 Lightnings from the Fifth, acting on radio intercepts, jumped a formation of Japanese aircraft approaching Bougainville in the Solomons. On board one of those planes was Admiral Yamamoto, the architect of the Pearl Harbor attack and the ranking commander in the Imperial Navy, who was killed in the ambush.

MacArthur's Operation Cartwheel against New Guinea and the Solomons got under way in June 1943, with close air support from the Fifth, sometimes called "the Jungle Air Force," and from the carriers of Admiral William "Bull" Halsey's Third Fleet. Kenney also sent his bombers against the strategic Japanese base at Rabaul on New Britain. In the Central Pacific, Nimitz's offensive, supported by Navy, Marine, and Army air units, proceeded through the Gilberts, with bloody landings at Tarawa and Makin in November, and northwestward into the Marshalls. In mid-February 1944 carrier-based aircraft from Rear Admiral Marc Mitscher's task force destroyed more than 200 hundred Japanese planes and sank eight warships in a major air assault against the important Japanese base at Truk in the Carolines.

Throughout the remainder of 1944 and into the new year Navy forces, joined by Fifth and Seventh AF planes, fought furious air battles across the Pacific. A spectacular encounter in June 1944 reflected the impact of the vastly improved American aircraft and pilots. When Admiral Mitscher's task force, operating in waters off the Marianas, were attacked by almost 400 Japanese planes, Mitscher's carrier-based aircraft downed 275 while losing only 29 of its own planes. The "Great Marianas Turkey Shoot," the pilots called it. Between August 24 and January 26 aircraft from Halsey's Third Fleet, supporting operations in the Western Carolines and the Philippines, destroyed over 4,000 Japanese planes and sank 82 Japanese combat vessels, while losing 445 of its own aircraft.

After the fall of the Marianas in the summer of 1944, the AAF hoped to undertake a massive campaign of daylight strategic bombing of Japan, as it was being practiced in Europe. The aircraft intended for that mission was the B-29 Superfortress. This "very long-range bomber" became available in early 1944 and was deployed to the Twentieth Air Force operating from bases in India and China. At that point in early 1944, China seemed to offer the best launching pad for operations against the Home Islands of Japan, but because of the difficulties of supplying the Twentieth (fuel and munitions had to be flown over the Himalayas from bases in India), the giant bombers were able to mount only sporadic raids during the summer and fall.

The first American attack against the Japanese Home Islands since the Doolittle raid in 1942 came on June 14, 1944, when 60 Superfortresses of the Twentieth AF attacked the iron and steel complex at Yawata. The attacking planes, flying at 30,000 feet, encountered cloudy conditions and very strong winds that made precision bombing extremely difficult. The cloud cover and the high winds at altitude—the Twentieth Air Force had discovered the jet stream—continued to be a problem in subsequent raids.

With the capture of the Marianas in June and July, 21st Bomber Command under Brigadier General Haywood Hansell began daylight raids launched from Tinian, Saipan, and Guam. Using the high-altitude precision methods honed in Europe, Hansell was determined to destroy the Japanese aircraft industry. The problems, however, continued. Accurate bombing proved almost impossible. The target areas in Japan were almost invariably obscured by overcast during daylight hours and had to be bombed using airborne radar. Moreover, the tremendous strength of the jet stream over Japan played havoc with bombsight calculations.

In January 1945, Arnold, impatient with 21st's meager results, replaced Hansell with Major General Curtis LeMay. LeMay had pioneered daylight strategic bombing in Europe, flying missions and introducing a number of tactical innovations to produce more accurate bombing. At first LeMay continued the precision raids on the aircraft industry, but after several missions he introduced a dramatic shift in American bombing policy. He scrapped daylight precision bombing and ordered his B-29s to attack at night. Cloud cover was thinner, antiaircraft fire would be less accurate (unlike German flak, it was not for the most part radar-guided), and the Japanese night fighter force was almost nonexistent. Under the cover of darkness, he argued, the B-29s could fly below the jet stream, dropping their bombs from as low as 5,000 feet. This would conserve fuel and allow for heavier bomb loads. Moreover, because Japanese industry was scattered throughout the urban landscape, with networks of small shops dispersed in residential neighborhoods, area bombing would be more effective. Finally, because of their many paper and wood structures, Japanese cities would be more highly vulnerable to incendiaries. It was a deadly combination.

The crews were skeptical about LeMay's breech of air force doctrine—especially the low altitudes and his order to strip the planes of their machine guns to allow for greater range and more bombs. But on the night of March 9-10, LeMay's views were vindicated when more than 300 B-29s appeared in the black skies over Tokyo and for over three hours disgorged thousands of incendiaries, turning a mixed area of factories and private dwellings into a

"My Mother's Name Was Enola Gay . . ."

I was in North Africa one day when my CO called me up to his office. He said, "I just got off the telephone with General Arnold. They're having trouble with the B-29." I said, "What's the B-29?" He said, "Well it's the latest bomber under contract. And they're having a lot of trouble with it. General Arnold wants me to send him my most experienced field grade officers." I was a lieutenant colonel field grade officer, so he added, "You answer the bill. You've got more experience than anybody else."

I went to Witchita and reported to the Commanding Officer. He looked at me and said, "Who are you?" I said, "Sir, I'm Lieutenant Colonel Paul Tibbets. I was sent here to fly a B-29 airplane." He looked out the window and said, "Well, there's three of the damn things sitting out there, go fly one."

Well, we went out and things worked out alright. I didn't have one minute's trouble with the thing. I fooled around with it. I stalled it. I put the flaps down. I did everything I could think to do with it to get the feel of it. After about two hours of flying, I said, "OK, I understand this airplane."

Later they gave me a full briefing of what the United States was doing with nuclear energy. They explained that we were building this bomb and that's why I was there. When the bomb was built, I would be flying it. On one occasion, Oppenheimer was explaining the differences between conventional bombs and this one. I said, "Doctor, over in Europe, I drop a bomb, I fly straight ahead, and the bomb explodes behind me." He responded, "Yeah, but you can't do that with this one. You wouldn't be here to talk about it." So I said, "OK, how do I get away from it?" He said, "Real simple. Turn tangent to the ever expanding shock wave, 159 degrees in either direction." I understood.

Our take-off was perfectly beautiful. We were exactly on schedule. I got to thinking that I've got to have more speed than normal. So I pushed those throttles forward and I watched that airspeed pick up past the point where normally we would have been taking off at that weight. I held it there until the airplane wouldn't stay on the runway, then I just let it alone and it lifted right off and we were on our way.

When the time came, it took Parsons and Jepson about 30 minutes to arm the bomb. They went into the bomb bay and I didn't hear anything for what seemed like maybe half an hour. Then Parsons came in and said, "It's all ready. Green plugs are in," meaning the bomb was activated.

The only thing I could think of all the whole time that I was out there flying was, "Have I made a mistake anywhere?" I counted the last fifteen seconds and the bomb left the airplane right with my count. I rolled the airplane off on its right side to bring it around in the 42 seconds I had before the bomb would explode. I didn't have time to think about anything else. I was flying on instruments. I kept reviewing everything in my mind. And I did that until the bomb exploded.

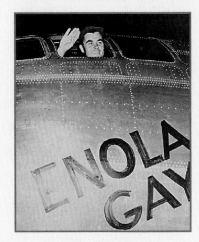

Paul Warfield Tibbets, Jr.,
Bomber Pilot, Fighter Pilot

How the hell could you get that much power out of something? I saw Hiroshima when we turned away. I wanted to get out over the Sea of Japan as fast as I could because I didn't think they'd have any fighters along the sea coast. That was my biggest safety consideration. I placed the airplane on autopilot so I could get a good look. I could see a black cloud hanging over the city, tumbling and boiling, with sparks flying out. I saw new fires starting. I thought, "That's one hell of a big bang." I didn't know how anybody could stand up to that weapon. Then I told the guys, "In case you don't understand it, you have initiated nuclear warfare today."

Where did the airplane's name—*Enola Gay*—come from? My mother's name was Enola Gay Heggard. I knew that the airplane would go down in history. There was no question in my mind about that, so I wanted it to have a good name, one that wouldn't be duplicated later on some other airplane. It was the rarity of the name.

What we did was teach the Japanese the futility of continuing to fight. Winning the war meant something else to me. It meant giving credit where credit was due, which was mainly to the women, the children, the people, the allies—everybody that did something to help us get that airplane to Japan on that day.

I don't think I should have any regrets. I was doing something I believed in. I believed that I was saving lives. I never lost a night's sleep over the whole thing.

raging inferno. A firestorm, on a scale to match the horrific raids on Hamburg and Dresden, raged across the city, consuming 16 square miles of urban landscape and killing more than 80,000 people. It was the most devastating conventional raid of the Second World War, and a terrifying preview of the coming campaign. In the following days, the 21st launched similar raids on Nagoya, Osaka, Kobe, Yokohama, and the campaign continued on into the summer.

By July, the B-29 raids were augmented by aircraft from a huge armada assembling off the coast of Japan. Planes from the Third Fleet undertook, in Admiral King's words, to "complete the destruction of the Japanese fleet, conduct a pre-invasion campaign of destruction against every industry and resource contributing to Japan's ability to wage war, and maintain maximum pressure on the Japanese in order to lower their will to fight."

With an invasion of the Japanese Home Islands looming in the late summer, and estimates of expected American casualties running well into the hundreds of thousands and Japanese casualties, military and civilian, as high as a million, President Harry S. Truman chose to employ a new weapon that held out the prospect of a quick end to the war. The atomic bomb had been tested on the night of July 15–16, 1945, in the desert near Alamagordo, New Mexico, and on August 6, the *Enola Gay*, a B-29 flying from Tinian, dropped the bomb over Hiroshima. In the shock waves and towering mushroom cloud, 60 percent of the city disappeared, and perhaps as many as 100,000 people perished, many vaporized in the blast. On August 9, a second atomic bomb was dropped on Nagasaki, killing another 60-70,000. Added to the grim totals killed in Tokyo and other Japanese cities since the first raids in March, these horrific casualties finally provoked the Emperor to act. The next day the Japanese government sued for peace.

TOURS OF DUTY

Each arena of combat—on the ground, at sea, or in the air—has its own distinctive forms of terror. Flying at altitudes of 20 to 30 thousand feet in a machine whose aluminum walls were so thin they could be punctured by a handheld screwdriver and at temperatures that often reached 60 degrees below zero, airmen faced death in a variety of hideous ways. Some planes, hit by flak or enemy fighters, simply disintegrated in a blinding flash of flame and debris, while others, their crew pinned helplessly to their positions by the centrifugal force, plunged in a sickening "graveyard spiral" to their death five miles below. As an Air Force flight surgeon reported in 1943, "Watching close-in and constant enemy fighter attacks, flying through seemingly impenetrable walls of flak, seeing neighboring planes go down out of control and at times explode in mid-air, returning with dead or seriously wounded on board and other such experiences imposed a severe and repeated stress which demanded a high degree of personal 'toughness' to tolerate."

Nor did the enemy pose the only dangers. Roaring down runways, loaded

to beyond capacity with 100-octane aviation fuel and tons of bombs, the planes had
little room for pilot error or mechanical
trouble. Aborting meant catastrophe. Once
airborne, assembling hundreds of aircraft,
often in dense cloud cover, was an arduous,
gut-wrenching part of every mission, and
close-formation flying, bucking in the tur-
bulent "prop wash" of a giant formation,
added to the tension. A single plane drifting
off course could set off a chain reaction of
calamity.

Conditions inside the aircraft added to
the hardships and anxieties of combat. As
the planes climbed above 10,000 feet, the
men went on oxygen, sometimes remaining
tethered to their masks for hours at a
stretch. At 20,000 feet, the temperature in-

Standing before the P-51 Lady Gwen II *a 353rd Fighter Group pilot describes his recent dog fight.*

side the planes plunged to –30 or –40 degrees Fahrenheit. Icy wind howled
through the turrets, the open windows in the waist, and the bomb bays. To
touch anything without gloves meant losing a finger or hand, and frostbite
was a constant danger. The men wore bulky flying clothes against the cold,
which made escape from the tight confines of a plane difficult. In the intense
cold, the clammy rubber oxygen masks routinely froze. After 30 seconds the
first signs of anoxia—oxygen deprivation—set in: a man grew woozy, his
judgment clouded, and his reflexes slowed. After a short time and with little
warning, he would lose consciousness. Only the B-29s, which went into
combat for the first time in the summer of 1944, were pressurized and
heated, but the mammoth planes suffered from persistent mechanical
problems—the giant engines had a proclivity to catch fire—making their
long-range missions over the Himalayas and the Pacific an exercise in un-
predictability.

If in the Pacific the cold was less a threatening presence than in Europe,
the ocean made up for it. Whether setting out from a ship or shore, flying for
hours over the trackless Pacific with no landmarks except the stars was
always fraught with peril. Battle damage hundreds of miles from base or a
simple navigational error, especially when trying to locate the position of a
moving carrier from the cramped cockpit of a Hellcat or Corsair, could mean
death. With bad weather and enemy action added to the mix, getting home, as
one Marine pilot put it, was often "by guess and by God." Hundreds of airmen simply vanished over the Pacific without a trace.

To deal with the unusual pressures and high risks of the war in the air, the
AAF and Navy developed a rotation system, determining what would constitute a tour of duty—an important distinction from the Germans and
Japanese, whose pilots flew until they were lost or the war ended. A tour of
duty varied from command to command and theater to theater. Fighter

commands measured a tour by the number of combat hours flown. In the Eighth and Ninth Air Forces, fighter pilots flew between 200 and 300 hours of combat; in the Mediterranean, around 300. Fighter pilots in the Pacific often flew between 400 and 500 combat hours. Carrier pilots generally flew for six months then rotated back to base to train new pilots before returning to combat.

Throughout the air war, the highest losses, both in absolute terms and in casualty rates, were suffered in Europe. In 1944, at the height of American air activity around the globe, 7,311 light, medium, and heavy bombers were lost or written off due to battle damage in Europe, 1,144 in the Pacific and Asia. The gap narrowed in 1945, with combat continuing in the Pacific into August, but the relative figures—reflected also in fighter losses—remained constant. In the Fifteenth Air Force, a tour for bomber personnel was set at 50 missions, though raids into Germany counted double. Crews in the Twentieth flew between 25 and 35. In the Eighth Air Force, a tour of duty

Crews begin to sift through the wreckage of a crash-landed B-24 Liberator, looking for survivors.

for bomber crews was initially 25 missions. But between August 1942 and August 1943 only 30 percent of bomber personnel actually survived 25 trips to the Continent. Thirty-seven percent were lost before they had completed five missions.

In January 1944, Doolittle increased a tour of duty in the Eighth to 30 missions, and later in the year, to 35. With more and more planes and crews arriving in Europe, the odds of surviving improved significantly, but casualties remained stubbornly high. In early 1944, the life expectancy of an Eighth Air Force bomber and its crew was only 15 missions. In fact, the absolute number of casualties rose dramatically until the summer of 1944, peaking in April-

Bomber crewmen who completed a combat tour became part of an elite "Lucky Bastard Club." Each bomb group had its own certificate design. The example shown is from the 94th Bomb Group of the Eighth Air Force.

May when the Eighth lost 671 heavy bombers. Even though the Luftwaffe had been severely weakened, flak continued to exact a very heavy toll. By war's end, antiaircraft fire claimed more American aircraft in Europe than did fighters. Under these circumstances, survival was a considerable accomplishment. Although the practice was unofficial and varied from group to group, each man who completed a tour was given a "Lucky Bastard Certificate," stating that he had flown 25 or 30 missions "in the Big Leagues of Aerial Combat and is going home to God's country, the lucky bastard."

How did the men cope? Some were fatalistic, assuming that they were living on borrowed time. Others simply denied the possibility of death. Death was something that happened to others. One gunner recalled that "if the briefing officer had told us that the mission was going to be particularly rough, that only two of us in the room would be coming back that afternoon, I would have looked around and wondered who the other guy would be." Most were superstitious; many carried good luck charms—St. Christopher's medals were a favorite—or developed rituals for every mission.

Everyone counted the missions but no one wanted to talk about it. In his memoir, *Combat Crew*, John Comer, a B-17 flight engineer in the 381st Bomb Group, wrote, "The trip would make twenty missions for me and should have been good news except for a strange phenomenon. Luck ran out for so many men…in the final quarter of the game….Why had so many men who approached the finish line met with disaster?" After all, "…what was luck? Was it an inexplicable thing available to a few at times but withheld from most men? Or was it a series of pure coincidences?" Some men and some crews "…wore a charm one could almost see. I could spot them around the operations area or the mess hall. I could spot others that I felt certain would never make it."

When his kid brother wrote to him from home in April 1945, asking how many more missions he had to fly, Howard Goodner, a radio operator in the

Fliers of the 15th Air Force in Italy, in the shadow of one of their P-51 Mustangs, August 1944.

466th, responded: "James, you ask how much I lack being through, well, that is something I never discuss. You see, I'm superstitious and so are all the guys who fly combat. You'll know when you see me next, so don't worry...because I'm alright and when you see me I'll be through." A week later Sergeant Goodner and his crew were lost over Regensburg flying the last B-24 shot down over Germany in the war.

The stress was intense. "They have been waking us up at 3 A.M. for breakfast," Lawrence Pote, a copilot in the 390th, recorded in his diary in March 1944, "then flight briefing, preflight check of airplane, assemble bomber formation, fly a 10-hour mission in formation on oxygen, return, debrief, eat, hit the sack about 9 P.M. and then being awakened again at 3 A.M. to go through the whole routine again. This has been going on for ten days now. The excitement and the fatigue really get to you."

The tension sometimes found expression in curious ways. As one group medical officer observed, "The men lived the battles in their sleep, with considerable mental disturbances. The other night the men went into the barracks and found Captain Fenton flying an apparently tough mission. Apparently his ship was hit and he exclaimed: 'Copilot—feather number four!' The lieutenant, sound asleep in the bunk beside him, answered him. Both of them, sound asleep, piloted the severely damaged Fort back home." (Quoted in Martin Caidin, *Black Thursday*)

The men who flew these missions were, with rare exception, not professional military men but draftees or young volunteers from all over the country, who rushed to join what was considered the most adventurous and most glamorous of the services. Most had never set foot in an airplane before entering service, but they were highly motivated (they had to volunteer for combat flying) and the training rigorous. As a group they tended to have a more extensive educational background (two-thirds of the AAF's enlisted men had graduated from high school) and scored higher on the Army's standard aptitude test than other branches of the military.

They were also exclusively male and almost exclusively white. Women did not fly in combat, but in 1943 the Women's Airforce Service Pilots (WASP) was created. Although not AAF personnel (they were civilian employees of

"We Were As Much American as White Americans"

I was born in Petersburg, Virginia. Every time I heard an airplane, I'd run outside and take a look at it. One day I saw some fighter planes flying across at a good clip—they were probably out of Langley—and I wished that I could do that. I was A-1 for the draft. If I hadn't volunteered for the Army Air Corps and pilot training, which is what I wanted, I'd have been drafted into the Army in the ground forces. I wanted to fly! Up until that time, there were no African Americans in the Army Air Corps. They were in the Army in segregated units, mostly in service units doing menial jobs that required very little intelligence. It had already been determined that we had no qualities of leadership.

Tuskegee Army Airfield in Alabama is where we did most of our training, but during the war we did not call ourselves the Tuskegee Airmen. We were the 332nd Fighter Group. We were part of an African-American experiment. The Army Air Corps expected that we couldn't fly the airplanes, and they were just doing this to let us prove to ourselves that we couldn't fly the airplanes.

I joined the 332nd Fighter Group at Ramatelli, Italy. The whole air base was African American. All the support people were African American. I flew 135 missions in P-40s and P-51s. We were dive bombing and strafing immediately in front of our ground troops, which required precision navigation so that we wouldn't kill our own people with what they call friendly fire. That's not too friendly.

We had about eight airplanes, P-40s at 8,000 feet, patrolling the Anjou beachhead. Anzio was only about a week old at that time. And we were called on the radio by the ground controllers, saying that there were many airplanes coming in at high altitude. They turned out to be FW-190s, fighter bombers, that were coming in to dive bomb the shipping in Anzio harbor. We couldn't stop them because they had a much faster airplane than we did. But then they went down close to the ground under us, and we jettisoned our auxiliary tanks that we carried under the airplane, and did a split S. We turned upside down, pulled through and went down. And I found myself sitting right behind the FW-190. I just shot him, and I never looked back.

Each one of the fighter groups had the tail assembly on the airplane painted a different color so that the crews in the bombers could know who was escorting them on a particular mission, and ours just happened to be red. The red tail was a symbol of the Tuskegee Airmen. And when some of the white pilots heard that African Americans were flying those airplanes, they didn't believe it. They knew it couldn't happen. Until they realized that whenever the 332nd with their red tails was protecting them from enemy airplanes, they were losing no bombers to enemy aircraft.

One mission that stands out in my mind was north of Naples in the mountains and we were to dive bomb and strafe artillery positions. And when we got to the target area, the target was obscured by low clouds. The clouds were so low there were peaks of mountains sticking up through them. And since I had never returned to base without finding a target, I didn't want to do it this time.

I weaved through the mountain, through the valleys and I found the target. I dropped the bomb on it, pulled back on the stick, and zoomed up through the clouds. To my surprise, the heat and the concussion of the exploding bomb blew a big hole in the clouds. And the other people were able to bomb through that hole. And that is what I got the Distinguished Flying Cross for. But it was a foolish thing to do.

We were in combat in Europe about two years, and during that time, 66 of our pilots were killed in combat. Another 33 were shot down or forced down in enemy territory and became prisoners of war. One of those prisoners of war came back and told us that when he was being interrogated after being shot down by German intelligence officer, that he was asked, "Why did you people fight so hard for a country that treated you so poorly?" He probably didn't have an answer, not a good one anyway. And of course he probably hadn't thought about it, like most of us hadn't thought about it. We didn't think that we were doing anything that we shouldn't have been doing. We felt that we were as much American as white Americans.

Second Lieutenant Howard L. Baugh,
One of the famed Tuskegee Airmen

the War Department), the WASPs were trained pilots who ferried military aircraft of all sorts from the factories that produced them to ports of embarkation. Some delivered the aircraft overseas. (See the section "Women in World War II")

The armed forces remained racially segregated throughout the Second World War, and bomber crews remained exclusively white. But in early 1941 the Air Corps created an African-American fighter squadron, which commenced its training at the Tuskegee Institute in Alabama. In late 1942, the 99th squadron arrived in North Africa, where it flew close air support missions for ground operations in Italy. In 1944, it was assigned to the newly arrived all-black 332nd Fighter Group and transitioned from Thunderbolts to Mustangs. The 332nd flew with the Fifteenth Air Force, and distinguished itself in escort missions over Italy and Germany. It was enormously popular with bomber crews, and for good reason: at war's end the 332nd could boast that it had never lost a bomber to enemy aircraft.

Black or white, the vast majority of men who flew were astonishingly young, between 18 and 25. Barely 24, Roy Allen, pilot of a B-17 in the 457th Bomb Group, was the oldest man on his crew and was dubbed, inevitably, "Pappy," by one of the 18-year-old-gunners. Jack Brennan, a B-24 waist gunner, pleaded with his parents to sign a release so that he might join before he turned 18. At 19 he was flying missions over Germany; he was killed in action before his 20th birthday.

What did these young airmen think of their chances? How did they evaluate their role in the war? More than 40,000 American airmen were killed in the Second World War. Despite the daunting odds, the men flew their missions; they did their part. Although they seldom agonized over the moral dilemmas of bombing operations, few relished their job or hated the enemy. If they thought at all about the political and ethical dimension of the war—and there is little evidence to suggest they did—they shared the national consensus that the defeat of the Axis regimes was a moral imperative that justified the mission they had been assigned. Although virtually everyone bellyached occasionally, and morale was subject to dramatic swings, most men found a way to deal with their fear and felt a tremendous loyalty to their comrades and considerable pride in their unit. They did their jobs, and those who came home knew how lucky they were.

The War on
the Home Front

⋆

HULL No. 227
WM. PEPPERELL
Keel Laid: 4-9-43
Launch: 5-24-43
45 DAYS

"They have given their sons to the military services. They have stoked the furnaces and hurried the factory wheels. They have made the planes and welded the tanks, riveted the ships and rolled the shells."

—FRANKLIN D. ROOSEVELT

THE ARSENAL
OF DEMOCRACY

Douglas Brinkley

There is no question that World War II was won on the battlefield, but it could not have been won had the United States lacked the wherewithal to unleash its enormous industrial capacity to arm itself and its allies. Friend and foe alike believed that should the Americans enter the war, their greatest contribution would be in the form of war materiel. As Japan's Admiral Isokoru Yamamoto confided to a friend in 1940, "I feel that if we're going to war with America we must accept the idea we're taking on almost the whole of the rest of the world."

The scale of the effort to convert a depression-era industrial workforce into what President Roosevelt called "the Arsenal of Democracy" was colossal. The number of people employed in factories and on farms dwarfed the 16 million Americans in the armed forces who relied on them to produce everything from food and medicine to bullets and ships. Industrial production was the result of both private and public initiative. The automotive industry was at the center of production for military materiel, building some 2.4 million trucks, as well as hundreds of thousands of jeeps (Willys-Overland built 360,000 jeeps, Ford 227,000). Nearly half of the 50,000 tanks built during the war were built by Chrysler at the government's Detroit Tank Arsenal.

A staggering 300,000 fighter aircraft were built between 1941 and 1945. Ford alone built more than 8,000 B-24 bombers at the mile-long Willow Run assembly plant near Ypsilanti, Michigan. General Motors converted assembly plants for Oldsmobiles, Buicks and Pontiacs in New Jersey, New York, and Maryland to produce 7,500 Grumman-designed Avenger torpedo bombers and nearly 5,000 Wildcat fighters. In addition, American industry produced 3.3 million rifles, 2.6 million machine guns, and 41 billion rounds of ammunition—not to mention 47 million tons of artillery ammunition.

Between the end of 1941 and 1945, more than 75 private and government shipyards and nearly 400 other companies, employing hundreds of thousands of workers, launched nearly 70 thousand vessels of all kinds. Maine's Bath Iron

Works alone launched 83 destroyers during the war—more than all Japanese shipyards combined. The total cost of war materials between 1941–1945 has been estimated at $183 billion.

In addition to assembling military hardware, American industry also fabricated a huge variety of raw materials, foods and medicines. In Utah, the 4,000 employees of the Geneva Steel Works produced 634,000 tons of steel plates and another 144,000 of shaped steel. Two years after its first successful use on a human, the government and private industry threw themselves into the mass production of penicillin. From a mere 231 billion units in 1943, production of the "wonder drug" antibiotic grew from to nearly 8 trillion units in 1945.

All Americans were affected by austerity measures such as rationing, the end of civilian car production, and recycling, but there were compensations in the form of increased wages, price controls, nearly full employment—between 1938 and 1944 unemployment fell from 19 percent to only 1 percent—and more widespread opportunity for all, including women and minorities. The lure of higher wages in industry resulted in huge internal dislocation as people moved in search of better opportunities. By mid-1942, an estimated 6 million people had walked off the farm for high-paying work in the factories of the Midwest and especially the West Coast, where the combined population of California, Oregon and Washington grew 49 percent in the 1940s—3.5 times more than the country as a whole. Efforts to recruit urban volunteers to work on the farm were organized by the Women's Land Army, and by the end of the war some 3 million women had enlisted for a "Victory vacation."—Lincoln Paine

MOTOR CITY MOBILIZATION: THE FORD MOTOR COMPANY, WILLOW RUN AND THE B-24 BOMBERS

In a radio address on December 29, 1940, President Franklin Roosevelt declared that America was the "Arsenal of Democracy." What he didn't say was that metropolitan Detroit was the vortex. And at the center of the vortex was Ford Motor Company—headquartered in Dearborn, Michigan, and given the task of building B-24 Liberators. The company stunned the world with its unprecedented manufacturing productivity from 1942 to 1945. Anything grand that happened in the United States's wartime industrial mobilization effort happened in an exaggerated way at Ford Motor Company, particularly at its enormous Willow Run plant near Ypsilanti, Michigan. A *Popular Science* article published during World War II summed it up best: "Willow Run is America's big all-out attempt to apply the technique of automobile mass production to the rapid manufacture of a four-engine bomber."

In 1940 war was raging across much of Europe, but in America the automobile business was strong and Detroit-Dearborn was buzzing with excitement. U.S. automakers—Ford Motor, General Motors, Chrysler, Packard, and Hudson, among others—were enjoying a banner year in vehicle sales, in part due to the very real fear that war would suspend new car production. However much these Michigan companies produced for the military, cars remained the greater priority. In the summer of 1941, Virginia Senator Harry Byrd sneered: "The U.S. in the past year succeeded in producing five thousand combat planes and five million automobiles. Something must be done to reverse those numbers."

President Roosevelt intuited the coming of U.S. involvement in the Second World War and had begun laying the groundwork for increased military production as early as 1940. He hired the Danish-born William Knudsen (1879–1947), who had served as chief of Ford's production team from 1911 to 1921, to help him retool the humming plants of Detroit-Dearborn into military mega-factories. Knudsen had left Ford to join Chevrolet in 1922, turning that company into a leading car manufacturer. In May 1940, when Roosevelt selected Knudsen to be a member of a small Office of Production Management (OPM) team whose responsibility was the conversion of American industry to war production, he was an established industrialist ready for the Herculean task. Under Roosevelt's direction, Knudsen, given the rank of Lieutenant General in the U.S. Army, soon coordinated the manufacture of all military equipment produced in America for use by U.S. and Allied forces from 1940 to 1945.

Knudsen had a lot of things to do in the new OPM, but the most urgent assignment was antithetical to everything he'd done before. He had to stop the auto industry from making so many cars. In August 1941, the OPM announced an average reduction of 26.5 percent for the remainder of the year and 50 percent for the first six months of 1942. Ford Motor Company, which had built 20.2 percent of the nation's vehicles in the 1940 model year and 18.1 percent the following year, was allotted a production quota equivalent to 18.6 percent of the industry for the '42 model year. Those percentages placed Ford in third place behind the Chrysler Corporation (23.1 percent) and General Motors (44.3). In real terms though, this meant that Ford would be allowed to make only 399,600 cars for the year, about half the number it had made the year before. Knudsen said of the legendary Henry Ford, a renowned pacifist and isolationist, "It's the not making automobiles that really stuck in his craw."

The attacks on Pearl Harbor and the Philippines in December 1941 changed the allotments. Suddenly the United States entered a two-front war in Europe and the Pacific. The pressure on American industry, and automaking in particular, increased overnight. Luckily for companies like Ford Motor, Chrysler and General Motors, the members of the United Auto Workers (UAW) were ready for the war. The UAW boasted 200,000 members in metropolitan Detroit. Many young men enlisted in the armed forces, but those union men who stayed in Ford factories such as the River Rouge and Willow Run would do their jobs so well that about 25 percent of all Allied war materiel—aircraft engines, artillery shells, bombers, jeeps, machine guns, tanks, and many other products essential to waging modern warfare—would be manufactured in the Detroit area. Blue-collar workers would transform Henry Ford's "Motor City" into the very epicenter of Franklin Roosevelt's "Arsenal of Democracy." As Japan continued its military rampage through the Pacific, the image of Willow Run (or The Run, as workers called the Ypsilanti factory) served as a real morale boost. "It is a promise of revenge for Pearl Harbor," the *Detroit Free Press* observed. "You know when you see Willow Run that in the end we will give it to them good."

On February 9, 1942, all automobile assembly lines in Detroit and other Michigan cities ceased production of civilian vehicles and manufactured only military vehicles until the end of the war. Ford Motor Company's River Rouge plant, for example, was converted into a tank arsenal. And starting on May 15, 1942, Ford's Willow Run plant started making B-24 bombers. The aluminum and other raw materials that entered at one end of the mile-long main building at Willow Run were stamped, stretched, milled, machined, or

A partly-finished halftrac scout car body is lowered on a chassis in a war plant operated by the Diebold Safe and Lock Company, Canton, Ohio. (December 1941)

Workers install single-row intake pipes on a new Pratt and Whitney airplane engine in one of the company's plants, dedicated exclusively to the production of powerful motors for Army and Navy aircraft. (June 1942)

riveted into parts: in all, 550,000 pieces went into a B-24, not counting the 700,000 rivets. The parts were constructed into sub-assemblies, which fed into two parallel, final assembly lines. By that point airframes progressed along conveyors, pulled by underground cables. As the planes emerged from the building, they were tested on the adjoining mile-long airstrip.

For all of the effort that went into the planning and construction of a factory so immense, and at the same time so complex, two early mistakes nearly scuttled the enterprise. They may have been apparent to experienced production men, but the Ford mystique was such that few outsiders questioned even the company's most unorthodox decisions. The mystique existed within the company, but even on the inside, managers were reluctant to question policies handed down from the top. Once inspiring, the mystique became as tight as a straightjacket on the question of Willow Run.

In the first place, Ford executives probably should not have opted to use steel-cast dies—11,000 of them—in the production of the B-24. Long-lasting but difficult to make, steel dies were appropriate for automobile models. Cars not only had production runs in the hundreds of thousands or even millions, but also were subject to relatively few design changes. The B-24, on the other hand, was expected to peak at about 5,000 units per year at Willow Run: a lot for an airplane in 1943, but not much for steel-cast tools and dies. Moreover, the B-24 design used by Ford to set up the new factory had never been tested in combat. Once the United States entered the war, actual experience resulted in a steady stream of design changes. To implement them meant long delays at Willow Run while new steel dies were cast. Because specified improvements took so long to show up in production, the Army took a drastic step in 1942, temporarily suspending the implementation of changes in Ford-made B-24s. Until the process was finally reorganized late in the year, Willow Run B-24s were restricted to use in training.

The second problem facing Willow Run was entirely Henry Ford's doing: the location of the plant made finding a wartime workforce extremely difficult. During the Great Depression, automakers had enjoyed a wide choice in hiring, drawing from a ready pool of experienced, reliable workers. That changed once the war started. Within months of Pearl Harbor, it was the workers who had their choice of factories. A bomber factory located 25 miles from downtown Detroit did not tempt many workers away from local plants operated by GM, Packard, Chrysler, Hudson, and even Ford itself. *The New York Times* noted with alarm on December 5, 1942, that Ford Motor Company was unable to maintain a workforce at Willow Run. Company representatives recruited heavily in rural districts in Michigan, where the choice of jobs wasn't as wide as it was in Detroit. "Some men came all the way from Algonac," recalled Clem Davis, referring to a small town northeast of Detroit. "That's over 100 miles back and forth to Willow Run." A commute that long would have been tough enough in peacetime, but when nationwide gas rationing started in December 1942, it required special permits or careful planning.

After canvassing the Michigan countryside, Ford officials fanned out to towns throughout the upper Midwest, even scouring hollows in Appalachia, looking for workers. Practically any able body would do. So many workers came from the Bluegrass State that Ypsilanti was jokingly referred to as "Ypsitucky." The recruiting drive drew farmhands, store clerks, and others who had never earned as much as an auto worker's wages. "A fellow called me up one day," recalled Tony Harff, who worked in Willow's administration office, "and said we had a fellow out there who came into work that morning and had no shoes on his feet. They didn't know whether to send him out into the plant or not without shoes, but they finally did." Willow Run didn't turn down many people. "The fellow said he never wore shoes in his life," Harff added, "and he wasn't going to start to wear them now, just because he was going to work inside a plant."

The only thing worse than trying to draw workers out to Willow Run was the frustration of trying to keep them there. Ford Motor Company couldn't be faulted for the training it offered inexperienced workers; in fact, its programs were probably too thorough. The company had had long experience in making production factory workers out of new immigrants, ex-convicts, and the disabled. During the war, it could and did teach factory skills to thousands of neophytes. Unfortunately, a high percentage of workers took what they learned in Willow Run's training programs and immediately secured work in Detroit or another big city. Another problem was that the U.S. government kept drafting workers to join the armed forces. "In January 1943," Harff said of Willow Run, "we hired 1,186 men and lost 1,669. . . . There was a terrific turnover."

Ford Motor Company contributed to the labor problem by refusing to cooperate with the government's efforts to build housing adjacent to the factory. The company was against the plan because

Partially completed twenty-eight ton M-3 tanks roll along the assembly lines at Chrysler's huge tank arsenal in Detroit, ca. 1944.

it felt the construction, estimated at two years, would drain employees from the plant. Henry Ford was adamantly opposed to a factory village, in some measure because he didn't want to populate a Republican county with voters who would cast ballots along union lines. Eventually, Ford Motor Company did build its own temporary housing complex near the plant. Composed of little more than wooden huts, the workers' quarters didn't invite permanent residency, further contributing to the high turnover. In order to encourage workers to drive in from Detroit, however, good, direct roads to Willow Run were built.

Henry Ford took only passing interest in the Willow Run facility, and rarely visited it or conferred with others about it. As the war work progressed, Henry Ford was embittered in many respects, all too aware that for the first time, his company had only one customer: the U.S. government. That had not been the case during World War I, when the company continued vehicle production alongside military work. But in 1942, the United States was mobilized for war to a far greater extent. New car sales ended and Ford Motor was, like all other automakers, an adjunct to the U.S. military. Hordes of officers and inspectors descended on Ford plants, especially Willow Run, making demands, inspecting paperwork, and generally examining operations at will. Henry Ford regarded it as a plot to assume control of the company. He was particularly acrimonious toward Bill Knudsen. "All he is here for is to take over our plants," Ford concluded.

Aloof and grumpy, the 79-year-old Ford had become a ghost of his former vigorous self. He was, in historian David Kennedy's apt phrase, "a crusty icon of industrialized America."

Henry Ford had always aligned himself with strong personalities. One favorite who was around Willow Run a great deal was Charles Lindbergh, whom Henry Ford hired in March 1942 as a test pilot. Because Lindbergh was deemed *persona non grata* by the Roosevelt administration due to his isolationist attitude, companies like Consolidated Aircraft snubbed him. Ford, in kind, snubbed the White House because to him Lindbergh was still the all-American hero. Upon seeing Willow Run, Lindbergh recorded in his diary that the facility was "acres upon acres of machinery and jigs and tarred wood floors and busy workmen . . . . a sort of Grand Canyon of the mechanized world." Ford asked Lindbergh to name his salary—he would pay it. The tarnished idol responded that he would accept only what a colonel received in the Air Corps: $666.66 per month.

Before long the Lindberghs, a very wealthy couple, settled into a cozy home in Bloomfield Hills, Michigan. Lindbergh started work inspecting and test-flying planes at Willow Run. "The government's attempts to stifle Lindbergh's wartime career increased his desire to prove himself a good soldier," biographer A. Scott Berg maintained. "He shifted his high-octane work ethic into an even higher gear, never allowing anybody to accuse him of goldbricking. He usually left for work before daybreak and did not return home until long after dark. He became his own harsh taskmaster, creating assignments for himself when he had exhausted those put before him." So

it was that America's two most infamous isolationists, Henry Ford and Charles Lindbergh, teamed up to do whatever they could to make America and Ford Motor first in airplane production.

On September 18, 1942, Franklin and Eleanor Roosevelt paid an official visit to the gigantic plant, intended to boost Allied morale by focusing attention on the biggest bomber factory in the world. The United States had not fared well in its first months of military engagement, and needed the news that long-distance bombers were about to start pouring out of the Ford plant. Until the Roosevelts brought their spotlight to Willow Run, people could still believe that the factory was operating according to plan. "We went to a lot of trouble in arranging that trip to make sure he saw as much as possible," recalled assistant plant supervisor Logan Miller. "We arranged to have his car driven down between the press lines and through the subassembly area. He saw with his own eyes what was going on."

Under increased pressure from the Army, Willow Run finally turned a corner in 1944. With the old Ford Motor Company bravura, it was finally producing first-rate B-24 Liberators, in line with the original schedule. Mead Bricker, general manager of the bomber plant, deserved a fair share of the credit. Under his brand of tough, logical leadership, the factory reached its potential and then some, going from the back of the pack to the leading edge. Working at Willow Run was a no-nonsense proposition. Music was banned, coffee breaks were non-existent, and smoking was out of the question. Workers learned the system, and moreover, the system learned to use workers without a great deal of experience, making up for high turnover rate. By the summer of 1944, Willow Run had produced 5,000 planes and was working at a much faster rate than any other B-24 factory. It was even assigned extra tasks—for example, making spare parts and modifications to older B-24s.

With technique tightening and morale rising, the transformation at Willow Run was dramatic. Inspectors found an average of 800 quality problems on each plane in 1942. By 1944, the number of "squawks," as the problems were called, was down to 20.

To motivate workers, the Willow Run plant newspaper printed accounts from pilots who flew the planes that the factory built. One was called *Yellow Easy* by its crew. "We never coddled that plane," said one of the captains, Richard A. Potter of Toledo. "Other planes would be housed up for the sub-zero nights with heaters blowing through their engines. But not *Yellow Easy*." The crew flew the long-range plane out of a base in Italy. "We hit Weiner Neusstadt on our third mission," Potter said of a German target. "*Yellow Easy* had one prop sheared completely off—another engine holed by flak, and she struggled home slashed to pieces. Two days later she was ready again and doing her stuff over a target in south France." *Yellow Easy* crashed on its 70th mission, over Vienna. With the engines on fire and one wing torn in half, it glided gently down, giving all 10 men on board time to parachute safely to the ground.

George Sunal, an engineer credited with creating the upper instrument panel in the B-24, recalled the horror of cleaning out cockpits of Liberators that had seen action. "Many were full of bullet holes," he said. "Sometimes we found blood inside, where crew members had been wounded or perhaps killed during combat. It was heartbreaking. And I thought I was doing a lot. You felt you were a part of each plane made. You were at the plant so much, you practically lived there."

A Curtiss-Wright representative who toured Willow Run at the time of the D-Day invasion wrote, "The Ford Willow Run Bomber Plant, flight operations area, with a shop personnel of approximately 420 employees divided into two nine-hour shifts, is delivering to the Army, at present, an average of 13.4 Liberator bombers daily. In light of our own experience this is an impressive record."

Some of the returning Liberators spoke more clearly of victory. Pilots frequently had mascots hand-painted on the fuselage. Cartoon characters and sexy women were favorites. But what cheered the workforce most were the tallies etched near the wings, signifying the number of successful bombing missions completed by a B-24.

The Army Air Force (AAF) launched a propaganda campaign designating the B-24 Liberators the greatest flying machines ever made. They could fly 3,000 miles without refueling, cruised at over 300 miles per hour, and held up to four tons of bombs. What they didn't say was that pilots had a brutal time steering the aircraft. However heroic the exploits of plane like the *Yellow Easy*, it was the ace pilots who made them great. Aside from the dangers inherent to combat, pilots faced a struggle just to fly and land them safely. Warplanes are not designed with the pilot's ease in mind, and the B-24 was no exception. There were no windshield wipers, so pilots were forced to stick their heads out the window in bad weather. There was no aisle or bathroom, and few safety features. Pressurization was a real problem, and pilots and crew often had trouble breathing. Chronic dizziness and nausea ensued. Oxygen masks were usually necessary. "Absolutely nothing was done to make it comfortable for the pilot, the co-pilot or the other eight men in the crew, even though most flights lasted for eight hours, sometimes ten or more, seldom less than six," Stephen E. Ambrose recalled in *Wild Blue: The Men and Boys Who Flew the B-24s over Germany*. "The plane existed and was flown for one purpose only, to carry 500 to 1,000 pound bombs and drop them accurately over enemy targets."

Senator Harry Truman (at right, with unidentified Ford employee) examines a recently-completed B-24 bomber at Ford's Willow Run plant in April 1942.

*(Next page)
On May 15, 1942,
the first B-24 rolls off the
production line at Willow Run.*

ROSIE THE RIVETER AND THE PEOPLE OF WILLOW RUN

Women constituted a large part of the Willow Run workforce, the most famous of them all being Rose Monroe, the celebrated "Rosie the Riveter." For a long time, confusion surrounded the identity of the real Rosie, and for good reason. Originally, the U.S. government distributed a poster by J.

Howard Miller entitled "We Can Do It!"; it showed a woman in denim overalls flexing her muscles, a bandanna on her head. There was no model for this poster—it was merely a composite symbol of women in the defense industry. Later, illustrator Norman Rockwell painted his own "Rosie the Riveter," using as his model Mary Doyle Keefe of Nashua, New Hampshire—a part time telephone operator who never riveted anything—for a *Saturday Evening Post* cover (the original artwork fetched an amazing $4.9 million at a Sotheby's auction in May 2002). Meanwhile, the song "Rosie the Riveter" recorded by bandleader Kay Kyser, was inspired by a New Yorker named Rosalind B. Walter. The song was heard all over the world, a big-band-era tribute to women fighting for democracy. Given all the publicity, an effort was undertaken to find a real worker to represent "Rosie" and help promote war bonds. They found her at Willow Run. Actor Walter Pidgeon, known for performances in such films as *Dark Command* and *How Green Was My Valley*, was touring the cavernous factory when he was introduced to an attractive riveter with curly brown hair, almond eyes, and a Midwestern demeanor, and assemblyline tools in her hand. "She was just perfect," Pidgeon recalled. "A real honest-to-God, hardworking lady whose name was Rosie." A native of Somerset, Kentucky, Rose Monroe, a self-labeled tomboy, had had a hardscrabble life. In 1940 her husband was killed in an automobile accident. After Pearl Harbor she joined the home-front effort, accepting employment at Willow Run. With daughters Vicki and Connie in tow, she headed for Ypsilanti, Michigan, in an old Model A, hoping for the best.

Never allergic to hard work, Rose Monroe carried sheet metal, fitted parts, and used jackhammers, all of which made her arms terribly sore. But she never complained. Her dream was to fly. Unfortunately, as a single mother, she was ineligible to join any military or civil aviation programs. (She did earn a pilot's license in the 1950s.) When Pidgeon stumbled upon her, she was doing her job with characteristic diligence. "Mom happened to be at the right place at the right time," her daughter Vicki recalled. All over America, in Pidgeon's famous promotional film, there was Rose Monroe for all to admire, building B-24 bombers that would help crush Hitler's army and Tojo's ships.

The most unexpected workers at Willow Run were the "little people," 12 midgets who could crawl into the tight spaces of B-24s under construction. They actually riveted inside wings and inspected rudders. One of the little people, Robert Hardy, even befriended Henry Ford. A native of Wyandotte, Michigan, Hardy had dropped out of high school and joined a New York musical troupe called Rose's Midgets. When World War II started, the 23-year-old Hardy heard through the grapevine that Willow Run needed a dozen "small statured" assembly-line workers. Hardy traveled to Detroit in the only suit he owned and was hired on the spot. "Ford sent me to school," Hardy recalled, "and gave me a course in rivet theory." He joined the UAW Local 50 and started inspecting planes. "Henry Ford would visit the line, come over and talk to me, and often would bring celebrities with him,"

Hardy recalled. "Once, he introduced me to Irving Berlin. Another time, he brought two young boys and wanted me to show them around to all the work the little people were doing." He was also introduced to Lindbergh, aviator Eddie Rickenbacker, and Vice President Henry Wallace.

Besides women and little people, an influx of African Americans found employment in the Ford factories during World War II. The sudden proximity of increased numbers of blacks and whites at work, on public transportation, and in parks kindled bigotry into violence. In February 1943, a white mob attacked several black tenants at the Sojourner Truth housing project in a heavily Polish north Detroit neighborhood. As tensions escalated afterward, nine whites were killed and thousands of people from both races were injured. Bands of vicious white youths roamed the streets, beating every African American they could catch, and soon the blacks reciprocated. Entire city blocks were destroyed while Mayor Edward Jeffries Jr., and Michigan Governor Harry Kelly were paralyzed by fear and indecision. Kelly even tried to stop federal troops from entering the city in hopes that his state forces could cool the situation. After a week of sporadic rioting, looting, and arson, however, the governor relented and allowed President Roosevelt to send two military police battalions into Detroit. By the time they arrived, however, the uprising had ended. More than 1,800 people had been arrested.

Willow Run wasn't the only Ford Motor factory producing materiel during World War II. Gliders were built in the timberland of Ford's installation

One of Ford's B-24 assembly lines at Willow Run, ca. February 1943.

at Iron Mountain on Michigan's Upper Peninsula. At the River Rouge plant in Dearborn, one of Ford Motor's most successful wartime projects was the quarter-ton 4x4 truck—the jeep. The American Bantam Company had designed the vehicle in 1940, in conjunction with the U.S. Army Quartermaster Corps. Although Ford passed on the initial invitation to bid on building jeeps in quantity, it soon recognized that the little battle car held terrific potential for use in the war and even afterward. Trying to make up for lost time, the company was accused of forcing its way into a contract. "Certain officials of the Defense Commission and the War Department had gone out of their way to favor Ford," wrote I.F. Stone in New York's crusading *PM* newspaper. The specter of a giant company shouldering aside the enterprising American Bantam Company ignited a Senate investigation chaired by Missouri's Harry S Truman—once a prospective Ford dealer. The findings were not conclusive, but the issue was hot, and so it was no surprise that the OPM's Knudsen recommended that Willys-Overland receive the contract. However, the Army Quartermaster Corps, wanting lots of jeeps as soon as possible, had much more faith in Ford Motor. Through its influence, Ford eventually shared the major portion of the jeep contract with Willys-Overland.

Jeeps, which could go anywhere and then go some more, were ubiquitous in World War II. Early in 1942, boxed jeeps from Dearborn waited on the docks in Rangoon, even as British and American soldiers searched for a way to race north to meet fast-moving Japanese troops. As soon as mechanics could assemble the jeeps, soldiers jumped in and drove into Burma's jungles and rice paddies to intercept the enemy. That is considered the first time jeeps entered battle, though the Soviets had been using them through the Lend-Lease program, since 1941.

Pulled by the government and pushed by the Army, Ford Motor Company ultimately fulfilled its potential, producing war materiel in almost exact proportion to its position in the peacetime economy. In fact, Ford turned in an exemplary record and so did Willow Run, once it was finally on track. "Although some aircraft manufacturers questioned whether the same results could not have been accomplished in less time and at smaller cost," the authors of *The Army Airforces in World War II* concluded, "it seems clear that the Ford experiment was ultimately successful." The greatest progress occurred in 1944, as Ford production finally responded to such pragmatic bosses as Mead Bricker, who put it on schedule and kept it there. "Every major wartime production effort of the Ford Motor Company benefited from Mr. Bricker's great manufacturing knowledge and skill," Henry Ford II noted. "In particular the output of 2,000-hp aircraft engines and the unprecedented heavy bomber production at Willow Run were personal triumphs of leadership." The availability of long-range B-24 bombers in large quantities certainly hastened the end of the war in Europe. During the war, Ford Motor produced 8,685 B-24 bombers, 57,851 airplane engines, 277,896 jeeps, 93,217 trucks, 26,954 tank bombers, 57,851 airplane engines, 2,718 tanks and tank destroyers, and so on, down a long list of heavy machinery. Major General James M. Gavin also praised Ford Motor for building 4,291 of the finest motorless gliders ever manufactured in the United States. Meanwhile, the Lincoln Motor plant contributed by manufacturing 24,929 nacelles (housings) for B-24 bombers.

The production output of the United States has often been credited with turning the tide for the Allies. But when the job was done, production abruptly ended. On April 17, 1945, the AAF and the War Production Board issued a notice of termination. "To the Employees of the Ford Willow Run Plant," it began. "Changing war needs and the rapid collapse of the German Luftwaffe have reduced requirements by the Army Air Forces. Consequently, production will be scaled down progressively and will cease not later than August, 1945."

World War II ended in August 1945 soon after the atomic attacks on Hiroshima and Nagasaki. Detroiters congregated along Woodward and Michigan Avenues to celebrate the Japanese surrender with parades and victory rallies. Most industrial companies were eager to return to business in peacetime—Ford Motor Company was no exception. Like all the other Detroit area automakers they were proud that they had been key pillars in transferring President Roosevelt's "Arsenal of Democracy" rhetoric of 1942 into historical reality in 1945. Now Ford Motor wanted to get back to doing what it did best: building cars.

SHIPBUILDING IN WORLD WAR II

Between the end of 1941 and 1945, more than 75 private and government shipyards and nearly 400 other companies employing hundreds of thousands of workers—many of them women—launched nearly 70,000 vessels of all kinds, from the 32-foot Higgins boats to Essex-class aircraft carriers that could carry 100 aircraft. American industrial capacity was the one thing that both German and Japanese strategists feared, but the scale of the effort to convert a depression-era industrial workforce into "the arsenal of democracy" was stunning. Maine's Bath Iron Works, for example, launched 83 destroyers during the war—more than all Japanese shipyards combined.

In shipbuilding, the roots of the effort lay in the National Industrial Recovery Act of 1933, part of which was committed to promoting naval and merchant marine shipbuilding. The former had been allowed to slip because of the nation's isolationist and pacifist tendencies, while the latter had been hobbled by the decline in world trade that accompanied the great depression. The focus on naval construction in the 1930s owed much to the efforts of President Roosevelt, who had been Secretary of the Navy under Wilson—and who famously declared, "You know I am my own Secretary of the Navy"—and Congressman Earl Vinson of Georgia. With the support of these two, in 1933 the Navy ordered 32 ships, including two aircraft carriers. While this represented progress of a sort, under a shipbuilding authorization passed the following year, the navy would have achieved "treaty strength—that is the number of vessels allowed under the London Naval Conference of 1930—only by 1942. A further problem was the doctrinal schisms between proponents of battleships and of aircraft carriers, and between proponents of large combat ships and of smaller vessels designed for convoy support and amphibious operations. As Roosevelt complained, "The Navy couldn't see a ship under a thousand tons."

Working his way around a reluctant public and Congress, between 1935 and 1939 Roosevelt helped enlarge the navy from 90,000 to 191,000, and in 1940, after the war had begun in Europe, the Navy won a $4 billion appropriation to construct an additional 257 ships—a 70 percent increase, and enough for an effective "two-ocean" navy.

At the start of World War II in the Pacific, the Japanese outnumbered the U.S. fleet in all classes of ships, most significantly in aircraft carriers. Over the next three years, 34 private and nine government shipyards turned out more than 2,500 large combatant, amphibious and auxiliary ships, including aircraft carriers, cruisers, destroyers, destroyer escorts, submarines, repair ships and landing ship, tanks (LSTs).

If the confrontation in the Pacific hinged on the Navy's raw combat

Even late in the war, Ford's Jeep assembly lines continued to roll out new Jeeps at a staggering rate. (August 14, 1945)

strength, the situation in the Atlantic was vastly different. As early as 1940, Britain's survival depended not on its ability to defeat the Germans; first it had to guarantee its own existence, which depended on a steady and large stream of food, arms and other necessities from Canada and the United States. With its own industrial capacity stretched to the limit, the British traded bases for destroyers, and ordered 60 Ocean-class ships from American shipyards.

By December 1941, American destroyers had been experiencing wartime conditions in the North Atlantic for nearly two years. Yet after Germany declared war following Pearl Harbor, the naval high command ignored whatever lessons it might have learned from the experience. In the first six months of 1942, U-boats sank 176 ships, including 63 tankers, in the Caribbean, Gulf of Mexico and along the East Coast. Once the Navy imposed convoys and coastal blackouts, only another 121 ships were lost here for the remainder of the war. The scale of these losses, which represented a greater strategic setback than Pearl Harbor, can be seen in the fact that as of 1936, there were only 374 U.S. merchant ships engaged in foreign trade, not including tankers. As part of its efforts to rebuild the merchant marine, the Maritime Commission had 127 dry-cargo ships and 12 fast tankers under construction by the end of 1939. In the aftermath of Pearl Harbor, the goal grew more than tenfold; and this was only a first step.

The existing pool of eight naval and nineteen private shipyards was incapable of satisfying this demand—which came on top of orders for combat vessels—so the Maritime Commission ordered the construction of twenty-one additional shipyards. The demand for such quantities of ships also required a new orientation to shipbuilding, with simple, inexpensive vessels capable of being built quickly by a relatively inexperienced workforce. For freighters this was satisfied by the famous Liberty ship, modeled on the British Ocean-class ships. By the end of the war, more than 2,700 of the so-called "Ugly Ducklings" had been built. Such output was only possible because of radical innovation in the industry, including prefabrication of parts and the use of welding rather than riveting. Credit for bringing mass production techniques to shipbuilding goes to Henry J. Kaiser, "America's boldest, most spectacular entrepreneur." A veteran of the Grand Coulee and Hoover Dam projects, Kaiser had never built a ship. Thanks largely to his methods, the average time to build a 441-foot, 14,000-ton Liberty quickly fell from more than 100 to under 50 days. All told, the Kaiser yards in Richmond and Los Angeles, California; Vancouver, Washington; Houston; and Providence launched nearly a third of the Liberty ships and 60 percent of the 550 larger Victory ships built for the war effort.

If capital ships, freighters, tankers and other vessels were essential for bringing the war across the oceans, the amphibious landings on the beaches of the Pacific, North Africa, and Europe would have been impossible without tens of thousands of smaller landing craft. Credit for the greatest innovation in this sphere goes to Andrew Jackson Higgins. A builder of workboats when the war broke out, Higgins quickly came up with an impressive collection of designs for PT boats, antisubmarine boats, dispatch boats, small supply vessels and other specialized patrol craft. More important still were his innovative concepts for a variety of landing craft, especially the Landing Craft Vehicle/ Personnel (LCVP). The 36-foot Higgins boat could deliver 36 troops or a light tank onto the beach, pull away and return for more.

THE HIGGINS BOATS

While Henry Ford was building B-24s at Willow Run Creek, Andrew Jackson Higgins, a burly, hard-drinking shipbuilder, was building 20,094 specially designed boats for the Allies at Higgins Industries in New Orleans. To put Higgins's accomplishment in perspective, consider this: By September 1943, 12,964 of the American Navy's 14,072 vessels had been designed by Higgins Industries. Put another way, 92 percent of the U.S. Navy was a Higgins navy. "Higgins's assembly line for small boats broke precedents," President Roosevelt's former adviser Raymond Moley wrote in *Newsweek* in 1943. "But it is Higgins himself who takes your breath away as much as his remarkable products and his fantastic ability to multiply his products at headlong speed. Higgins is an authentic master builder, with the kind of will power, brains, drive and daring that characterized the American empire builders of an earlier generation."

The roots of Higgins's wartime success lay in the fleet of schooners and brigantines he built to carry his lumber. In 1937 Higgins owned one little New Orleans lumber yard where 50 or so people worked. By the time Japan bombed Pearl Harbor, he was designing prototype landing craft in a warehouse behind his St. Charles Avenue showroom and owned a massive boat manufacturing plant in New Orleans. A perfectionist obsessed with good workmanship, he was also positioned to rapidly accelerate his shipyard pro-

(Next page)
The Liberty Ship Ethan Allen, *built by the South Portland Shipbuilding Corporation, is launched on August 16, 1942, just seven months after its keel was laid. The ship, chartered by the Army Transportation Service, could transport 550 troops.*

Inside the Higgins Industries shipyards in New Orleans, Louisiana.

Men working on the hull of a U.S. submarine at the Electric Boat Company, Groton, Connecticut, August 1943.

duction to produce shallow watercraft, or even aircraft—whatever was needed. "The sad state of war," he said, "has made it my duty to build."

And build he did. Higgins Industries expanded into eight citywide plants, employing more than 20,000 workers able to produce 700 boats a month. With a labor pool diminished by the young men drafted to fight, Higgins became an equal-opportunity employer by default, hiring women, blacks, the elderly, the handicapped—anyone he could find to build boats. Everyone who had the same job was paid the same wage, and together they set homefront production records. Winning the Army-Navy "E"—the government's highest award for a company—was commonplace for Higgins Industries.

In his book, *Andrew Jackson Higgins and the Boats That Won World War II*, the historian Jerry E. Strahan recounts the frenetic boat-building mania that swept over the Port of New Orleans under the Higgins name. Higgins Industries constructed two kinds of military craft during the war: high-speed PT boats and various types of steel-and-wood landing craft to transport fully armed troops, light tanks, and field artillery. It was this latter class that made the D-Day landing, on June 6, 1944, feasible. "Without Higgins's uniquely designed craft," writes Strahan, "there could not have been a mass landing of troops and materiel on European shores or the beaches of the Pacific islands, at least not without a tremendously higher rate of Allied casualties."

No less an authority than General Eisenhower agreed. Higgins is "the man who won the war for us," he said. Ike's personal assistant Harry Butcher recalled his boss's saying in March 1943 that when he was buried, his "coffin should be in the shape of a landing craft, as they are practically killing [me] with worry." But a year later, because of Higgins Industries, there were enough LCVPs (or Higgins boats, as soldiers called them) for Ike to plan the D-Day invasion with one less worry. "Let us thank God for Higgins Industries' management and labor which has given us the landing boats with which to conduct our campaign," he told the nation that year in his Thanksgiving Day address. So crucial was Higgins's amphibious warfare that a disgruntled Adolf Hitler called him the "new Noah."

THE WAR ON THE
HOME FRONT

Terry Golway

War had been raging in Europe for more than a year when morning broke across the United States on October 16, 1940. It was to be a day like none other in American history. More than 16 million men between the ages of 21 and 35 would be assembling at more than 6,000 offices to register for the nation's first peacetime draft.

Just four days earlier, on October 12, President Roosevelt told an anxious nation that America must be prepared "to repel total attack from any part of the world." So now, on this fall morning in the midst of a presidential campaign, millions of young men put aside their chores, postponed appointments, and otherwise changed their routine to conduct their business with the United States government. They stood in long lines—rich and poor and middle class alike—waiting to sign up. When they did, their newly convened draft boards assigned them a number. Two weeks later, President Roosevelt would call out a number—158—chosen from a glass bowl, and the process of building a conscript army began. Those men holding number 158 became the first Americans ever drafted in peacetime.

The Japanese attack on Pearl Harbor was still more than a year away, but on October 16, 1940, life in America changed. The marshalling of the nation's manpower had begun. And so had a collective enterprise that would challenge and then change long-established notions of American individualism. Total war would mean total mobilization, and that would require centralized planning, unprecedented government intrusion in the marketplace, and strict rationing of the nation's resources. The war's outcome would depend not only on the bravery of front-line soldiers, but also on the sacrifices, hard work, and morale of the nation's rear guard—the men, women, and children at home who harvested crops, built bombers, bought bonds, and collected scrap metal, all in the name of victory.

No other experience in American history compares with the war years at home. Never before had the nation been as united, and never before had so much of the nation's energy and resources been directed toward a common goal. Never before had the federal government assumed such an all-powerful role in society and in the marketplace—the federal budget grew from $9 billion in 1939 to nearly $100 billion by war's end. And not since the 1860s had a generation of Americans been so heavily influenced by the tragedy and transforming power of war.

THE WAR AND THE NEW DEAL

From a military perspective, America was woefully unprepared for global conflict in 1941, even after thousands of civilians began trading in their tools and briefcases for backpacks and rifles in the fall of 1940. But from a political perspective, the nation had come a long way from the days when presidential candidate Herbert Hoover condemned what he called the "centralized despotism" of the federal government during World War I. During his successful race for the White House in 1928, Hoover spoke longingly of "the American system of rugged individualism," which, he said, was responsible for the country's "unparalleled greatness." The candidate condemned trends toward "state socialism" and "paternalism," saying that centralized control would lead to "the destruction of self-government."

Adolf Hitler's father, an illegitimate child, bore his mother's name, Schickelgruber, for nearly 40 years before he established a claim to the Hitler family name. Der Führer's questionable genealogy is thus gleefully emphasized by these spirited Army recruits, who wave a banner announcing their readiness to take the fight to Germany just after enlisting at the Philadelphia customhouse in January 1942.

Hoover's vision of America was taken from the pages of the celebrated 19th century writer Ralph Waldo Emerson. Whatever the merits of "self-reliance" were in pre–Civil War America, Emerson's ideas made for a thin gruel when the nation was plunged into the Great Depression. Americans rejected Hoover and his version of rugged individualism in 1932, turning to Franklin Roosevelt's promise for a New Deal. Faced with an economic emergency of historic proportions, Roosevelt brought centralized government to Washington in ways Hoover could not have imagined. New federal agencies were established not to manage a war, but to reorganize the nation's economy. An array of new agencies—the National Recovery Administration, the Civilian Conservation Corps, the Works Progress Administration, and many more—filled the power vacuum left by the collapse of the unregulated economic individualism of the 1920s. Through Roosevelt's first two terms, the federal government expanded its role in the nation's economy and in the lives of ordinary citizens. The WPA brought work to tens of thousands of unemployed. The CCC introduced the notion of national service (in fact, the Army ran the CCC). The nation's capital, a sleepy southern city of fewer than a 500,000 people when

Roosevelt took office, suddenly became a magnet for young, idealistic public servants who became known as the "whiz kids."

And so, when the unavoidable war finally arrived on American soil on December 7, 1941, Washington was prepared to assume greater and even more-unprecedented power, ultimately serving as the arbiter of supply and demand, the regulator of prices and wages, and the supervisor of goods and services. The rugged individualism of Emerson and Hoover became one of the war's earliest casualties.

Even as the nation's young men began disappearing from the farms, towns, and cities of America, those left behind soon learned that they, in their own way, had been conscripted into national service, too. They were to provide the muscle, labor, and money for the gigantic, all-encompassing enterprise known as world war—and they would be expected to make do with less for the sake of their loved ones in uniform.

Within weeks of the Pearl Harbor attack, the Roosevelt administration put together a new federal agency known as the War Production Board. This was to be more than just another New Deal bureaucracy set up to bring electricity to rural areas or to build public works projects. The WPB had near absolute

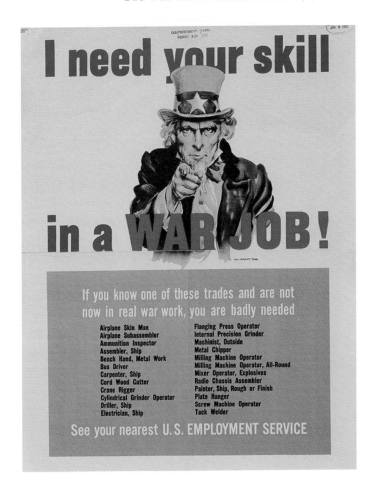

power over nothing less than the nation's economy. The WPB's head, a one-time top executive at Sears Roebuck named Donald Nelson, was given the informal title of production czar. He supervised the conversion of America's industrial capacity to all war, all the time. In a sign of just how ruthless this transformation would be, the WPB immediately shut down production of new automobiles, the very symbol of American affluence, mobility, and technological wizardry. Americans would have to get by with the 27 million cars they already owned—those assembly lines and factories were needed for war materiel.

The WPB did not stop there. It scoured the nation's marketplace and found more than 300 consumer items that simply had no place in the wartime economy. There would be no new bicycles, no new coat hangers, no new washing machines, and for those citizens who were planning on replacing their archaic icebox with the latest consumer miracle, the refrigerator, they would have to rely on their icemen for the duration of the war. The laws of supply and demand gave way to the rigors of wartime necessity, and the WPB decided what was necessary, and what wasn't.

The government-enforced conversion of the American economy produced astonishing results. Between 1941 and 1945 the U.S. manufactured hundreds of thousands of planes and tanks, millions of trucks and jeeps, as well as thousands of ships and tens of thousands of landing craft (see "The

Arsenal of Democracy"). Less celebrated, but just as productive, were the nation's farmers, whose crops fed troops and civilians alike. Even though some 6 million people left the nation's farms during the war—some to serve in uniform, others to find factory work—agricultural productivity increased by more than a third.

To deliver the tools of war to far-flung battlefields, plants worked day and night, providing work for any civilian who wanted it, and then some. Unemployment during the war years shrank to an almost negligible 1.3 percent, and the number of jobless fell from 9 million to about a million during the war. Membership in the nation's labor unions expanded along with the workforce, from about 10 million in 1941 to almost 15 million in 1945. Union membership brought union wages and benefits—including overtime pay. Factory workers saw a real increase of nearly 30 percent in their wages. For a nation that had suffered for so long during the Depression, wartime America seemed unimaginably prosperous.

UNITY AND SACRIFICE

The war truly touched the lives of all Americans at home. Just as wealth, celebrity, and influence offered little protection from the draft board, fear and anxiety, whether for a friend, a relative, or for the nation's future, crossed regional, cultural, religious, and racial boundaries. Though racial and labor tension had not been legislated away—there were race riots in Detroit, and nearly 15,000 strikes nationwide during the war—unity and sacrifice were the home front's watchwords. Sacrifice was bearable because it was perceived to be shared. If the heavyweight champion of the world, Joe Louis, was in uniform, if baseball hero Ted Williams was flying fighter planes, if movie stars such as Jimmy Stewart and Clark Gable were in actual combat, and if you and your neighbors were cooking meatless meals and reusing coffee grounds so the troops were better fed, it was easy to believe that everybody was doing his or her share.

And, for the most part, everybody was. Civilians too old for military service volunteered for civil defense, serving as air-raid wardens or making sure that homeowners and businesses complied with blackout regulations. More than 6 million men and women volunteered for the armed services, and more than 11 million were drafted. (About 6 million were rejected for medical or psychological reasons.) That's not to say some men didn't try to evade the draft, or that some didn't receive dubious exemptions, or that some civilians didn't work the system to thwart government-imposed rationing. But they were the exceptions. Americans understood that their nation was in mortal peril, and, even amid some grumbling, they acted accordingly.

Americans at home soon learned that good jobs and decent wages did not mean they could indulge in luxuries previously denied them. It followed that if the federal government could control production, it could also regulate consumption. And so it did. To conserve everything from rubber to metal to even such a mundane pleasure as coffee, Washington imposed on the home front a bewildering and often unpopular system of rationing. Rubber was a particular priority, since Japan's military successes in Asia had cut off 90 percent of the country's supplies. In mid-1942, Roosevelt asked the home front for help in supplying the armed services with rubber, and civilians responded by collecting tires, garden hoses, boots, gloves and the occasional garter belt. The government imposed a "Victory Speed Limit" of 35 miles an hour to conserve tires, which were strictly rationed, and installed businessman William Jeffers as the nation's "rubber czar"—the war effort would require more than just one "czar" to oversee the economy. Rubber was so precious that some drivers resorted to driving on wooden wheels when their tires wore out, and the Texaco oil company promoted the Victory speed limit and other measures designed to conserve, rather than consume.

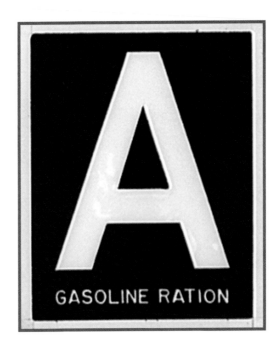

An "A" gasoline ration sticker.

Indeed, wasteful consumption was the declared enemy of the home front, and to guard against it, Roosevelt's Washington set up another new agency. The Office of Price Administration was charged with the obvious—administering prices to ward off ruinous inflation. But it also served as the bureaucracy Americans loved to hate, for it oversaw an unprecedented system of centralized rationing. As the war progressed, the OPA became a favorite target of radio comedians and citizen grumbling, thanks in part to its complicated, points-based system of food rationing. Foods, from canned goods to meat, were assigned points depending on their availability—for example, in late summer, 1943, a pound of porterhouse steak cost consumers 12 points, while a pound of spareribs were valued at just two points. Individuals and families received ration coupons of varying values every month. Grocery shelves featured the price of goods as well as their point value.

Food rationing started in mid-1942 with limits on sugar and coffee—the latter sacrifice inspired both President Roosevelt and New York mayor Fiorello La Guardia to publicize their personal recipes for reusing old coffee grounds. The reaction was somewhat less than enthusiastic. On his Sunday night radio program, Fred Allen "interviewed" actors playing ordinary citizens who had tried the homemade brews. Housewife Pansy Nussbaum, played by actress Minerva Pious, reported that "the president's coffee is tasting like low tide at Coney Island" while "the mayor's coffee could be somebody putting shellac in the Pepsi Cola."

Things only got worse for Mrs. Nussbaum and the rest of home-front America. Soon canned goods were rationed, then meats, dairy products—everything worth eating, and maybe some things that weren't. To conserve beef to feed the troops, the government allowed the sale of horse meat on the consumer market, leading one clever butcher in Newark, N.J., to start a business called the Man O' War Packing Company, named after the famous

Singer Bing Crosby pitches in with a box full of golf balls, gathered for a scrap rubber drive in June 1942. The worldwide shortage of rubber led the U.S. government to halt production of golf equipment for the duration of the war.

thoroughbred. Horse meat was not rationed, so it cost buyers no prized coupon points. (One of Fred Allen's guests reported that after eating horse meat for three weeks, he was able to run the mile in one minute, 38 seconds.)

Meat sometimes was simply unavailable, even after strict rationing. The Department of Agriculture published a leaflet entitled "Ninety-Nine Ways to Share the Meat." It took time to produce meat, the pamphlet explained, noting that it took "longer to 'build' a good beef steer than to build a destroyer." And when that beef became available, the men "in the fighting forces naturally have first call …" It was time, the government said, to "share and share alike" for that was, after all, "the American way." Americans, familiar with want after years of Depression, took these shortages with good humor. On the Fred Allen show in early 1943, Allen's wife, Portland Hoffa, described her New Year's Eve feast: She treated herself to "breast of shrimp" and a sandwich named in honor of Leon Henderson, who ran the OPA. And what was a Leon Henderson sandwich? A piece of lettuce on a ration card.

Americans were less willing to laugh about gasoline rationing, which severely limited their prized mobility. Washington was well aware of the grumbling, and countered it with a series of propaganda posters reminding disgruntled drivers of the true cost of driving. One widely circulated poster showed a crippled oil tanker about to sink—the victim of a Nazi torpedo. "Should brave men die so you can drive?" the poster asked. To encourage car pools, another poster featured a man behind the wheel with a chalklike figure of Hitler beside him. "When you ride alone, you ride with Hitler," the poster read.

Most American motorists sported an "A" sticker on their cars, meaning that they drove mostly for pleasure and so were entitled to just three to five gallons a week. Emergency workers, clergy, and others were allowed higher allotments.

The war entailed other daily sacrifices—nylon was needed for parachutes, so women went without stockings. To make up for food shortages, Americans planted vegetables in Victory gardens—some 20 million of them, occupying open space in backyards as well as in city parks and accounting for about a third of the American wartime harvest. Smokers rolled their own cigarettes, rather than wait on long lines where they were limited to just two packs per purchase.

In case people forgot why they were forced to endure such sacrifices, a poster reminded them. Featuring a picture of a healthy, happy GI lifting a metal cup to his mouth, the words read: "Do with less—so they'll have enough."

The message resonated with civilians who desperately wished to be a part of the struggle, a participant—not a detached, ironic observer—in the great national cause. Though they were far from the battlefields, they, too, had a vital role to play, as they were reminded by the Office of War Information, which helped shape the national message of unity and sacrifice. Making do with less was one way to speed the troops to victory. But there were other, more active, ways to serve on the home front. Children organized scrap drives to collect pots, pans, tin foil, and anything else that might be of use to the troops. Families were even encouraged to collect grease and fat from cooking materials, leading the radio poet, Falstaff Openshaw, to compose this ditty:

> *My little niece is saving grease*
> *To help to beat the Japs.*
>
> *To help defeat the Nazis*
> *She's collecting bacon scraps.*
>
> *The drippings from each mutton roast*
> *She knows make ammunition.*
>
> *The donuts that my niece collects*
> *May bomb a Jap position.*

Children, in fact, were very much a part of the effort on the home front. Just as women stepped in to fill jobs men formerly held, teenagers—male and female—streamed into the workforce. Some 2 to 3 million teenagers took jobs during the war, thanks in part to measures that suspended or eased laws regulating child labor. However, the stream of minors into the nation's factories brought back unpleasant memories of a time in the not-so-distant past when the nation's factories were filled with children, a practice that had been outlawed in the social reforms of the 1920s. In 1943, the Children's Bureau of the Department of Labor (run by the nation's first woman cabinet member, Frances Perkins, who had campaigned for child labor laws in New York) put out a pamphlet calling for a "Children's Crusade—a 'Back to School' Crusade."

"We must find the words to convince adults that the unplanned child labor we are permitting now is the most expensive way possible of meeting labor needs," the pamphlet read. The jobs children were performing were temporary, the pamphlet implied. But the damage to postwar America would be permanent if they stopped going to school.

BRINGING THE WAR HOME

Unlike the people of Germany, Poland, Russia, Britain, France, China, Japan, and so many other nations, Americans at home were not eyewitnesses to war. They saw it on newsreels, heard about it from Edward R. Murrow and other radio news reporters, and read about it in dispatches from Ernie Pyle, Ernest Hemingway, Walter Cronkite, and hundreds of less celebrated war correspondents. There were no air raids on American cities, no tank battles in the deserts of the Southwest, no trenches dug into the soil of the Great Plains, only the occasional sighting of a burning merchant ship offshore in the early days of the war. Nevertheless, the war was an overpowering presence in the lives of 130 million Americans. Even if they sought an escape, either from anxiety for a loved one or from the rigors of wartime discipline, relief was hard to come by.

...give her a war bond—
and anything by Charles of the Ritz

LUCKY STRIKE GREEN HAS GONE TO WAR!

So here's the smart new uniform for fine tobacco

CIGARETTES

LUCKY STRIKE

Radio, the most popular medium of the day, played a major role in producing a sense of national unity. In addition to President Roosevelt's "fireside chats," enormous numbers of war bonds were sold over the air on special programs hosted by stars such as Bing Crosby, Bob Hope, and Jack Benny—Americans bought $135 billion in bonds during the war. Almost every commercial contained a message to buy bonds, or to observe rationing rules, or to remember "the boys overseas." Many of the most popular serials involved their characters in the war, some in silly ways (as when Superman saved Lois Lane from the clutches of the "Japs") but some in moving, realistic ways (as when Ma Perkins's son, John, was killed "somewhere in Germany"). On his radio program, comedian Jack Benny somehow managed to capture Nazi General Erwin Rommel, the "Desert Fox," in late 1942.

In Hollywood, director Frank Capra produced a series of classic propaganda films entitled *Why We Fight*. Hollywood, of course, also churned out war movies and movies with wartime themes by the dozens, from the ridiculous (Abbott and Costello's *Buck Privates*) to the sublime (Humphrey Bogart and Ingrid Bergman in the classic *Casablanca*.) Hollywood drafted Sherlock Holmes into the war effort, transporting the great detective, played by Basil Rathbone, from Victorian London to wartime Britain. And even the cartoon characters went to war—in a short called "Falling Hare," Bugs Bunny battles a rascally gremlin intent on sabotage at an Army Air Force base. (A sign outside the base reads: "*Location: Censored. No. of planes: Censored. No. of men: Censored. What Men Think of Top Sergeant: CENSORED!*) When Bugs confronts a suspicious-looking character near a blockbuster bomb, he wonders aloud if he has, in fact, found the gremlin. "It ain't Wendell Wilkie," the smart-aleck gremlin replies.

Many of the best-known films were made about actual battles and wartime experiences (*Bataan*, 1943; *Guadalcanal Diary*, 1943; *30 Seconds Over Tokyo*, 1944; *The Sullivans*, 1944; and *Back to Bataan*, 1945). Reminders of the war—at home and abroad—were everywhere. Store windows displayed posters encouraging civilians to buy war bonds, to postpone unnecessary automobile or train trips, and to watch what they said in case the enemy was

This is one of the most famous ads from the war era. The makers of Lucky Strike changed the color of the pack to show, they said, what they were doing for the war effort. Hundreds of ads with war messages appeared in all the major magazines and newspapers.

listening. One bond poster showed a smiling, confident pilot and the words: "You buy `em, we'll fly `em!" Another, darker poster depicted a limp, obviously dead paratrooper, with the blunt warning: "CARELESS TALK ... got there first." Broadway featured such shows as Irving Berlin's *This is the Army*, featuring a cast of 300 soldiers.

Popular music also featured war themes, highlighting the common aspects of military service ("Coming In On a Wing and a Prayer," "Boogie Woogie Bugle Boy"—the latter by the enormously popular Andrews Sisters); or the longings felt by millions ("We'll Meet Again," "When the Lights Go On Again All Over the World"). But in typical raucous American style, many songs insulted Adolf Hitler ("In the Führer's Face"—spit, that is—by Spike Jones; and a woman's lament about the lack of available men, "They're Either Too Young or Too Old"). But it was the American master songwriter, Irving Berlin, who in 1938 produced the great anthem that will, for the war generation, always be associated with World War II, "God Bless America," which, as sung by the extraordinary Kate Smith and played continuously over the radio, became a communal prayer for all Americans.

Baseball, reigning supreme as the nation's pastime, also contributed to the war effort in both tangible and intangible ways. The 16 major league teams were a source of healthy, young American males, and they certainly put their country ahead of their careers. More than 500 major leaguers served in the armed forces during the war, and about 3,500 minor leaguers. The most famous ballplayers to wear Uncle Sam's uniform were Ted Williams, Joe DiMaggio, Bob Feller, Yogi Berra, Warren Spahn, Jerry Coleman, and Hank Greenberg (who would celebrate his return to the Detroit Tigers by hitting a pennant-clinching grand slam against the St. Louis Browns in 1945).

But the game did more than supply troops. It served as an important distraction for millions of fans. Legendary baseball commissioner Kenesaw Mountain Landis had seriously considered suspending baseball in the aftermath of Pearl Harbor, and wrote to President Roosevelt asking for his advice. FDR, in a letter dated January 15, 1942, replied: "I honestly feel that it would be best for the country to keep baseball going. There will be fewer people unemployed and everybody will work longer hours and harder than ever before. And that means they ought to have a chance for recreation and for taking their minds off their work even more than before." The president noted that baseball games do not "last over two hours or two hours and a half" and "can be got for little cost."

Roosevelt foresaw that the "actual quality of the teams" would be "lowered by the greater use of older players." He was right about that. Not just older players, but players who would never have been given a chance to play in the major leagues, most famously Pete Gray, a one-armed outfielder with the St. Louis Browns. The Browns themselves were a wartime anomaly—a sad-sack franchise that won its only American League championship in 1944. In the World Series, the Browns lost to their hometown rivals, the St. Louis Cardinals, in a series played entirely in Sportsmen's Park.

"It Was a Very Sad Time..."

I've only seen my dad cry a few times, and the first time was on the 7th of December, because he couldn't understand why the land of his birth was attacking the land of his heart. The second time was when we boarded the trains to leave San Jose to go off to the camps. We were all raised as Americans. We were told about our uncles and aunts, grandfathers and grandmothers in Japan, but other than that, we really had no connection with anything Japanese.

After Pearl Harbor, there were many stories being spread about Japanese Americans being spies, and so there was this kind of "get the Japs out" kind of mentality, and Earl Warren, who was then the Attorney General in California, was leading the effort to get the removal of Japanese Americans from California and to have them interned in camps. Large posters were stapled and nailed on the sides of buildings and utility poles saying "Attention, all those of Japanese ancestry, alien and nonalien," so they weren't even referring to us as citizens. After the posters had been put up, then more specific orders started coming out as to when we would be leaving for camp. Everyone had to sell their goods or store them because all you could take to camp was what you could carry. Many people lost their homes during that time period.

We left on the 29th of May, 1942. We boarded the trains at the freight station which happened to be close enough to my grammar school that my classmates from the 5th grade came down during the lunch hour to see all of us off. And to me it was wonderful to have all these friends of mine coming down to say goodbye, even though it was a very sad time. Once you got into your car, you couldn't move from car to car, and all the blinds were drawn. I had a baseball, baseball glove, and a baseball bat, and as I got on the train, the MPs confiscated my bat because it could be used as a lethal weapon.

The army had commandeered all the race tracks and the fairgrounds in Washington, Oregon, and California because they had built-in sleeping quarters—namely, horse stables. We were assigned to Santa Anita Race-track, near Los Angeles but because we were one of the last ones to be interned, luckily for us, the horse stables had all been occupied. So then they took us to our barracks building where six of us were put in one room (roughly 20 x 20), mom, dad, my two sisters, my brother and myself. We had barbed wire all the way around the camp and about every 200 - 300 feet, there were armed guard towers with machine guns and search lights.

There were very bitter reactions. As Japanese American citizens, we couldn't understand why the American government was doing this to us. They weren't doing it to those of German ancestry, Italian ancestry. Here was a small population group of 120,000, all of a sudden, forcefully evacuated and interned for the duration of World War II in camps where the death rate was high. Despite this treatment some decided to volunteer for the armed services and the 442nd Regimental Combat Team was formed. The 442nd Regimental Combat Team became the most highly decorated Army unit of its size in the history of the Army.

After the war there were acts of violence against Japanese Americans coming back. Farms and homes were being burned. A veteran who had lost his arm in Italy and was at the Veterans Hospital in Stockton, California, left the hospital one afternoon to go get a haircut and was shot and killed in downtown Stockton. So here he had gone all the way through World War II, fighting with the 442nd, and then he got shot and killed in California because he was of Japanese ancestry.

When I was in Congress I introduced legislation with a number of others to have Congress apologize on behalf of the nation to the Japanese Americans and to also pay a nominal redress, and it took ten years to pass that bill. The bill was called the HR 442 in honor of the 442nd Regimental Combat Team. It was a great moment because the Bill passed the Congress on September 17, 1987, which was the 200th Anniversary of the signing of our Constitution.

—Norman Y. Mineta, Former U.S. Congressman
and Secretary of Transportation

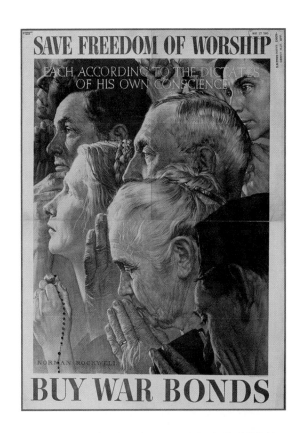

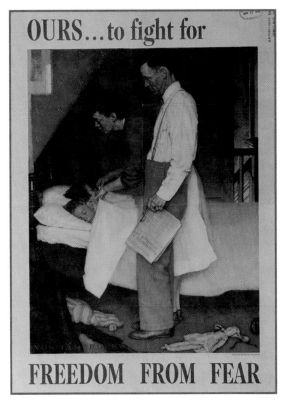

On January 6, 1941 President Roosevelt delivered his historic "Four Freedoms" speech to Congress. His vision of a world inspired by American ideals so moved the famous illustrator, Norman Rockwell, that in 1943 he created this series of paintings that became the centerpiece of the massive U.S. war bond drive.

STRUGGLING TO KEEP OUR VALUES

For some Americans, however, even the simple pleasures and distractions of baseball or the movies were unavailable. Hustled away from their homes and crowded into makeshift internment camps, about 125,000 Japanese-Americans spent the war behind barbed wire in their own country. President Roosevelt approved the roundup two months after Pearl Harbor, and few voices were raised in protest. While some German Americans and Italian Americans were subjected to curfews, the nation burned with anger over the Japanese attack, and seemed convinced that Japanese-American farmers, tradesmen, and businessmen on the West Coast were plotting further attacks on U.S. soil.

So they were taken away, often on short notice, and installed in such places as the famed Santa Anita racetrack in California. The treatment of these innocent civilians seemed at odds with Franklin Roosevelt's famous enunciation of the principles that united the world's democracies. They were the Four Freedoms—freedom from fear, freedom from want, freedom of worship, and freedom of speech. Artist Norman Rockwell drew four popular wartime posters illustrating these ideas, and reminding Americans why they ought to buy war bonds. But those freedoms stopped at the gates to America's internment camps.

For the most part, however, the nation's democratic institutions and traditions, and its commitment to the Four Freedoms, survived the necessities of a wartime emergency. Elections proceeded as scheduled, in contrast to Great Britain, where elections were suspended until 1945. Roosevelt did not set aside the Constitution, as Lincoln had done during the Civil War when he suspended *habeas corpus*. The presidential election of 1944 saw a vigorous challenge to Roosevelt from a young Republican named Thomas E. Dewey, who implied that it was time for a change.

Dewey lost, but he was not altogether wrong. America had, in fact, changed a great deal during the war years, and more change would come with victory, the return of the troops, the emergence of the United States as a superpower, and the implementation of the G.I. Bill of Rights, passed during the war. Women had experienced the workforce, and would soon demand a greater role in society. Blacks had fought and died for the Four Freedoms, but in a segregated military. That, too, would change, as would segregation itself. The American way of life was introduced to nearly every corner of the globe, in some cases replacing traditional culture with the movies, music, and consumerism of pop culture.

The home front from 1941 to 1945 saw the promise of the American Century become reality. In a moment of unity and purpose, Americans came together and perhaps surprised even themselves by all they accomplished.

WOMEN IN
WORLD WAR II

★

Emily Yellin

"Women who stepped up were measured as citizens of the Nation, not as women...This was a People's War and everyone was in it."

—COLONEL OVETA CULP HOBBY

When we look back at American women during World War II, the image comes to mind of a soldier's noble wife or mother left behind on the home front while the men go off to battle, or of a diligent female defense industry worker like "Rosie the Riveter," who represented the women behind the men who fought the war. To be sure, those enduring images embody a general spirit among American women at that time, as well as significant roles many women played in the war effort. Most of the more than 12 million men who served in the armed services during the war had mothers, wives, or both, at home. And approximately six million women worked in factories during the war, manufacturing the planes, ships, weapons, and ammunition that made the United States into the "arsenal of democracy." But to understand the magnitude of the part women played in World War II, it is important also to look beyond these familiar icons to the actual women behind them, to their everyday lives and their individual acts of courage, sacrifice, and patriotism during the all-consuming conflict.

While so many men were fighting on the front lines, women were asked to take on roles in American society that they had never been invited or allowed to assume before. The seemingly temporary steps women took to support or fill in for the men at war became an inadvertent social revolution in America. Necessity transformed both society's vision and the perception of women themselves about what they were capable of at home, at work, and in the military. After that, for better or worse, there was no turning back. During World War II, women realized more fully than ever before their rights and their responsibilities as citizens of the United States. Those four years expanded forevermore the way half of this country's population participated in and contributed to American society.

WOMEN IN THE MILITARY

Until World War II the only way women could be a part of the military was to work as nurses. The Army and Navy Nurse Corps had been formed at the beginning of the 20th century. But at the beginning of World War II there were only a few thousand nurses serving. When Pearl Harbor was bombed on December 7, 1941, only 119 military nurses were stationed in Hawaii, and they worked nonstop for days treating the thousands of wounded and dead. "All morning the work went on," reported one nurse on the scene. "Occasionally a nurse rested her tired back by stretching and looking out at the ships blazing in the harbor, took a deep breath to clear away the stench of charred flesh, then returned to the job."

Nurses were arguably the least sheltered of all American women from the horrors of war. Not only did they see the results of war first-hand, but they were sometimes even a part of the battle. For instance, 77 Army and Navy nurses were among the Americans taken as prisoners of war by the Japanese when the Allies lost the Philippines in the beginning of 1942. They were not freed until 1945 when the Allies regained the Philippines.

By the end of the war, 70,000 nurses had served with the Army and Navy. Of those, 35,000 nurses served overseas and 16 nurses died abroad. Lieutenant Frances Y. Slanger was an Army nurse serving in Belgium in October 1944 when she was killed by German shell fire. Hours before she died she had written a letter to the military newspaper *Stars and Stripes* expressing her admiration for the soldiers she was treating, in spite of the hardships military women endured. "Sure we rough it, but in comparison to the way you men are taking it, we can't complain.... We have learned a great deal about our American soldier ... the patience and determination they show, the courage and fortitude they have is sometimes awesome to behold."

The letter was published after Slanger died and hundreds of soldiers replied. One soldier pointed out that nurses, because they were not drafted but volunteered, deserved more credit than anyone for weathering the rigors of war. In what remains a poignant eulogy to Lt. Slanger, and a homage to all nurses, he said, in part, "We are here because we have to be. You are here because you felt you were needed. So, when an injured man opens his eyes to see one of you ... concerned with his welfare, he can't but be overcome by the very thought that you are doing it because you want to ... you endure whatever hardships you must to be where you can do us the most good."

In many cases nurses were the only women allowed in military areas. And despite the accolades they received for their work, they did not have full military status. They were considered civilians serving with the military, not in it. That meant that during the war, they would receive few, if any, military benefits, and would not be classified as veterans after their term of service was over. It took a female legislator to begin to change that. But she had to start with getting women into the Army as soldiers. After some failed attempts through the years, Massachusetts Congresswoman Edith Nourse Rogers finally pushed through a bill that granted women the right to serve as soldiers with the Army in May 1942. The first women's branch, the WAAC (Women's Army Auxiliary Corps), was established. But just as the nurses had always been, women soldiers still were not considered full members of the Army, only auxiliaries.

The Navy was the first branch to grant women full status in the military. A few months after the WAAC bill passed, new bills passed establishing three women's branches under the auspices of the Navy: the WAVES (Women Accepted for Volunteer Emergency Service), the Coast Guard's SPAR (*Semper Paratus*, Always Ready) and the female Marines, who had no acronym but were simply Marines. All three bills specified that the women would be considered full members of the military, with the benefits accorded their male counterparts. Within a year, the Army relented and allowed its women full military status. In 1943, the WAAC shed its auxiliary standing and became the WAC (Women's Army Corps).

Margaret Porter Polsky was among one of the first few groups of women to go through WAAC officer training in Fort Des Moines, Iowa, in 1942.

U.S. Army nurses line the rail of their vessel as it pulls into port in Greenock, Scotland, on August 15, 1944.

She came from Missouri, where she had been a schoolteacher before the war. Upon joining the Army she realized that she had entered "a whole new world" for women. "I was a part of something that was new and different," said Polsky, "radical to a lot of people, questioned by a lot of people." But Polsky watched the women's branch of the Army blossom before her eyes and felt proud to be part of it. Approximately 150,000 women served in the WAC during World War II. They mainly worked in clerical jobs and communications. Polsky said that so many women "did their jobs so efficiently and so well. And at the same time they were being productive for the nation, for the war effort, they were also realizing a personal sense of contribution and fulfillment."

The WAC was the only women's branch of the military that sent its members overseas to areas in the Allied war zones. Not until the last year of the war did the Navy allow its women members to serve outside the continental U.S., but only in U.S. territories. WACs served in administrative capacities throughout the European, African, and the Pacific war theaters, but by law, no women were allowed in combat.

In a letter home in 1943, Miriam E. Stehlik, who worked on General Eisenhower's staff in North Africa, told how even the most routine tasks had a sense of excitement and purpose about them for the first American women to serve overseas. She said she knew in her "heart that 'paper work' is just as important in this business of war, as is ammunition and supplies—and no day is too long for me to work."

The WAC was also the only one of the women's services to admit African-American women to its ranks from the beginning. Late in the war, the Navy allowed some African-American women to serve. The entire military was racially segregated during World War II, with African-American men, as well as African-American women serving in separate units. Approximately 6,500 African-American women served in the WAC during World War II. And of the 440 women in the first WAAC officer training class in 1942, 39 were African-American.

Charity Adams was one of only two African-American women promoted to the rank of major during World War II. She commanded the only African-American WAC unit to serve overseas during the war, a battalion of more than 800 African-American women, who were sent to Britain and later France to sort through huge backlogs of mail to troops in the European theater of war. Their first assignment was supposed to take the battalion six months to complete. But working around the clock on three eight-hour shifts the women sorted the mail and got it to its recipients within three months instead. Those kinds of successes became standard

WAACS
(Women's Army Auxiliary Corps)
on parade ground going through the
company drill, Des Moines, Iowa, 1942.

in Adams's unit. Even with limited opportunities, the women "were proud and had every right to be," said Major Adams.

On the home front, approximately 86,000 women served in the WAVES, 11,000 women in the Coast Guard's SPAR, and about 20,000 female Marines pioneered in the military doing work that, as in the WAC, was supposed to free military men for combat jobs. Ruby Messer Barber was one of six sisters who grew up in La Grange, Georgia. As soon as she heard about the WAVES she knew it was something she had to do. "It was a choice of adventure," she said. "I didn't have any brothers, and I thought that's something I can do, one way I can make a contribution." She worked in person-

"How Could I Forget?"

I graduated from the University of Pennsylvania Nursing School. I worked about a year and then I got a letter the government sent to all nurses asking if we would join the Army. I was sent to Camp Claiborne, Louisiana. I worked in surgery there. I'd worked there a year when President Roosevelt said we had been bombed and that war was declared, so I knew I was in for the duration.

I was put in the 2nd Auxiliary Surgical Group, a group of surgeons who had been hand picked from all over the United States, and all the nurses really knew their way in surgery. We left February the 28th, 1943, we sailed for nine days and we landed at Casablanca. The natives all thought we nurses were concubines because the French carried their own concubines with them.

We were really kept busy all the time. We had drill, we had to learn French, and we had to take our medicines in case we got malaria. We found how to use our helmets to bathe. One helmet a day, we were given. And surprisingly, we managed very well.

Next I was sent to Italy. We went to bed one night and everything seemed fine, but then we got awakened in the morning to the noise of a plane diving and hitting the ship. It gave quite a thud! We all jumped up and started to get dressed. We tried the doors, but they were jammed. We couldn't get out. And this sailor said, "You girls better get out of here. This ship's on fire!" When we got to the deck, it was really blazing. He took us over to the side. There was a rope ladder there, going down to a little boat.

We were taken back to Africa to be outfitted. I was assigned to the 16th Field Hospital in the Po Valley. We were sometimes maybe a mile from the front. In fact we had a German doctor one time who was brought in as a prisoner, who was amazed to find that we nurses were up that far to the front. He said in Germany nurses are not allowed within 100 miles of their front.

When the boys would come in, it was so sad. They were so cold. They would have frostbite, they would have frozen feet. It was just everything. A lot of 'em would step on mines. And you know they would have wounds on the front of 'em. But you had to turn 'em over and take all the shrapnel and work on their backs, too.

We were in the Po Valley for about a year, and then I was told I was going on another hospital ship. We went out to pick up patients who were badly hurt. They would bring the fellows out on boats and load 'em onto the ship, and then we'd operate on them as much as we could. When we

got a full load of boys, we'd take 'em back to Naples, and then we'd go back again, and keep pickin' 'em up.

Captain Laura Ruth Balch Nurse, Africa and Italy

Now, every time we'd go up to Anzio the Germans would shoot at us. And this one morning, we wanted to pick them up but we couldn't because it was so bitter cold and the water was so rough that they couldn't bring the boats out with the fellows in them. So we were going out to sea for the night. The rules are you don't bomb hospital ships or anything with the red cross. But the Germans bombed the hospital ships.

We were going to bed when a plane dived on us. It sounded like a thousand china closets falling over. All the lights were out and everybody was screaming at the top of their voices. Somebody said, "Get in the lifeboats." Well, you couldn't get in. It was so full, you couldn't get another person in it. And that was the last I knew of the ship because I looked up and the mast was just falling over towards me, and the next thing I knew, I was in the water. I kept going down with suction for a long time. I got my wits about me and I thought, "I'm going to die. That's all there is to it, because I have to have a breath of air." And when I thought that, swoosh, I started going up just as fast as could be, my head came out of the water! This one officer yelled, "Hey Ruthie—is that you?" And I said, "Yes, yes." He said, "Well, you swim towards me, and I'll swim towards you. And we'll get on the same log," which we did. And we got a patient on with us." Everybody's screaming and yelling. And it was so cold. It was January. The waves were rough and it was good just to have somebody to talk to, but we just hung on. We were on the log for about two hours when we looked up and we saw lights of a ship.

When the ship arrived to pick us up, this fellow said to me, "Can you pull yourself up?" I couldn't do it. I just didn't have the strength. And then I thought I would die. I just thought I wouldn't live. I was so cold. So he took us back to the ship and gave us good warm blankets. And, of course, the British would give you Scotch and I fell right asleep.

I received the Bronze Star and the Purple Heart. A man asked me not long ago, "Can you remember all that back to World War II?" And I said, "How could I forget?"

WAAC Captain Charity Adams of Columbia, North Carolina, who was commissioned from the first officer candidate class, and the first of her group to receive a commission, drills her company on the drill ground at the first WAAC Training Center, Fort Des Moines, Iowa, in May 1943.

Technical Sergeant Tommye Berry looks over her WAC's at Camp Shanks, New York, the Transportation Corps staging area of the New York Port of Embarkation. (April 16, 1945)

Jane Straughan completes a flight in an AT-6 at Houston Municipal Airport.

Ethel Finley stands in front of a BT-13 at Avenger Field, Sweetwater, Texas.

nel and lived in the barracks at the Atlanta Naval Air Station for two years. "I was doing a job that needed to be done," said Barber, "for my country."

The women airplane pilots in the WASP (Women Air Force Service Pilots) took over some of the most unglamorous and sometimes dangerous military piloting jobs on the home front. Some of the nearly 2,000 women who primarily transported planes from the factories that made them to air bases in the continental U.S. were already highly experienced pilots before the war. Others were trained by the WASP during the three years of its existence. Some of the women also worked towing targets for the men who were learning to shoot at planes from the air and ground. The women flew planes with targets attached to a long line, like a kite, behind them and the men being trained would shoot at the targets. This was dangerous work and many male pilots refused to do it. But the women of the WASP took it on.

The WASP was disbanded in 1944, before it ever gained full military status within the Air Force. Thirty-nine women pilots died in the line of duty, but they were considered to be civilians serving with the military not in it. So they were not given military burials and their families received no death benefits. None of the women in the WASP were given any benefits or the title of veteran as a result of military service until 1977, when they were belatedly granted military status.

WOMEN AT HOME

Mary O'Keefe heard that her boyfriend, Bill Dwyer, was going off to war in January of 1944. They were both only 17 years old and had not thought much about life after high school. But it wasn't long before Mary got a letter from Bill in April of 1944, just after he arrived in Australia for duty in the Navy, telling her he loved her and asking her to marry him when he returned home. Mary was surprised since the two had never spoken of such serious things before. "I always said," Mary remembered, "he had to go 3,000 miles away to find out he was in love." She gladly accepted his proposal by mail, and they agreed not to make any more plans until the war was over.

The uncertainty of war had raised the stakes in relationships all over the country. Warnings went out to unmarried young people from parents and clergymen to postpone marriage until after the war since the future was so unsure. Many like Mary and Bill listened. But many did not. Hasty war weddings were a feature of the World War II home front, along with food and gas rationing, blackout curtains, and war bond drives. Approximately 1.8 million couples married in 1942, the first year of the war, over 200,000 more than in 1940. But 1942 was also when women began watching their husbands, boyfriends, sons, and brothers head off to faraway, unpredictable places, while they navigated the unfamiliar terrain of the wartime home front. Many women whose husbands were away at war became, in effect, single mothers, finding ways to care for their children and run their households without their husbands' support. Their mothers and sisters often stepped in

(Opposite)
Mrs. John Gagne, the first "Gold Star Mother" of Lynn, Massachusetts in World War II, places the gold star flag in her front window, following the news of the death of her son, killed in action during a bombing of Hickam Field in Hawaii. December 14, 1941

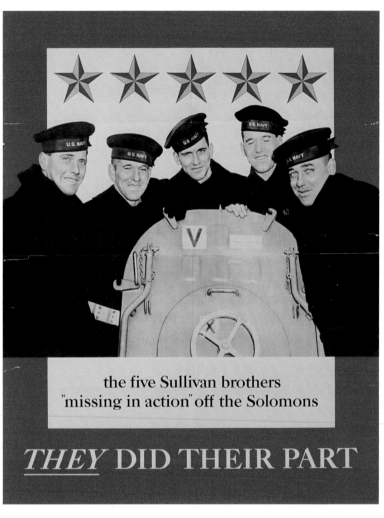

the five Sullivan brothers
"missing in action" off the Solomons

THEY DID THEIR PART

to help, since day care was not readily available. Other wives followed their military husbands for as long as they could while the men were in training here in the United States. Mary's sister, Margaret, was one of those women, called camp followers, who moved to be near her husband when he was stationed at a Colorado air base. She ended up having her first baby there.

Mary's brother, George, who was a just a few months younger than Bill, also went off to serve in the Navy in 1944. "We were all frightened and concerned for their well-being," Mary said, "but we knew they had to go, and accepted the fact and prayed to God that they were going to come back safe and sound." Having such a stake in the war, meant Mary and her family, like so many people all across the country, felt more strongly than ever that they wanted to do all they could to support the war effort. So in the summer of 1944 they each took jobs at the same factory in New York City, where they lived, making spark plugs for military planes. Mary and George's girlfriend, Nancy, worked the day shift. Mary's mother and aunt worked from afternoon to midnight, and her father worked the midnight to eight a.m. shift. "We had it all covered," said Mary. It was one way they felt they were helping Bill and George come home from the Pacific war sooner.

Mary's brother and boyfriend did come home alive. She and Bill married in 1947 and had two children. But the effects of a head wound after Bill's ship was attacked by a Japanese suicide bomber meant he had seizures for the rest of his life. Bill died in 1956 after a particularly strong seizure. Even though her husband came home seemingly intact, his death was the result of a war injury, so Mary was considered a war widow. "I went to bed one night and I had a husband and two children," said Mary, "and I woke up the next morning and I was a widow." Mary met other women who had gone through some of what she was facing when she joined Gold Star Wives, an organization for war widows started at the end of World War II by Marie Jordan Speer, a woman in New York who had lost her husband in the war. The group was inspired by the American Gold Star Mothers, a group that had formed after World War I. The Gold Star in both groups' names came from a tradition that began in World War I. When families had a loved one in the military, they hung a blue star in their window as a symbol of him. If their loved one died in the war, families hung a gold star in their windows. Both groups are still active today with members all over the country.

For the wives, mothers, and sisters of the men who went away, World War II demanded a particularly self-sacrificing kind of courage. They had to make sense of and accept the ways, both great and small, that the war had turned their lives upside down. They were missing their husbands, sons, boyfriends, and brothers with a fury they had never imagined possible. They also had pressures of their own in maintaining their homes, families, and lives while living with constant uncertainty. In magazines, on the radio, and in their communities, women were urged to remain cheerful and upbeat in the face of it all. For many, that proved a useful coping strategy. But their real tests of courage came in their more private moments, when those who lost so much to the war had to learn to go on in spite of the inevitable feelings of anger and doubt that accompany longing and loss.

Alleta Sullivan's five sons went off to war, all joining the fight for democracy together, with zeal and conviction. Their mother was proud but couldn't help feeling some fear as well. Her worst nightmares were confirmed when news came from the Navy that the ship on which all her sons had served, the USS *Juneau*, had been sunk in the Pacific just after the battle of Guadalcanal in 1942. All five of her sons died on that ship. "It seemed as if everything I had lived for was gone," she said. "I couldn't eat or sleep, and I cried a lot." Trying to make some sense of her loss, she and her husband and daughter, Genevieve, agreed to tour the country in 1943 visiting war production plants and encouraging the women and men there to work especially hard to make sure her sons did not die in vain. "I knew that it had been God's will that my boys should die," said Mrs. Sullivan, "and I felt that it must be His will that we should, in some way, carry on the work they had begun." In that same spirit, Genevieve joined the Women's Army Corps in 1943. In addition, the family's story was made into a feature film during the war years, called *The Fighting Sullivans*, meant to inspire those on the home front to do all they could for the war effort.

WOMEN AT WORK

In the early 1940s, America's factories emerged from the economic depression of the decade before by signing lucrative government contracts to build the machinery of war. At the same time, young male factory workers were being drafted or voluntarily joining the military. Industry had a labor shortage and America's women became a large part of the solution. Women who already were working before the war were the first to take the step up from traditionally female jobs of housekeeping and waitressing, to higher-paying industrial work. The government mounted an all-out public relations effort to change attitudes toward women in jobs outside the home, in hopes of easing the transition for many women and the men in their lives. Posters began appearing with smiling women working and captions like "I'm proud ... my husband wants me to do my part!" Gradually, single women and even

"Oh I Married That Young Ensign"

Sylvia Rindskopf, wife of submarine Captain Morris Rindskopf, poses for a family portrait

I graduated from Connecticut College in 1940. I met my husband to be in July of '40. We were married during my spring vacation, as I worked. My boss said to me, "Well, Sylvia, what did you do during your spring vacation?" and I said, "I got married!" And he said, "Oh that's wonderful. Who did you marry?" I said, "Oh I married that young Ensign I've been going—" "Oh my god!" he said, "don't you know we're going to have a war? Why would you do that?" I was in love! That was a silly question.

When my husband and I were first married, he would go out in the morning, and he'd come back in the afternoon. And I thought, well this is how it's going to be for the rest of our lives. Instead of going to the bank or to an office, he's going to go out in the water for the day and come back. Little did I know that things were going to be different.

I came home and lived with my parents during the war. People I'd gone to school with would come up to me and they'd say, "We're not in the war, Sylvia, but we're working at the electric boat company." Or "I had a bad back and they wouldn't take me," or "my ears are not good." People were apologetic for not participating in the war. Everybody asked me all the time, "What do you hear from your husband? We're so sorry that we're not fighting, too." The spirit was incredible.

We used to have to stand in line to get toilet paper; nylon stockings were a luxury. We were all feeling as if we were doing our part for the war. We were issued tickets for how much gasoline we could get for our automobiles. We had food rations. We had black curtains that we had to put on our windows at night, in case we were attacked.

My brother worked during the day with my father. They were in a real estate and insurance business. And at 5:00 p.m. he would come home and have some supper, and then he would go to work at the Electric Boat Company, and he would work until midnight. And he did that 7 days a week, all during the war. Everybody felt that we had to defend our country. There was this tremendous feeling of unity that I have not seen since.

After my husband had been in the Pacific for a year, they let him come home for two weeks. He was coming back on a train and I went to New York to meet him in Penn Station. While I was sitting there, a young woman, my age, started talking to me and she said, "Are you waiting for your husband?" And I said, "Yes." And she said, "What does he do?" And I said, "Well, he's in a submarine." And she said, "Oh my god! How can you stand it?" And I said, "Well, you just do. What does your husband do? Are you waiting for him?" And she said, "Oh, yes. He's a Marine aviator." And I thought, oh my god, how can you stand it?

I went back on the train with him to San Francisco. We were there for five days. We would go up to the top of the Mark Hotel in San Francisco, and look out on the water to see if the boat was there that was gonna be taking him back to Pearl Harbor. And he would sometimes have to go out in the evening. And one night, he didn't come back. And in the morning, there were two other wives from the Drum, we went up to the top of the Mark, and all the tables were full of empty chairs turned over, you know what it's like. And we looked out on the water. The boat was gone. And we knew that our husbands were gone.

We listened to the radio all the time. You just had to believe that everything was going to be all right. And if you lay in bed and thought about submarines being lost all the time, you'd go out of your mind. We didn't actually get the word until after the war. We didn't know at that time how many submarines had been lost.

You know it wasn't easy in many instances for the women who had been on their own, paying the bills, running the household, as it were. All of a sudden you have your husband come back and take over, being pushed aside as it were. But it's amazing that there weren't more divorces.

married women and older women took jobs in the factories and offices of war production.

The fictional "Rosie the Riveter" became a pervasive symbol of the six million women who joined the workforce during the war. Her fable was first advanced in a song that gave her her name, and spoke of her boyfriend, "Charlie," fighting overseas while she made the airplanes that would help him and his fellow soldiers win the war. Then in 1943, artist Norman Rockwell depicted a rugged-looking Rosie on the cover of the magazine *Saturday Evening Post.* Finally, the war department produced a poster with a more feminine-looking worker, bearing plucked eyebrows, lipstick, and well-manicured fingernails, in a red bandana and blue work shirt, flexing her muscle with a now-famous caption that read, "We Can Do It!" She embodied the ideal that women were able to step into men's jobs temporarily, all the while maintaining their womanly appearance.

Real-life female war workers took jobs in airplane factories, shipyards, munitions plants, and various other industries involved in war production. Lee Turner Foringer went to work at Douglas Aircraft in Long Beach, California, in 1942 and worked as a riveter on B-17 bombers after her husband volunteered for the Air Force. She had seen an ad in the newspaper asking for female workers. "I thought, 'gee that's great,'" said Lee, 'they need me.' Douglas Aircraft employed nearly 22,000 women dur-

A woman welder at the Inglewood, California plant of North American Aviation works on part of a tank for a B-25 bomber. ca. October 1942.

during the war years and was one of the largest producers of warplanes. Lee worked on the assembly line using a rivet gun to drive the bolt-like rivet into a pre-drilled hole and secure the parts of the plane together. "I really looked forward to going to work each day," she said. Lee worked there for nearly two years. During one of her husband's leaves, she got pregnant but kept working as long as she could until she quit to have her baby.

Unlike the airplane industry, which was relatively new in the 1940s and therefore less tradition-bound in its opposition to women workers, the shipbuilding industry was as old as the country itself, and had always barred women from its ranks. For instance, it was not until 1942 that the Brooklyn Navy Yard lifted a 141-year ban on hiring women. But World War II began to change that. On the West Coast, a maverick shipbuilder named Henry Kaiser introduced mass production to the industry and began turning out cargo ships in record time. He also hired women by the thousands, especially at his Kaiser Shipyard in Richmond, California, outside of San Francisco.

Women also headed to work in munitions plants making bombs and bullets for the Allies. And as the war progressed, and more and more men joined the military, women took over such traditionally male civilian jobs as bus drivers and train conductors. Those jobs also came to be considered war work when women did them, because they kept the home front going.

In professional work as well, doors that had always been closed started to open for women. As men were drafted, women began to break into journalism, reporting on aspects of the world they had never been allowed to cover before. For instance, the number of female newspaper and magazine reporters accredited to cover the House and Senate in Washington, D.C.,

Women shipfitters on board the USS Nereus *at the U.S. Navy Yard in Mare Island, California, as they near completion of part of the engine room floor (from left to right: Betty Pierce, Lola Thomas, Margaret Houston, Thelma Mort, and Katie Stanfill). ca. 1943*

"We Regret to Inform You . . ."

During the war Bedford County, Virginia was a fairly rural county. Most families farmed for a living. We raised our lots of vegetables and had chickens and hogs and cows. Churches were a part of the community at that time, more so than they are now. And the town was very patriotic. People spent time rolling bandages. Lots of the women went to work making gas masks. Some went to Newport News to work in ship-building. Some were raising victory gardens and I remember that, even when I was in school, we were trying to buy savings stamps towards a bond. But there was just a real emptiness in the community because almost all of our young men had gone away to war.

My brothers had been inducted into service in February of '41. My older brother, Bedford, was very outgoing and, if you were around him, you would know he was there. He liked to play poker with the other men. Bedford never did things that he was supposed to do. He was busted in the Army I don't know how many times and died a private—he'd been a sergeant several times. He was so different from my younger brother, Raymond, who was very quiet and reserved. Raymond joined the National Guard just because his big brother did. Raymond was a staff sergeant, and he did exactly what he was supposed to do all the time.

On D-Day, I believe that the entire community of Bedford was apprehensive and worried and very, very upset. The Bedford Presbyterian Church was overflowing with people who had gone to pray for the men. And I'm not sure my parents knew for sure that my brothers were involved, but they knew this huge military operation was taking place and so I think they were worried that my brothers were involved.

We received our first telegram on a Sunday about the middle of July as we were getting ready to go to church. It had been a good while since we had heard anything from my brothers and, in fact, some letters had already been returned saying "Undeliverable." The Sheriff came by and my father answered the door and the sheriff handed him the telegram. The telegram just read, "We regret to inform you that your son, Bedford T. Hoback, has been killed in action." My father came in and was with my mother for a while, and then the children were called in and we were told what had happened. My parents were devastated at the news. That was the loss of their first son.

We were very active in Centerpoint Methodist Church, so when we didn't show up for church that morning, the church just came over because they realized what had happened. And my mother and father went to Bedford's fiance's house to tell her what had happened.

Somehow we made it through the day and then, on Monday, my sister and I thought, we would make Mom and Dad feel better. We'd make some ice cream. We had the ice cream freezer out, and were cranking away, when the second telegram came saying my younger brother, Raymond, was missing in action. And from then on, I can't remember what happened that day. It was just such a blow to receive a second telegram.

Lucille Hoback Boggess, sister of two soldiers who died at Normandy

My parents were so distraught. My father would often go out to the barn to cry because he didn't want us to see him. My mother just spent all her time crying. And the entire community was crying because there were telegrams coming in every day. The first week there were nine telegrams delivered where the men had been killed, and they kept coming in. Bedford was hit really hard. Nineteen young men from Bedford died on D-Day. This community lost more men on D-Day than any other community in the United States.

A few weeks after my parents received the telegrams, my mother received a package in the mail. When she opened it, it was my younger brother Raymond's bible. My mother had given him that bible for Christmas in 1938, and he had carried it with him ever since. I suppose when he was shot, he dropped his pack and the bible fell out in the sand. A soldier from West Virginia, walking on the beach D-Day-plus-one, saw the bible lying in the sand and picked it up. He wrote my parents the most beautiful letter. As he explained in the letter, "As anyone would do, I picked it up to keep it from being destroyed." My mother always treasured that bible.

In a real way, those who don't go to war suffer too. My mother was never the same after my brothers died. She went on and tried to carry on, but she was never like the mother I had known prior to their death. Bedford's fiancé was heartbroken for a long, long time. And many soldiers returned home with guilty feelings because these men died and they lived. The impact is huge not just on a family, but on a community and on the nation.

tripled from 33 before the war to 98 by 1944. And by 1945, the military had accredited 127 female reporters and photographers to cover the war overseas.

One of the most famous was the photographer Margaret Bourke-White, who was the first woman to be accredited in World War II, and covered major stories for *Life* magazine. In 1941, she was the first American to photograph scenes of World War II in Russia, when the Nazis bombed the Kremlin at night. She photographed the Allied invasion of North Africa and took combat photos in Italy and photos of air raids over Germany. She also had one of the most gruesome assignments in the war. She marched with General George Patton to cover the first liberation of a Nazi concentration camp at Buchenwald where at least 40,000 died. "I saw and photographed piles of naked, lifeless bodies," she said, "the human skeletons in furnaces, the living skeletons who would die the next day." And she photographed the German citizens whom an irate General Patton forced to come and view the more than 1,200 dead and charred bodies lying unburied on top of one another near their villages.

In the more secretive aspects of the war's operation, more than 4,000 American women worked for the Office of Strategic Services, precursor to the CIA during the war. Only a few were involved in the most clandestine work, spying. Among them all, a standout was Virginia Hall, a Baltimore native. In her late 30s during the war, she had attended Radcliffe and Barnard colleges and worked for the State Department in the 1930s in embassies in Poland, Estonia, Vienna, Turkey, and Italy. As the war heated up in Europe, she went to France in 1939 and joined the French Ambulance Service. Once France was conquered by the Nazis she headed to Great Britain and worked for their intelligence operation the Special Operations Executive (SOE).

Since she was fluent in French, the SOE sent Hall to France as a spy in 1941. Her cover as an American reporter for the *New York Post* let her send back such valuable information that she earned a Member of the British Empire medal for bravery after she was ordered out of the country by Nazi occupiers in 1943. Hall then joined the American OSS office in London and was sent back into France, this time disguised as a milkmaid. Hall's codename inside the OSS was Diane. But she was known more widely as "the limping lady," since she walked on a wooden leg after a hunting accident in Turkey had caused her leg to be amputated. Despite what should have been a noticeable handicap, Hall was never captured. But it was not for lack of trying on the part of the Nazis. The Gestapo called Hall "one of the most valuable Allied agents in France," and even put a drawing of her on a wanted poster with a caption that said, "We must find and destroy her." Yet Hall's disguises cleverly eluded the Nazis, and for more than a year she was able to work with French resistance workers, providing the Allies with valuable information in planning the D-Day invasion. At the end of the war, the U.S. government awarded Hall the Distinguished Service Cross, the second highest military award for bravery after the Medal of Honor. She was the only civilian American woman to receive that honor in World War II.

(Previous page)
Men and women work side by side building A-20 attack bombers at the Douglas Aircraft plant in Long Beach, California, ca. October 1942.

Women made smaller strides in medicine and the law during the war, even though some law schools and medical schools (including Harvard) still did not admit women at the start of World War II. But those barriers were broken in most places by the end of the 1940s. When the minor league baseball season was cancelled because players went to war, women stepped in to form the first women's professional baseball league. And a huge influx of women descended upon Washington, D.C., in the war years to work in clerical jobs. They came to be called "government girls." Before that, women were not welcome in many offices in the nation's capital.

Women had only gained the right to vote in 1920. So two decades later, when World War II began, relatively few had been appointed to key government positions or run for office. But some women managed to make their way into the seats of influence in American government. One such early female government pioneer was Frances Perkins, the first female cabinet member, who served as Secretary of Labor for the entire Roosevelt administration. She helped to create Social Security and to institute the minimum wage and the 40-hour workweek. Her main champion was the one of the most influential first ladies of all time, Eleanor Roosevelt.

Though not an elected official, Mrs. Roosevelt redefined the role of first lady in much the same way other wartime women were redefining women's roles throughout the country. At one point, early in the war, Mrs. Roosevelt served briefly as a deputy director of the Office of Civilian Defense, encouraging citizens to volunteer for useful work on the home front. But because of her high profile, she received more attention and criticism than

Clerical workers processing forms for production requirement plan, Priorities Division, War Production Board (WPB), October 1942.

most mid-level government officials, getting in the way of the work to be done. So she soon resigned, and found other ways to have an impact on the war effort. She conducted major tours of war zones, visiting with Allied troops and leaders and boosting morale. And she used the media to instill a sense of duty in American citizens, especially women. In a radio address on December 7, 1941, the evening of the attack on Pearl Harbor, Mrs. Roosevelt included a special admonition to the women of the country saying, "When we find a way to do anything in our communities to help others, to build morale, to give a feeling of security, we must do it. Whatever is asked of us I am sure we can accomplish it."

Mrs. Roosevelt fought for the rights of minority soldiers and women to serve in the military, and she worked hard to secure job opportunities and support for minorities and women who wanted to work at war jobs on the home front. The first lady was a key force in establishing some of the country's first day care centers, a new concept at the time and one designed to allow women to choose to work in war jobs without sacrificing their children's welfare. She also worked in the face of some opposition to help children escape from Hitler's Germany and become refugees in the United States. And even after the war, and her husband's death, she continued to influence the social and political affairs of the nation and the world when she was appointed by President Truman to serve as an American representative to the United Nations.

Montana Congresswoman Jeanette Rankin was another of the first women to break down the gender barriers in the higher levels of government when she became the first woman elected to Congress in 1917. She was able to win because Montana had granted women the right to vote and run for office before the country as a whole had done so. Rankin's first vote in Congress came when America was deciding to join World War I. Rankin, a lifelong pacifist, was in the minority who voted against American involvement in the war. Then, in December of 1941, when President Roosevelt asked Congress to declare war against Japan, Rankin was the lone vote in either the House or Senate against war. "As a woman I can't go to war," said Rankin, referring to the fact that women were not allowed to serve in the military in 1941, " and I refuse to send anyone else."

WOMEN IN THE SPOTLIGHT

When the war began, entertainers were unsure what role they might be able to play in the all-out effort to win. But it was not long before their services became vital to the morale of the troops and the nation.

Jean Ruth was one of the first women disc jockeys on the radio during World War II. Her show, *Reveille With Beverly*, was broadcast at home and abroad on Armed Forces Radio. She was able to bring a bit of the music and spirit of the home front, and the comforting voice of an American woman, to lonely U.S. soldiers around the world. Before the war, women's voices had

"A Niece of Uncle Sam"

When the War started, everybody's life changed. I went to work for North American Aircraft in Grand Prairie, Texas, a suburb of Dallas. They sent me to riveting class. They called me at the office and said, "You don't belong in riveting, you have experience." So I went to the main plant in Grand Prairie as a drill press and punch press operator.

The punch press was a machine that formed the pieces. In other words, you would have a set up and you would put your aluminum on the machine, absolutely flat. When that piece came out, it was formed. We did our own setups, a lot of them. We did our blue print reading, and we worked on aluminum and stainless steel. We were constantly working on parts that were going into the planes. Sometimes we'd see P51s in formation, and we'd say, "Ooh! We worked on those!"

Drill press and punch press was hard work, and a lot of the parts were very heavy, sometimes it took two people to lift some of the equipment that when we would do a new set up on the punch press. We had a lot of standing, but no one complained. We didn't complain. We didn't go around moping and groaning. You didn't say, "Well, gee, I have to go to work." You didn't feel that way. You went to work because you were needed and you wanted to do it. We did have some laughter there at times, but everyone was definitely there to work. We didn't stop and think about the sadness or why we were there. We were there so the men could do the fighting.

No one seemed surprised that women could do these jobs. We were healthy and able to do them. And no one resented anyone to the extent that we were there.

We had such a variety of women, and we had to dress accordingly in pants and tops with no frills and no jewelry, and you also had to cover your heads. Nothing was exposed, because the hair and clothing could interfere with the machines. The machines could be a little bit dangerous.

Nobody worried about being beautiful and this, that, or the other. We didn't worry about our hands or our nails. We were people. Some were very beautiful women, but they weren't there for the glamour. They were there to do what we had to do and we got our faces dirty. We got our hands dirty. We got our clothes dirty.

The men never threw it in saying, "Gee, now I'm the man, you're the woman." They didn't do that. Everybody was equal, yet we were women and they were men. We never ever said, " I'm a woman, you treat me such and such" because they treated women with respect at that time.

I think the ones that were out on the front risking their lives, they were the ones that were there for us. We in the defense industry worked to keep things going for the ones that were out there fighting for us. We can't even visualize what some of these experiences were like.

I never considered myself "Rosie the Riveter," because that was a job. But I considered myself a niece of Uncle Sam.

Margie Grant Munn
Drill Press Operator,
North American Aircraft,
Grand Prairie, Texas

(Opposite page)
The original "Rosie the Riveter"
poster was created in 1943 by
J. Howard Miller for the War
Production Board. This illustration
was not based on an actual person but
when the image became so popular
Norman Rockwell did his own version
using a live model. (See the section,
"The Arsenal of Democracy"
for more information.)

General Millard F. Harmon, Eleanor Roosevelt, and Admiral William "Bull" Halsey in New Caledonia, September 15, 1943.

not been thought authoritative enough for radio. "I was reaching out to 54 countries and 11 million possible listeners," said Jean. "I didn't talk too much about the war." Instead she tried to keep her tone upbeat and relaxed. "My voice was the thing, and the music of the day was the other that made it all hang together."

Women in the films provided important role models onscreen for other women, with such actresses as Katharine Hepburn, Greer Garson, Claudette Colbert, and Lauren Bacall portraying noble women dealing with the rigors of the war. Actresses became symbols of American womanhood for troops overseas as well. Betty Grable's famous pinup picture, along with countless other such photos of actresses such as Rita Hayworth, Veronica Lake, and Lena Horne were credited with lifting the spirits of many an American soldier abroad and reminding him what he was fighting for back home.

The United Service Organization, which was formed in 1941, sent professional American performers all over the world to put on live shows for the troops. Many female Hollywood stars performed in USO touring troupes both at home and abroad, including Rita Hayworth, Betty Grable, Ann Sheridan and Marlene Dietrich. But many of the women who went overseas with the USO to perform were relatively unknown and spent years on what was called the foxhole circuit. An unnamed female USO performer in New Guinea described the conditions under which they performed in a letter home. "We've played to audiences, many of them ankle deep in mud, huddled under their ponchos in the pouring rain (it breaks your heart the first two or three times to see men so hungry for entertainment).... We've played with huge tropical bugs flying in our hair and faces; we've played to audiences of thousands of men, audiences spreading from our very feet to far up a hillside and many sitting in trees." She also told of the reaction of the men, which was often quite profound. "A mighty spontaneous roar went up when the girls pranced on the stage.... The din was terrific—months of pent-up emotion blew out in one instant.... To these men who have suffered intolerable tortures from Mother Nature and the Japs—it was a miracle—a temporary Shangri La—where their cares could be dispersed.... A half hour after the performance the men were still sitting in the rain, still applauding."

WOMEN VOLUNTEERS

Marlene Dietrich and Rita Hayworth serve food to soldiers at the Hollywood Canteen, November 17, 1942.

Most of the women who volunteered during the war effort did so in addition to other roles they had taken on. Single working women and married women with children alike volunteered as hostesses in the more than 3,000 USO-operated clubs in the U.S. They danced, played cards, and socialized with soldiers at bases around the country. Other women volunteered in many of the activities of the Office of Civilian Defense, which coordinated volunteer activities and organized war bond campaigns, scrap metal salvage drives, and child care services in neighborhoods all over the country. Nearly 3.5 million women volunteered in various divisions of the Red Cross as well, working as nurses aides, shipping care packages to prisoners of war and soldiers at home and abroad, and collecting some 13 million pints of blood by war's end from donors at blood drives around the country. The blood and plasma were essential in treating wounded troops around the world.

When male farmhands went off to war the nation's farms suffered a labor shortage in the same way that industry did. So once again, women stepped in to keep the production of crops and livestock going. The U.S. Department of Agriculture even created the Women's Land Army, a quasi-military civilian organization that trained and sent approximately half a million urban and suburban women to work on farms. One woman said, "I decided not to join the WACs or WAVES, but to do farm work and help in farm production. I believe this is just as important to the men in the armed forces."

One of the most adventurous volunteer jobs for women was in joining the

Red Cross for service overseas. About 7,000 women did so, serving in all the theaters of war, staffing 1,800 Red Cross clubs providing rest, food, conversation and dancing near wherever troops were stationed. Red Cross girls, as they were called, had to have a college education and be at least 25 years old. They needed the maturity it was reasoned, because they had to be able to handle the pressures of being so close to the front and in places where the ratio of men to women was sometimes 250 to one. Some Red Cross girls in the North African and European war theaters also staffed clubmobiles, traveling kitchens from which they served coffee and doughnuts to the fighting men. These women were often the closest to the battle front of any American women and 16 Red Cross women died while on overseas duty.

Jean Archer was a schoolteacher in New Jersey before joining the Red Cross and serving in Guam. In a letter home to her parents in 1945 she said, "My work consists of taking turns doing everything at the club....The sailors are grand and appreciate the club. It is always full, never enough chairs for all. We are busy every single moment, playing cards, Ping-Pong or just talking, but we never stop talking and listening. I've seen hundreds of pictures of best girls, wives, children. I've had any number of boys say to me, 'Do you know you are the first girl I have talked to in 22 months?' ... I wouldn't be any place else. It is the hardest and most tiring job I've ever had, not even a rest hour, but it is also the most interesting and satisfying."

After the war, many women gladly left their wartime work and took their place as homemakers in the postwar ideal for which many people felt the war had been fought. Most of the women who had worked in the factories went home to become full-time wives and mothers, and the suburban lifestyle began to take hold all across the country. Seeds planted during World War II, however, eventually came to fruition in the decades that followed. Women's wartime foray into the workplace and the military in particular, would forever change the idea that women could not handle such work. And in the professions, politics, and entertainment, women continued to rise to higher and higher positions. For better or worse, World War II was the first time women proved in such diverse ways that they could handle and thrive in what had traditionally been considered societal roles only suitable for men.

In 1942 Eleanor Roosevelt wrote in her syndicated newspaper column: "If the war goes on long enough and women are patient, opportunity will come knocking at their doors. However, there is just a chance that this is not a time when women should be patient. We are in a war and we need to fight it with all our ability and every weapon possible. Women pilots, in this particular case, are a weapon waiting to be used."

Mrs. Roosevelt was advocating for the formation of the WASP when she expressed that sentiment, but her words might also be seen as a tribute to the mix of fortitude and boldness that American women in all walks of life had to exhibit during World War II when they stepped up so adroitly to their rightful place as fully contributing citizens of the United States.

PART III

CREATING
THE MEMORIAL

Making History on the Mall

Robert Uth

The National Mall in Washington, D.C., tells the nation's story. The Capitol Building, the Washington Monument, the Lincoln Memorial, the Jefferson Memorial, the Korean War and Vietnam Veterans' Memorials, are all important chapters in the American experience. But the Second World War, one of the most important episodes in our history, has been missing. That has changed now with the creation of the World War II Memorial. How the memorial finally came into being—nearly 60 years after the war's end—is a lesson in the way Americans choose national symbols to reflect their history, values, and aspirations.

Some point to a moment in 1987 as the birth of the memorial to World War II. At a public gathering in Jerusalem Township, Ohio, a World War II combat veteran named Roger Durbin asked Congresswoman Marcy Kaptur (D-Ohio) why there was no such memorial in the nation's capital. She, as many Americans might have done, pointed out the Iwo Jima Memorial. Durbin, an army veteran of the Battle of the Bulge, correctly reminded her that this iconic sculpture was a tribute to one service, the United States Marine Corps. A historian and urban planner with deep family ties to the Second World War, Kaptur introduced legislation that year to remedy the situation. After six years of congressional wrangling, Public Law 103-32 was finally signed by President Clinton in 1993 authorizing the creation of a national memorial to the World War II generation. But creating a national memorial is a deliberately complicated and lengthy process, and for good reason. Once built, these memorials must stand the test of time and be recognized as worthy representations of historically significant events and individuals, helping to define the nation's principles and ideals.

FUNDING THE NEW MEMORIAL

The American Battle Monuments Commission (ABMC), an independent agency of the executive branch of the federal government, was directed by Congress to build the memorial and to raise the majority of the funds from private sources—an uncommon task for a federal agency. National memorials are primarily built with private funds with varying degrees of assistance from the federal government. ABMC received about $10 million from the Department of Defense World War II 50th Anniversary Fund and the public sale of 50th Anniversary commemorative coins, but the majority of the money would have to come from the public. The task of organizing the fund-raising effort fell to ABMC Secretary Major General John P. Herrling, USA (retired). In early 1997, he met with former senator Bob Dole, who agreed to serve as the national chairman of the fund-raising campaign. Federal Express founder and CEO Fred Smith joined Dole as co-chairman in August 1997, giving the campaign a strong tie to the corporate world. But fund-raising didn't jell until the summer of 1998, when the commission was able to take advantage of several timely happenings: Steven Spielberg's movie *Saving Private Ryan* generated a reawakening to the courage and sacrifice of those who fought in the Second World War; and newscaster Tom Brokaw introduced the public to what he called "The Greatest Generation." The effect of these popular cultural products was amplified by a growing awareness of how rapidly the nation was losing its World War II veterans—an alarming 1,100 each day. Of 16 million who had served in uniform during the war, fewer than 6 million were alive in 1998. (Fewer than 4 million still survived when the memorial was dedicated in 2004.)

In 1998, General Herrling again reached out for high-profile assistance, asking Oscar-winning actor and *Saving Private Ryan* star Tom Hanks if he would volunteer his time to serve as the campaign's spokesman. Hanks agreed without hesitation, and his message that "It's Time to Say Thank You" to America's World War II generation struck a responsive chord. A series of public service ads generated $90 million of donated advertising from print, radio, and television outlets. In the end, ABMC would receive more than $195 million for the World War II Memorial: $16 million from the federal government; $15 million in earned interest; and $164 million from hundreds of corporations and foundations, all of the major veterans groups, dozens of civic, professional, and fraternal organizations, the 50 states and Puerto Rico, 1,200 schools, and more than 500,000 individual Americans.

SELECTING A SITE

Congress did not specify an exact location in Washington for the new memorial, and its current location on the National Mall was not the obvious choice in 1993. In contemporary terms, the Mall generally means the swath of space stretching from the Capitol to the Lincoln Memorial. Surrounded by museums and memorials, it forms, with the White House and Jefferson Memorial, the centerpiece of the capital's monumental core. It is the preeminent public space of the nation.

However, as envisioned by the Franco-American architect Pierre L'Enfant in his 1791 plan, the Mall was to be a broad promenade only from the Capitol to the Washington Monument. Beyond were extensive marshes and tidal flats bordering the Potomac River. Recognizing the need to accommodate the memory of important national events and persons, L'Enfant deliberately built into his Washington plan numerous opportunities for memorial construction throughout the city. The Mall would be reserved for the most important subjects, beginning with the monument to President Washington.

For the first half of the 19th century, existing conditions discouraged any development on the Mall. Despite its faults, the centrality of the Mall began to assert itself, and the first federal building was completed in 1851 on the Mall's south side—an imposing structure for the newly created Smithsonian Institution. A leading landscape architect prepared a planting plan for the Mall, the Washington Monument grounds, and the White House. Slowly, the Mall took on a sense of civic importance with the establishment of extensive public gardens.

Despite a growing civic interest in the Mall, its unfinished appearance continued to be an embarrassment. Of primary concern were the unsanitary conditions of the tidal marshes covering the current sites of the Lincoln, Jefferson, FDR, and World War II memorials. Because of the magnitude of the problem, Congress brought in the Army Corps of Engineers. In 1883, the Corps began to create a massive landfill from dredging operations in the Potomac River and the Washington Channel. During the course of this work, more than 600 acres of new lands were created, including what today are known as East and West Potomac Parks.

With the approach of the capital's centennial in 1900, there was a growing interest in the nascent science of urban design, along with a revival in classical architecture inspired by the Chicago World Exposition of 1893. Known as the City Beautiful Movement, it would eventually touch many American cities, but none more so than Washington. There was talk of "aggrandizing" the capital city, of building block-long museum complexes and a new and larger White House. The Mall, however, continued to be the major focus of attention.

In the spring of 1901, an elite group of professionals (five in number—two architects, one landscape architect, one sculptor, and one legislative aide) was authorized by a Senate commission to undertake preparing a new plan that would bring distinction and prestige to the capital as it entered a new century.

Known as the McMillan Plan, the most important features included:

✦ The extension of the Mall westward on recently filled land—nearly doubling the length of the original Mall.

✦ Anchoring the far end with a major architectural element, the Lincoln Memorial, mirrored in a reflecting pool that would extend toward the Washington Monument, the grounds of which were to contain elaborate formal gardens.

✦ To the south of the White House, a new axis leading to additional lawns and a monumental grouping of buildings dedicated to honoring national heroes. The site is now occupied by the Jefferson Memorial and the Tidal Basin.

In presenting a plan with so many new and bold ideas, the members of the Senate commission were careful to point out that it was a framework for future growth, not a prescriptive document where every detail was to be developed as shown. Their efforts were met with widespread approval.

In 1910, Congress created an agency, the Commission of Fine Arts, to undertake the long-term implementation of the plan and oversee all federal architecture on the Mall and elsewhere in the capital. Its very first task was the Lincoln Memorial.

Over the next 20 years, many of the Mall's prominent features began to take shape: the Reflecting Pool, the elm-lined walkways, and the last major feature, the north-south axis through the White House, completed in the late 1930s. A long-simmering debate on who would be memorialized at this critical spot finally came to a head, with Jefferson prevailing over Theodore Roosevelt.

With the passage of time and numerous efforts to create new monuments and memorials, concerns began to rise that the Mall was becoming overbuilt. An adopted policy to deny more memorials was short-lived with the construction of the Vietnam Veterans' Memorial in 1982. The Korean War Veterans' Memorial followed in 1995, the same year the ABMC set out to choose a fitting place for the World War II Memorial.

The ABMC reviewed a number of sites offered by the National Park Service. Interestingly, all of the sites identified were located off the main visual axis of the Mall. Constitution Gardens, an English landscape of informal paths and a natural lake on the north side of the Mall, emerged as the favorite of the six sites made available. But J. Carter Brown, chairman of the Commission of Fine Arts, was not satisfied with any of the available sites. He and the Commission's secretary, Charles H. Atherton, thought that to place the World War II Memorial in the same context as the Vietnam or Korean War memorials, off the central axis of the Mall, would literally and figuratively define these events as having comparable historical significance. Further complicating the issue, the Constitution Gardens site was considerably smaller than those of the Vietnam or Korean memorials. To the surprise of many, Brown suggested that the ideal selection would be to shift the entire memorial site just south of Constitution Gardens to the 7.4-acre Rainbow Pool site on the east end of the Reflecting Pool. Here, situated between the Washington Monument and the Lincoln Memorial, the World War II Memorial would achieve the historic connection it demanded.

Though initially dismissed by the Park Service, it gradually appeared that there could be an extraordinary linkage between the major memorials on the Mall's main axis: the Washington Monument, the 18th-century icon representing the establishment of a union of states; the Lincoln Memorial, symbolizing the 19th-century struggle to preserve that union; and, completing the composition, the World War II Memorial, the 20th-century celebration of the overwhelming unity of the states.

Citing its prominence and spaciousness, its highly relevant surroundings, and its easy access to the mainstream of visitors to the Mall, ABMC made a compelling argument for its approval. The National Park Service dropped its previous opposition, and on October 5, 1995, the National Capital Planning Commission followed the Commission of Fine Arts in giving its approval. President William J. Clinton officially dedicated the site on Veterans Day, November 11, 1995. By his side stood Roger Durbin, the World War II vet from Ohio who had started it all eight years earlier.

CREATING A DESIGN

Nearly every memorial and monument on the National Mall has been controversial. In 1879, *American Architect* called the Washington Monument "the ugliest monument in the world." The powerful Speaker of the House, Joseph G. Cannon, led a bitter fight to prevent the Lincoln Memorial from being constructed in its current location. A memorial built there "might shake itself down with loneliness and ague," he said in 1921. The Commission of Fine Arts has never approved the design of the Jefferson Memorial. President Franklin Delano Roosevelt directed that it be constructed before there was a legislative process that now prevents such autonomous decision-making. In 1981, the now beloved Vietnam Veterans' Memorial was labeled "a black gash of shame and sorrow, hacked into the national visage that is the Mall." And so the tradition continued with the World War II Memorial.

In 1996, an open design competition attracted some 400 entries, many from the most prestigious artists and architects in the world. A 10-member independent design jury and a 12-member architect-engineer evaluation board selected six finalists to compete in a Stage II closed competition. In the end, the jury and board each unanimously selected the design of Friedrich St.Florian, a naturalized American citizen born in Austria and a former dean of the Rhode Island School of Design.

St.Florian's design met all the basic criteria. It created a unique "place" on the Mall, captured the theme of "unity" by composing two semicircles of columns around a reconstructed Rainbow Pool, and, most important, it did not interrupt the critical visual axis between the Washington Monument and the Lincoln Memorial. This was achieved by lowering the new Rainbow Pool 16 feet below grade. And though not a prerequisite, the design echoed the longstanding tradition of classical architecture on the Mall.

Critics of the St.Florian design expressed concern about the memorial's large scale, believing it detracted from the Mall's natural setting. A few even went so far as to compare it to totalitarian styles of architecture of the 1930s. And for others, still opposed to the memorial's location, no design was appropriate.

The initial concept was by no means perfect. The Commission of Fine Arts (CFA) and the National Capital Planning Commission (NCPC) looked favorably on St.Florian's underlying concept of a lowered plaza surrounding a reconstructed Rainbow Pool, but they believed the overall design to be too massive for its location. St.Florian was sent back to the drawing board, a step that echoed the creation of national monuments in the past. His revised design was submitted to the CFA for approval in May 1998. Though greatly reduced in scale, it maintained the same architectural geometry of a lowered plaza encircling a reconstructed Rainbow Pool. The original design's large earthen berms with their interior exhibit space were replaced with two memorial pavilions on the north-south axis. The colonnades of rounded pillars were reduced in size and a series of architectural screens were positioned between them. The new architecture embraced a smaller plaza that would now sit comfortably within the existing double row of elm trees. The plaza would be raised from 16 feet to 6 feet below grade, and on the western side of the plaza a Light of Freedom would rise from a broken plane between two waterfalls. The CFA approved the revised concept, as did the NPCP in July.

One year later, in the summer of 1999, ABMC took the next step in the approval process, submitting a preliminary design for approval. More changes had taken place. The architectural screens had been replaced with 56 pillars adorned by bronze oak and wheat wreaths. This was a stronger architectural representation of the states and territories. The unique "stripped classical" pillars had an opening down their center to make the memorial more transparent to the natural surroundings. Two bronze baldacchino sculptures of four American eagles, holding aloft a suspended laurel wreath, were placed inside both of the memorial's arched pavilions; and a cenotaph (a symbolic tomb) was added to the plaza in front of the Light of Freedom to represent the more than 400,000 Americans who died during the war. The preliminary design was approved by the CFA in May 1999 and by the NCPC two weeks later in June.

When ABMC and Friedrich St.Florian took the final architectural design for the World War II Memorial to the CFA in July 2000, it closely resembled the previous year's preliminary design, but with one dramatic difference. The ensemble of broken plane, Light of Freedom, and cenotaph in the plaza's western precinct had been replaced with a single, striking element: a curved Freedom Wall with a field of 4,000 sculpted gold stars, honoring the more than 400,000 Americans who gave their lives for their country and for freedom. During World War II, families received a gold star to hang in their windows when a family member perished in the war.

The CFA approved the final design unanimously and the NCPC gave its blessing on a close 7-5 vote, clearing the way for a ceremonial groundbreaking on Veterans Day, 2000—five years after the site dedication ceremony. ABMC would need 10 more public hearings to finish the design approval process. Construction finally began in September 2001. In just 31 months the memorial was completed and opened to the public in April 2004, a month prior to the formal dedication celebration over Memorial Day weekend.

BUILDING THE
WORLD WAR II MEMORIAL

Robert Uth

T he building of the World War II Memorial represents a coming together of history, ancient traditions, modern concerns and tastes, architects, artists and sculptors, engineers, and thousands of craftsmen and tradesmen, as well as the support and good will of the American people.

Compared to other monuments, the time to construct the Memorial was relatively short—only 31 months. Some have taken decades. The Washington Monument took more than half-a-century. And this is due in great measure to the organization and commitment of the American Battle Monuments Commission (ABMC), the federal agency charged to build the memorial.

Because of the extraordinary location and subject, it was determined from the outset that this memorial would be constructed to withstand the physical test of time. Only the best quality materials, highly skilled labor, and state-of-the-art technology would be employed. Redundancy would be built into all the engineering so that the memorial would stand long into the future. For instance, it would have been easier and less expensive to construct the memorial by hanging granite veneer off of poured-in-place concrete. But the design architect insisted, and ABMC agreed, that the construction should be monolithic, i.e. built of solid stone.

ABMC, famous for the construction of memorials and military cemeteries around the world, approached the task like a military mission. The motto was "Get the memorial built right, get it built on time, and get it built within budget." The logistics involved were no less intricate than a battle plan.

Over 500 workers—builders, craft workers, and stonemasons—contributed to the monument both on location in Washington and in quarries, foundries, and studios across the nation. They transformed a plan on paper into an actual memorial, a space that visitors experience with their bodies, hearts, and minds.

A number of local companies had worked on monumental Washington for many decades. Together, the firms that helped build the memorial had

Major General John Herrling of American Battle Monuments Commission (foreground) turns a spade with other dignitaries during the official groundbreaking, November 11, 2000.
(all photographs in this chapter are by Richard Latoff)

over 135 years of experience on national projects including the Washington Monument and White House restoration, the FDR Memorial, and even the original Reflecting Pool and the National Gallery of Art.

Time itself was the greatest challenge. The goal was to have as many World War II veterans as possible see it—and they were dying at a rate of nearly 1,100 per day. Moving fast but not sacrificing quality or taking short-cuts meant abundant overtime for crew and staff.

The official groundbreaking took place on Veterans Day 2000. Numerous dignitaries were among the 15,000 who attended. Site mobilization began in September 2001, and included activities such as placement of on-location project offices for the government and general contractor, perimeter fencing, tree-protection zoning, and installation of utility lines. So hallowed was the Rainbow Pool site and vista, members of the Commission of Fine Arts and the National Capital Planning Commission went to the location and stood on boxes and ladders at various heights to assure themselves that the memorial would in no way obscure the view between the Washington Monument and the Lincoln Memorial.

GEOLOGY   The challenge of building on the National Mall is the site itself. The soil beneath the Mall is actually reclaimed marshland. Geologically it is an invention, and as a result it has the worst soil structurally for building. Ground water is another problem. In some places it is only six or seven feet below ground level. And the excavation for the memorial was going to be 30 to 40 feet deep. On top of this, the memorial's site is in a flood plain, so it had to be designed to withstand the statistical "twenty-five year flood"—one of which nearly occurred while construction was underway.

To overcome these geological constraints, the first major phase of construction involved the installation of a two-foot wide reinforced concrete wall down to bedrock. This "slurry" wall followed the memorial's perimeter and was keyed into the bedrock below. In essence, it became a gigantic bathtub. But the function of this bathtub was to keep the groundwater *out*.

Though not glamorous in an architectural sense, the completion of this foundation wall was a major engineering accomplishment. Completed in June 2002, it allowed the contractor to begin foundation piling and general excavation.

EXCAVATION   The Memorial Plaza and reconstructed Rainbow Pool are the principal design features of the memorial. But first the old Rainbow Pool had to go because the new design called for it to be lowered six feet below the level of the Reflecting Pool and reduced in size by 15 percent. This was opposed by some architectural conservationists, but in fact the Rainbow Pool had been in a serious state of disrepair for many years. Demolition of the old pool began in June 2002. Then major excavation began to make room below for 18,000 square feet of tunnels and vaults beneath the memorial plaza.

FOUNDATION   The structural concrete work that would ultimately provide the base for all architectural finished stonework started in September 2002. About 600 steel piles (more than 14,000 linear feet) were driven into bedrock to support the concrete slab foundation. Miles of steel bars, called 'rebar,' were wired together for reinforcement. Then a continuous flow of concrete mixers began to roll in and ultimately poured more than 44,000 metric tons of concrete. Hundreds of concrete workers trudged through the muck looking like so many soldiers slogging through mud. Many of the workers on the site were veterans, or had parents who were veterans, and for them the work had special significance. And above it all swung the tower crane, with a huge American flag fluttering in the wind. Best of all, the project was ahead of schedule and on budget.

Then came the wettest period in recorded D.C. history, with rain falling for 40 out of 50 days. Production schedules began to slip. Then a real blow came. The site superintendent, Jimmy McCloskey, admired and liked by all, died suddenly. His death had a profound effect on all the workers on the site. He had chosen this as his last job before retiring because he wanted to help build the World War II Memorial. It would take weeks to get the momentum back and mourn a

(Next page)
The shape of the memorial can be seen from the Washington Monument in June of 2003. Most of the vertical stonework is finished, and the plaza foundation is nearing completion.

Pouring a section of the southwest corner of the plaza. A row of pillars and the Freedom Wall are taking shape in the background.

lost comrade. But by April 2003 the final section of the first layer of concrete for the plaza foundation had been poured.

STONE   The memorial required almost 17,000 pieces of precisely cut stone. The volume exceeded 100,000 cubic feet. Granite was chosen for its aesthetic appeal, superior strength and durability. Granite is very hard to cut, but it does not splinter. It withstands temperature variations. It is more permanent than marble. And it has been used to make memorials for thousands of years.

The memorial's design architect, Friedrich St.Florian, wanted a gray granite with a specific character—not too white, not too gray, and with a hint of color. Working with memorial advisors, he chose Kershaw from South Carolina for the walls and pillars, and Green County from Georgia for the main plaza stone. In addition, Mount Airy from North Carolina was selected for the coping stone around the Rainbow Pool; Academy Black from California for the of the Rainbow Pool; and Rio Verde and Moss Green from Brazil for accents on the plaza.

Stone Fabrication   Imagine a three-dimensional jigsaw puzzle about the size of a football field with thousands of moving pieces that had to be collected from different parts of the country and the world. That was the challenge the builders of the memorial faced. Here the team had an advantage over previous monument builders. This memorial was created first on a computer. By drawing the entire project in 3-D CAD (computer-aided design), every piece could be examined down to the smallest detail, and for overall aesthetics.

The geometric shape of the memorial is composed of segments of circles, so almost no stone involved a simple square cut. This required the highest technology available and computer driven saws.

Initially it was suggested that the stone be cut in Italy because of the Italians' renowned ability in this area. But the obvious cost, and a natural inclination to "buy American," led ABMC to tour the major stone cutting facilities in the United States to determine if American manufacturers had the capability. They did, and plants in Vermont, Massachusetts, Rhode Island, North Carolina, Minnesota, and one plant in Canada were selected. Each facility received a different portion of the job.

It is remarkable to watch a rough-hewn chunk of granite arrive by truck from the quarry and in a few hours or days be transformed into an object of art. Enormous machines and cranes lift mega-ton blocks through a series of processes that involve cutting, shaping, cleaning, detailing, grinding, surfacing and polishing. The powerful saws with diamond-tipped blades cut

William B. Owenby, WWII Memorial Project Executive, inspects an acre of fabricated stone before it is shipped to the construction site.

Massive blocks of "Mount Airy" granite awaiting fabrication at the quarry in North Carolina.

through one of the hardest substances on earth as if it were a block of wood. Watching this process, it is difficult to imagine that at one time it was all done by hand. And like the construction site, pride of working on the project could be seen in the faces of the stonecutters. In fact, the only World War II veteran who actually worked on the project was a healthy 80-year-old Chet Wachowicz, responsible for quality control of the stonework. "Working on this job," he said, "is my crowning glory."

Stone Assembly   On the 3rd of February, 2003, the first stone was put in place. This was the balcony stone for the south pavilion. The 35,000 pound block was cut like an inverted "L" out of a stone that originally weighed 80,000 pounds. Now an army of stone masons swarmed in, many of them of Italian origin. How to course the stone was the first decision—that is, the shape of the concrete joint made between the blocks.

A critical moment securing the keystone arch of the Pacific pavilion.

A V-joint as opposed to a more traditional rounded strut-joint was selected to enhance the shadow lines. This simple choice creates a powerful visual effect on the stonework as the sun rises and sets every day.

Soon the 56 granite pillars representing all the states and territories during the war began to rise from the foundation. Simultaneous with the pillars, the fountain walls, ramparts and stone benches that surround the plaza were pieced together. Gently sloping ramps leading into the plaza from the pavilions were designed with access for the disabled in mind, so there is no need for landings or handrails.

Every piece of stone in the memorial was given a number that followed it from manufacturing to the site. This numbering system was used to keep track of production and a corresponding stone setting schedule.

Soon, the tops of the granite towers of the pavilions began to creep up to their 43-foot height. Last to go in was the keystone in the pavilion arches. For the design architect this was a great moment. For the first time he could see the actual scale of his design on the Mall site—up till now it was a matter of faith. "It's perfect," he exclaimed.

ART   Behind the scenes of the construction, another major industrial activity was taking place. In the Maryland studio of sculptor Ray Kaskey, more than 200 separate pieces of sculpture were being created for the memorial. It

Construction progress seen from the tower crane as of September 2002.

would take nearly five years to execute all the work.

The choice of bronze was a joint decision between the architect and the sculptor. Bronze is a traditional material used in memorials. It is 90 percent copper with other alloys. The advantage of bronze over other metals is that it looks better with age and lasts for thousands of years. It is a very malleable and workable metal. And it is very warm in appearance compared to steel, nickel or aluminum, which are also subject to rust.

Another consideration was the visual relationship between the granite and bronze materials. A "cool" color relationship was preferred. In the end a bluish-green patina was selected.

Some of the sculpture was mass-produced, including the 56 wreaths of oak and 56 wreaths of wheat that ornament the memorial's pillars. There are also 52 sections of sculpted bronze rope placed in between each pillar, and 4,000 gold stars mounted on the Freedom Wall. There are also several thousand feet of sculpted drain grate.

The major works of commissioned sculpture are two sets of four American eagles holding a large victory laurel. One set is placed in each pavilion. In classical architecture this is known as a baldacchino, essentially a decorative canopy inside another building. Kaskey's design was inspired by a work he observed in Rome where small angels, *putti*, held a wreath above their heads. His choice of American eagles needs no explaining.

The dimensions of each baldacchino are truly monumental. Each rises approximately 29 feet into the air. Each 11-foot eagle rests on an 18-foot bronze column. And suspended from the eagle's beaks as if floating in air is a 5,000 pound wreath. This was as much a work of engineering as it was of art. In this case, the sculptor's best friend was his piping contractor. Beneath the bronze skin of the eagles is an intricate network of tons of heavy-duty bronze armature and stainless steel.

Then came the challenge of finding a way to suspend the giant wreath that made it seem to float in air. Kaskey created a ribbon motif, and the piping engineers devised an ingenious system that rolled a half inch by six inch piece of steel around a roller in a way that created a spiral approximating a ribbon. Naturally, a test was required to make sure it worked.

A new role for sculpture was introduced about half way through the project. It was thought that some use of human figures and simple storytelling would bring more emotional content to the memorial. A series of twenty-four bronze relief panels were created depicting scenes from the Atlantic and Pacific theaters of war, as well as the home front. Approximately 2 x 5 feet in dimension, these bas relief panels were placed along the

balustrades of the ceremonial entrance and represent the mobilization of the United States during World War II.

First, a series of detailed cartoons or storyboards was created. This took more than a year with many trips to the National Archives for inspiration. Then the sculptor and his team began to carve the full-sized panels in clay. Because it is art in the making, the scenes went through many modifications, each sculptor adding a personal touch. To lend the spark of life to the subjects, a team of World War II re-enactors posed with period uniforms and equipment for many of the scenes. The panels were created six at a time, and were reviewed and approved by ABMC and the Commission of Fine Arts before moving on to the foundry.

And there was still more sculpture to be created. On the floors of the pavilions, beneath the baldacchinos, are two 58-inch reproductions of the famous victory medal received by every veteran of World War II. In addition,

At his Maryland studio, Ray Kaskey points out a detail on the clay model of one of 24 bas relief panels to members of the Commission of Fine Arts looking on.

Molten bronze is poured to mold a section of one of the massive laurel wreaths that will be held aloft by four American eagles.

two 12-foot high bronze flagpole bases with six military service seals on each base flank the memorial's ceremonial entrance.

Foundry At the foundry, art and molten metal came together in dramatic ways. The size of the project required two foundries—one in Pennsylvania and one in Oregon. Sculptures were created with both sand casting and the "lost wax" casting processes. This process is more laborious and expensive and is used to preserve the greatest detail in complex forms such as the bas reliefs and wreaths. Rubber molds were made of the clay models. In this mold, wax is laboriously brushed on to the thickness of the metal desired, about a quarter of an inch in this instance. The rubber mold with wax is then cut into pieces that will fit the furnaces. The rubber mold is removed and a ceramic shell is molded around the wax replica of the sculpture. It is then fired in a furnace, which hardens the ceramic material and, at the same time, melts the wax out, hence the name lost wax. Into this hollow ceramic shell, the molten bronze is poured at about 2,000 degrees F. When it has cooled, the ceramic shell is broken off and the various pieces are sandblasted and welded together. Considerable handwork is necessary to grind the welds away and create an even texture over the seams.

Inscriptions Nick Benson is a third generation stone carver and letterer from the John Stevens shop in Newport, Rhode Island, founded in 1705. His father John left his mark on such national treasures as the FDR Memorial and the National Gallery of Art. Benson began by designing an alphabet specifically for the application. It employs a Roman-style letter, with thick and thin edges appropriate for the granite. The complete design process for the type and inscriptions took about two years.

In inscription work, little is left to chance. First an acetate sheet with the precise lettering is placed over the stone to ensure that it properly fits the space designated. Special attention is paid to the points where lettering must cross mortar joints. A rubber stencil of the laid-out lettering is then prepared, and an initial outline of the text is sandblasted into the stone to a depth of about 3/8 of an inch. The carver then uses a pneumatic hammer to shape the U-cut letters, and finishes them with a hand chisel. To increase legibility, the cut lettering is then stained with a black lacquer using a broad-edged brush, a process called lithochroming.

There are more than 3,000 individual letters carved in the memorial. These include 13 inscriptions and quotes; the names of significant battles, engagements and places; and 8 geographic theaters of the war.

Surfaces   A great deal of thought and design went into the paving of the memorial's plaza and walkways. The layout of the plaza creates interesting stonework patterns because the plaza is an oval, not a circle. The radial patterning of the stonework shifts. Laid out first by computer, no two adjoining blocks are the same. It is an amazing achievement in stone cutting and fitting. From a distance, the shift in the pattern creates a dynamic yet uniform space.

Art Installation   Installation of sculpture in the memorial pavilions began in the fall of 2003. First, the bronze ropes were installed between the pillars. About 5 feet in length, the ropes range from 7.5 to 16 inches in thickness. Because the allegory of the rope is the binding together of the states and the territories, the stone fabricator adjusted each of the plinth blocks so that the rope appears to penetrate the stone, which it does to a depth of 3/8 of an inch.

By far the most challenging task was assembling the large American eagle baldacchinos in the memorial's north and south pavilions. This process began in October of 2003 and took several weeks to complete. With little room for error, two of the eagles on columns had to be lowered through an opening in the tops of the pavilions. Here the skill of the crane operator is greatly appreciated. One mistake could spell disaster. The sight of the large metal eagles swinging in the air in front of the Washington Monument was stunning. Alignment of the columns was critical because the distances between the eagle's beaks had to be precise to fit and balance the wreaths. Here laser

Portions of an eagle's wings are welded together at Laran Bronze in Chester, Pennsylvania.

measuring devices proved indispensable. Once assembled, the pieces were welded together and the seams x-rayed and examined to ensure the integrity of the welds. "I feel about 20,000 pounds lighter now that the eagle has landed," said the exhausted sculptor when it was all over.

Smaller bronze wreaths were installed on both sides of the 56 pillars. These were installed in two phases. First, a specially made bracket was mounted between the two uprights of each pillar. Then the installation crew moved rapidly down the rows hanging a wreath every hour or so. The softening impact that this sculpture had on the granite forms was immediately apparent.

In the winter of 2004, another powerful sculpture was installed in the memorial—the Freedom Wall, covered with 4,000 gold stars. The stars were pre-welded onto 23 bronze plates, approximately 40 x 80 inches in size, then hung in sheets from brackets installed in the masonry. The stars are made of stainless steel and electroplated with gold.

To finish off the pavilions, large sculpted WWII victory medal replicas were installed in their floors, surrounded by the words "Victory on Land," "Victory at Sea," "Victory in the Air," and the years "1941–1945."

LIGHTING   One of the indelible images of the National Mall is the view of the major monuments gleaming at night. The World War II Memorial will enhance that sight. Lighting design was planned before construction began to accommodate the placement of fixtures and the running of electrical conduit and lines.

Lighting is a distinct discipline in the architectural world. Computer simulations were made during the design phase to determine the overall look and effect, as well as the types and number of fixtures that would be necessary—several hundred in the end.

All the light fixtures in the memorial are connected to rheostats, so the overall lighting effect can be adjusted to exactly what is required. A central light board will also make it easy on National Park Service engineers, letting them know when a light has gone out.

CEREMONIAL ENTRANCE   Early in 2004 the memorial's front door, the Ceremonial Entrance on 17th Street, began to take shape. A massive announcement stone was laid into place in mid-February. It gave the first hint of what visitors would experience on entering—an awe befitting the subject.

The broad granite steps descending to the memorial plaza were set in place in February and April. Two elab-

In a dramatic shot, an eagle on a column is flown through an opening in the top of the Pacific pavilion called an oculus.

orate flagpoles that frame the ceremonial entrance, and are embellished with the seals of the military services and Merchant Marine, were installed in April 2004.

Then the series of 24 bronze bas relief panels, depicting scenes from the war, at home and overseas, were inset along the ceremonial entrance balustrades to complete the overall effect—that of entering a place at once beautiful, solemn and filled with meaning.

PLAZA AND FOUNTAINS   Plumbing had been underway since the early stages of construction and there had been numerous challenges. The tunnel and vaults below the memorial plaza contain a maze of stainless steel pipes ranging from 4 to 30 inches in diameter—about 2.2 miles in all. The general contractor drew the position of every utility element in 3-D CAD to minimize errors and make installation more efficient.

Water cascades over two waterfalls flanking the Freedom Wall and enters a lower pool. Water also falls from an upper to a lower pool at both pavilions. Seven large pumps recirculate and filter the water to all of the pools and fountains continuously. The fountains in the Rainbow Pool are a work of kinetic art and plumbing virtuosity. One hundred small jets are positioned about the outer edge of the pool and spray continuous arcs of water toward the center. Two large cluster jets at both ends of the pool shoot dramatic sprays 10-15 feet in the air.

LANDSCAPING AND BLENDING WITH NATURE   Making the memorial fit into the natural environment was an integral part of the design. Even the green granite paving laid into the memorial's surfaces and walkways complements the natural greenery surrounding it. Two-thirds of the 7.4-acre memorial site is landscaping and water, designed to enhance the Mall's park-like setting.

Landscaping is also an architectural discipline. The plan called for 150 new trees, 20,000 new ground cover plants, 40,000 bulbs and 650 new shrubs. Every detail was sketched and considered including the color of the flowers—primarily pale green and white.

PUBLIC OPENING   In April of 2004, the perimeter fence was pulled back and the public was allowed to enter the World War II Memorial for the first time. The final work is a testament to the commitment and dedication of architects, artists, engineers and craftsmen, and to the American Battle Monuments Commission, and the many governing bodies involved. Though it remains to be seen how the memorial will be received by future generations one thing is certain—it will stand the test of time.

ACKNOWLEDGMENTS

The editors would like to thank the following organizations and individuals for their invaluable assistance: **Disabled American Veterans:** Arthur H. Wilson, Alan W. Bowers, Richard E. Patterson, David W. Gorman, Nancy L. O'Brien, Gary P. Burns, Gary Weaver, Joseph A. Violante, Christopher Clay, David Autry, Jim Chaney, Jim Hall, Rob Lewis, Alice Bersch, Doreen Lawson; **Ford Motor Company:** Sandy Ulsh, Sandra A. Nicholls; **American Battle Monuments Commission:** General P. X. Kelley, Major General John P. Herrling, Kenneth S. Pond, Barry Owenby, Mike Conley, Rosemary Fritz; **Smithsonian Books:** Don Fehr, Caroline Newman, Carolyn Gleason, Emily Sollie; **General Services Administration:** Darrell Brown; **Leo A. Daly:** Darren Zehner; **Tompkins/Grunley-Walsh Joint Venture:** Jimmy Walsh, Ken Terry, Dave Tweedie, Victor McCoy, Kurt Frevert; **Gilbane Building Company:** Greg Dunkle, Larry Rebel, Fred Dickson, Kent Mosmiller, Bob Wilson, Joe Kleiner, Stefano Terricola, Barbara Cameron, Bart Pixton, Merrill Lambert, Chet Wachowicz; **Commission of Fine Arts:** Harry G. Robinson III, Charles H. Atherton, Frederick J. Lindstrom, Susan M. Raposa, Sue Kohler, John P. Lukavic; **PBS:** Pat Mitchell, Jacoba Atlas, John Wilson, Steven Gray, Sandy Heberer, Shawn Halford, Cara Liebenson, Marcia Diamond, Lindsay Hess; **National D-Day Museum; City Museum of Washington:** Jill Connors Joyner, Laura B. Schiavo; **Individuals:** Friedrich St. Florian, Ray Kaskey, Nick Benson, John S.D. Eisenhower, former Senator Bob Dole, Congresswoman Marcy Kaptur, Captain James E. Wise, Major Steven O'Connor, Evelyn M. Monahan, Rosemary Neidel-Greenlee, Paul T. Sharp, Susan Packard, Peter Thomas, Dan Toohey, Elisa Rosen, Peggy Parsons, Paul Durbin, Perry Carsley, Aaron Sykes, Joanna Blake, David Seitz, Nicholas and Joshua Uth.

PHOTO CREDITS